Recent Research in Financial Modelling

Contributions to Management Science

Ulrich A. W. Tetzlaff
Optimal Design of Flexible Manufacturing Systems
1990. 190 pages. Softcover DM 69,–
ISBN 3-7908-0516-5

Fred von Gunten
Competition in the Swiss Plastics Manufacturing Industry
1991. 408 pages. Softcover DM 120,–
ISBN 3-7908-0541-6

Harald Dyckhoff/Ute Finke
Cutting and Packing in Produktion and Distribution
1992. 248 pages. Hardcover DM 120,–
ISBN 3-7908-0630-7

Hagen K. C. Pfeiffer
The Diffusion of Electronic Data Interchange
1992. 257 pages. Softcover DM 85,–
ISBN 3-7908-0631-5

Evert Jan Stokking · Giovanni Zambruno (Eds.)

Recent Research in Financial Modelling

With 9 Figures

Physica-Verlag
A Springer-Verlag Company

Series Editor
Werner A. Müller
Peter Schuster

Editors
Evert Jan Stokking MBA
University of Groningen, Department of Business
Administration and Management Siences,
P.O. Box 800, NL-9700 AV Groningen, The Netherlands

Professor Dr. Giovanni Zambruno
University of Milan, Faculty of Political Sciences,
Via Conservatorio 7, I-20122 Milano, Italy

ISBN 3-7908-0683-8 Physica-Verlag Heidelberg
ISBN 0-387-91448-X Springer-Verlag New York

CIP-Kurztitelaufnahme der Deutschen Bibliothek

Recent research in financial modelling / Evert Jan Stokking;
Giovanni Zambruno (ed.). - Heidelberg : Physica-Verl., 1993
(Contributions to management science)
ISBN 3-7908-0683-8
NE: Stokking, Evert Jan [Hrsg.]

7100/7130-543210 - Printed on acid-free paper

Contents

RECENT RESEARCH IN FINANCIAL MODELLING

This volume contains a selection of revised papers that have initially been presented at the meetings of the EURO Working Group on Financial Modelling, held in Sirmione, Italy (April 1990) and Gieten, The Netherlands (November 1990). These papers have recently been revised, taken into account the comments of the referees and the ongoing discussion on these subjects during the meetings of the Working Group every six months. This volume is therefore an interesting collection of readings covering the main topics of the Working Group. These topics are Corporate Financial Management, Banking, Financial Market Models, Security Evaluation and International Finance. These papers have been accepted for publication after being refereed by a group of leading academicians, whose kind cooperation the editors gratefully acknowledge.

The two 1990 meetings have been a great success. The attendance was large and qualified. The charming environment of the villages Sirmione and Gieten contributed to the establishment of a friendly atmosphere among the participants and to the benefit of formal and informal scientific conversations. This is in the style of the EURO Meetings on Financial Modelling, in which both finished and unfinished research is presented.

If the index of this volume were interpreted as providing an "unbiased statistics" of the research areas currently explored by European scholars, one could easily perceive a dramatic expansion of streams of analysis on the microstructure of capital markets. Actually, the many contributions on this issue provide evidence that the price dynamics of financial assets can only be explained - and modelled - on the basis of a careful examination of the decision process which leads traders to interact and fix the equilibrium prices. The papers by Peccati, Luciano, Ferrari and Cornaglia belong to this category, and help considerably understand the performance of markets which are relatively far from perfection (owing to thinness, frictions, taxation and the like). This is indeed the case for some European Exchanges.

The very foundations of quantitative financial analysis have been discussed in the contributions of Luciano, Canestrelli, Uberti and Van der Meulen. The classical - although recent - advances on the pricing of derivative securities have been analyzed and applied by Kremer, Hallerbach and Jensen-Nielsen, thus demonstrating that established theories still provide space for a deeper investigation.

Another major topic of interest relates to empirical studies about how markets behave with respect to theoretical models. In this respect, the contributions of Viren, Bradfield and Wilkie-Pollock are quite significant. They present evidence based on real data discussed in the light of advanced statistical techniques.

Surprisingly enough, models for the corporate financial policy have not been discussed extensively. Apparently these issues do not attract the interest of researchers the way they deserve. Yet it is apparent that Corporate Finance and Capital Markets are becoming more and more related and interacting with each other. Two remarkable exceptions are the contributions by Bergendahl, on the management of banks, and by Van der Horst Jansen, specifically intended to demonstrate the many advantages of a proper use of Artificial Intelligence models.

This quick summary of the content of this book is a representative but not an exhaustive enumeration of the topics currently investigated by the members of the EURO Working Group on Financial Modelling. Their activity is more and more expanding, academically and professionally.

Evert Jan Stokking

Giovanni Zambruno

BANK MANAGEMENT AND THE FINANCIAL SERVICE INDUSTRY

Göran Bergendahl*
Department of Business Administration
University of Gothenburg
Vasagatan 3, S-41124 Göteborg, Sweden

1. Assumptions

The financial service industry is assumed to be a collection of firms that serves the economy with financial transactions and financial intermediation. Most banks form a subset of these firms with the special privilege of serving customers with deposit accounts. Bank Management may then be seen as the management of transaction and intermediation in banks.

Economic theory has provided us with many reasons for that financial institutions are competitive. Santomero (1984, p. 577) has listed three of them:

a) They are competitive as asset transformers.

b) They have a central function in a monetary economy.

c) They may be engaged in risky arbitrage across markets.

This means that banks as financial institutions transfer deposits into loans, work as payment institutions and are willing to trade with risks.

Friedman (1985, p.4) has taken a similar view:

> "Three basic rationals typically motivate the reliance on financial intermediaries in the modern economy: benefits of size and specialization, when there are economies of scale in gathering information or in processing transactions; diversification of specific asset risks, when asset holders are risk averse; and pooling of liquidity or other risks, when asset holders themselves face uncertain contingencies".

The industry that performs financial intermediation is called the Financial Service Industry. Following Friedman this industry may be defined as the set of firms that produce three main classes of activities

- lending and depositing
- payment services
- optional service contracts

Lending and depositing concerns contracts to lend or to deposit a predefined amount of money over a limited or an unlimited time period to a defined interest rate. Loans and deposits

---

* I am indebted to the Nordbanken, Stockholm for financial support and to an anonymous referee for constructive comments.

may be either on accounts or as marketable instruments (bonds, notes etc). One reason for that special firms are utilized in order to manage loans and deposits on accounts is that there is a need for having them "tailor-made" at the same time as *risk may be transformed from depositors and diversified among borrowers.*

Payment services relates to a transfer of money in two ways, One is from an account to cash or reversely. The other is from one account to another. The service includes the *transfers* as well as the *information* about when the transfers were made. The charge for a payment service may be either a fee or an interest charge on the accounts affected by this service (e.g. current accounts, NOW accounts and Super NOW accounts).

Optional service contracts are used here as a collective name for many kinds of payment contracts with conditional clauses. Life insurance is such a contract, where the insurance company is willing to pay a prescribed amount of money if the customer dies. Motor insurance is another example, where the insurance firm pays an amount if the customer has a car accident. Currency options are contracts where the customer have the right to obtain a certain amount of money in case the exchange rate moves over a certain level. Guarantees are contracts where banks are willing to pay a customer a specified amount in case a borrower is unable to pay back a private loan. The Financial Service Industry may be willing to sign such contracts in order *to pool liquidity and other risks.*

A *bank* differs from other financial service institutions through that it is allowed to serve customers with deposit accounts. Some of these accounts may be used for payment purposes (i.e. as money).

2. Demand for and Supply of Financial Services

Above we assumed that the market for financial services may concern three classes of services:

a) Lending and depositing (unconditional contracts)
b) Payments (unconditional contracts)
c) Optional services (conditional contracts)

Lending and depositing activities increase when liquidity widens. Payment services are related mainly to trade. More trade gives more payments. Optional services will be directly dependent on the associated risks as for credits, interest rates, exchange rates, etc.

Lending, depositing, payment services and optional services are provided by different financial service organizations like banks, building societies, financial companies, pension funds and insurance firms. There exist several theories of these firms. From the point of view of cost accounting, the production approach and the intermediation approach are two of the most interesting ones for banking (see Berger et al 1987 p. 508, Hörngren 1988 pp 32-36):

> "Under the production approach, banks produce accounts of various sizes by processing deposits and loans, incurring capital and labor costs."..."Under the intermediation approach, banks intermediate deposited and purchased funds into loans and other assets." (Berger et al 1987, p 508)

The two approaches differ concerning how bank products are formed. In the case of the production approach, both deposits and loans are viewed as products, while capital (in terms of branches, computers, etc) and labor (salaries) are viewed as input. In the case of the intermediation approach, loans are the main bank products, while capital (in terms of branches, computers, etc), labor and deposits are viewed as inputs.

In both cases the number of accounts (N) and the account size in money terms (A) may be used as output "metrics" for a product (Baltensperger & Milde 1987 pp 244-5, Berger et al 1987, p 508). For the purpose of cost accounting and price differentiation in banks (as well as in other financial organizations), the production approach seems to be most appropriate and will be used onwards. General principles for the use of the intermediation approach has been developed by e.g. Lawrence & Shay (1986, pp. 58-62).

The financial service industry is unique in the way that a loan is both a product or a service and an asset. In a similar way, deposits are both a product and a liability. For example, Humphrey (1985, p. 749) has proposed "seven broadly defined bank functions": Demand deposits, savings deposits, purchased funds, securities and investments, commercial and industrial loans, installment loans, and real estate loans. They were all chosen for the purpose of cost control. Seen from the view of a balance sheet, a bank may be associated with product groups that corresponds to classes of assets and liabilities according to Table 1.

Table 1: Classes of Assets and Liabilities for a Bank

Assets (i)	Liabilities (j)
Cash	Customer current accounts
Interbank loans	Customer deposit accounts
Customer loans, domestic currency	Purchased funds
Customer loans, foreign currency	Dated loan capital
Government and other securities	Undated loan capital
Certificates of deposits	Reserves
Investment securities	Share capital

Most payment services of a bank are performed in association with a current account (to a certain extent also with savings deposits, NOW-accounts, etc.). Therefore, payments and current accounts may be treated as joint products, where the administrative costs of payments as well as the float from these payments may be associated with the corresponding current accounts.

From now we will address the classes of products by numbers i = 1,2,.., m for assets and j = m+1, m+2,..., n for liabilities. Then the volume of loans of a class *i* can be given as an asset (x_i) and the volume of deposits of a class *j* as a liability (y_j), where:

$$x_i = N_i\ A_i \qquad (1)$$
$$y_j = N_j\ A_j \qquad (2)$$

Now assume that the operating expenses of a bank may be divided into two groups:

a) running costs, which for a class (i or j) of accounts may depend on the number (N_i or N_j) of these accounts as well as on their average sizes (A_i or A_j). The main part of these short-term costs concern telecommunication and computer services, office space, and personnel.

b) fixed costs, which will cover premises, computer and other equipment, certain staff of personnel, etc.

One may expect that the only short-term way in which a bank may expand or contract the volumes of assets (x_i) and liabilities (y_j) is by increasing or decreasing the number of accounts (N_i or N_j). First in the longer run one may expect to attract customers with another average size (A_i or A_j) of account. Therefore, we will assume that the short-run administrative costs of producing these assets and liabilities will grow by the number of accounts (N_i) for given average sizes (A_i) of these accounts (cf. Baltensperger & Milde 1987, pp.40 & 244-5). Consequently, these administrative running costs may be approximated as:

$$c(x_i) = c(N_i, A_i) = a_i\ N_i \qquad (3)$$
$$c(y_j) = c(N_j, A_j) = a_j\ N_j \qquad (4)$$

where a_i and a_j are unit costs specific to each class (i or j) but assumed to be independent of the production volumes (N_i and N_j). Simply, the operating cost is divided by the number of deposit or loan accounts (c.f. Humphrey 1985, p. 753) Such an assumption will disregard the existence of economies of scale what concern the production of different services (i or j).

Following the production approach, the analysis will be based upon the existence of a marginal market rate (r), i.e. an interbank rate (such as LIBOR) at which lending (x_i) may be funded and deposits (y_j) may be placed. The cost $c_i(N_i)$ of funding a category i of loans on the interbank market will then depend on the amount of accounts (N_i) as well as the average size (A_i) of an account of category i:

$$c_i(N_i) = r\ A_i\ N_i \qquad (5)$$

In the same way one may calculate the revenue $r_j(N_j)$ from placing the proceeds from a category j of deposits on the interbank market as being dependent on the amount of accounts (N_j) as well as of the average size (A_j) of a deposit in the category (j):

$$r_j(N_j) = r\ A_j\ N_j \qquad (6)$$

There exist two basic procedures for the control of income and expenditures (see Horngren 1981, p. 372) : 1. to allocate costs to departments for planning and control, and 2. to allocate costs to products for product cost calculation. Then strategic issues to be determined concern (compare Holm & Thorburn (1990), pp 5-6):

a) if the cost for a certain service may be reduced,

b) if prices (internally in the institution or externally towards a customer) exceed the costs of providing these services in order to generate a sufficient margin to cover fixed costs and profit,

c) if it is feasible and efficient to introduce, expand, reduce or eliminate certain services on an established market, and

d) if short-term investments should be done in order to expand capacity In the next section, these issues will be transformed into two "standard banking allocation problems".

3. Two Short-run Standard Banking Allocation Problems

Let us now formulate a set of two short-run Standard Banking Allocation (SBA) problems. A bank that would like to become efficient may analyze them in terms of two steps A and B.

A. To Control the Short-term Net Interest Margins.

First assume as given a set of "market lending rates" (L_i), each referring to the rate at which loans of category i are supplied. Here customers may be grouped into different categories according to how risky projects they represent. Defaulters may be treated separately and charged a higher interest rate than others (see e.g. Stiglitz & Weiss 1983, pp. 912 & 918).

Furthermore, assume as given a set of "market borrowing rates" (D_j) also referring to the rate at which deposits of category j are provided. Then the bank may estimate:

a) the interest income of asset account i ($L_i A_i N_i$).

b) the interest expenses of liability account j ($D_j A_j N_j$).

c) fees, charges, and other income of account i ($p_i N_i$) and j ($p_j N_j$).

d) running costs of account i ($a_i N_i$) and j ($a_j N_j$).

This means that the bank is recommended to calculate net margins M_i and M_j for each product category i and j as:

$$M_i = \underbrace{(L_i - r) A_i N_i}_{\text{gross lending margin}} - \underbrace{(a_i - p_i) N_i}_{\text{- running costs + fee income}} \tag{7}$$

$$M_j = \underbrace{(r - D_j) A_j N_j}_{\text{gross borrowing margin}} - \underbrace{(a_j - p_j) N_j}_{\text{- running costs + fee income}} \tag{8}$$

The calculations of (7) and (8) give net margins in money terms. For a banker it seems to be of a greater value to analyze net interest margins (NIM) in percentage terms (m_i & m_j). Revell (1980) has been a pioneer in calculating net margins for different banks on the basis of accounting data. This study may be seen as an effort to expand his analysis in order to develop principles for product costing. The margins will be obtained by dividing the net margins for each class (i & j) by the corresponding production volumes ($A_i N_i$ or $A_j N_j$). They should give a large enough contribution to cover fixed costs:

$m_i = M_i/A_i N_i$	$= L_i - r -$	$(a_i - p_i)/A_i$	(9)
net interest margin for lending (%)	lending rate, market rate	running costs - fee income	
$m_j = M_j/A_j N_j$	$= r - D_j -$	$(a_j - p_j)/A_j$	(10)
net interest margin for borrowing (%)	market rate, deposit rate	running costs - fee income	

An operational objective for a profit maximizing bank would then be to specialize in those classes of loans and deposits, which generate the highest NIM:s. However most banks operate in such a competition with others that the market segments are rather limited (at least in the short run).The implication will be that out of these market segments any bank would aim the number of accounts (N_i & N_j) of different classes of credits (i) and deposits (j) where an Aggregated Net Margin (ANM) will be as large as possible. Consequently, a bank would maximize:

$$ANM = \Sigma_i M_i + \Sigma_j M_j =$$

$$= \Sigma_i \left((L_i - r) A_i N_i + (p_i - a_i) N_i \right) + \Sigma_j \left((r - D_j) A_j N_j + (p_j - a_j) N_j \right) \quad (11)$$

subject to "demand capacities", that is the notion that a bank cannot attract in the short run more that a limited number of credit accounts or deposit accounts. A given number of branches with a given configuration of computers, manpower, and associated facilities will influence these constraints. However, we disregard any capacity constraints that occur in the central production of a bank as well as in its retail network. In mathematical terms, the constraints will be defined as:

a) upper limits (W_i) of the number (N_i) of credit accounts (i) that the bank may attract. This implies (for each class i):

$$N_i \leq W_i \quad (12)$$

b) estimated amounts (W_j) of the number (N_j) of deposit accounts (j) that may be demanded in the short run. This implies (for such classes j of liabilities only):

$$N_j \leq W_j \quad (13)$$

Here, we have assumed that the control of product composition concerns lending and borrowing only. Thus, the bank may choose the best of these activities that it may manage subject to the demand constraints. There is no requirement that the corresponding assets and liabilities will match, but that the residual will be financed from or placed on the interbank market (to the rate r). Thus, the problem of maximizing the short term profit subject to capacity constraints will be formulated as to maximize (11) subject to (12) and(13). By doing so we have considered a) placement revenues (from lending both to customers and on the money market), b) funding costs (both from borrowing of depositors as well as on the money market), c) administrative costs and d) capacity constraints. The corresponding dual solution (∂_i,∂_j) to this short-run maximization task for the Standard Banking Allocation problem A (SBA:A) will then stipulate that the Net Interest Margin (NIM) per account has to be equivalent to the marginal cost of demand capacity:

$$L_i - r - (a_i - p_i)/A_i = \partial_i / A_i \quad (14)$$

$$r - D_j - (a_j - p_j)/A_j = \partial_j / A_j \quad (15)$$

[NIM] = [Capacity Cost per Account]

Figure 1 will illustrate the concept of net interest margins for a bank with four classes of assets (i=1,2,3,4) and six classes of liabilities (j=5,6,7,8,9,10). Both the assets and the liabilities are ranked in a decreasing order of Net Interest Margins, which results in the staircase structure. (For principles of staircase structures see e.g. Turvey 1971, p. 64).

Figure 1: Net Interest Margins for a General Bank

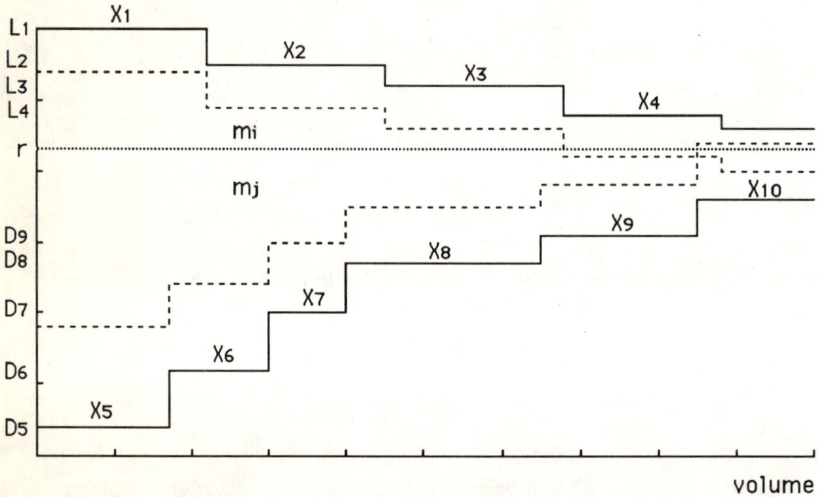

Legend

L_i	= lending rates (%)
D_j	= deposit rates (%)
$(a_i-p_i)/A_i$	= running costs - fee income per size of account (%)
m_i & m_j	= net interest margins (%)
x_i & x_j	= volumes of assets and liabilities

In this case asset no. 4 and liability no. 10 have gross interest margins that are positive, as the deposit rate (D_{10}) lies below and the credit rate (L_4) lies above the market rate (r). Still they are not profitable, as the gross interest margins and the fee income are not sufficient to cover running costs. Consequently, one ought to eliminate these activities from the bank. In principle, a bank has two ways of performing such an elimination. Either it stops offering the product to the customer, or it will price it out by increasing the actual lending rate or the fee as well as decreasing the corresponding deposit rate.

B. To Control the Balance Sheet and the Economies of Scope

Now we will expand our analysis of a bank in order to control not only loans and deposits but the whole balance sheet. Such an action will imply a simultaneous control of all assets and liabilities what concerns both risk and return. For risk analysis only, it has been a well established activity in banks in terms of Balance Sheet Management, BSM, or as Asset & Liability Management, ALM (see e.g. Bergendahl 1989).

For the Allocation Problem A we have assumed that the net surplus between lending and borrowing was financed to a market rate (or invested in case depositing is larger than lending). By doing so we were able to estimate the competitive advantage to produce services based on such a market rate r. Now we expand the analysis and replace the funding at a market rate r with a set of alternative assets i and liabilities j by assuming:

a) a surplus may be placed in other assets (i) than customer lending,
b) a deficit may be funded from other liabilities (j) than customer deposits.

Consequently, we will be more general than before by not only considering loans and deposits but all kinds of assets and liabilities in a bank. Therefore let L_i stand for the rate of interest income from asset i (in per cent) and D_j the rate of interest expenses from liability j (also in per cent).

For example, at least one asset (say i=2) will stand for interbank lending and at least one liability (say j=25) will concern interbank borrowing. Consequently, we no longer base the analysis on a single interbank rate (r), but on one interbank lending rate (here L_2) and a corresponding interbank borrowing rate (here D_{25}). One may expect that the resulting interbank margin (L_2 - D_{25}) will increase by bank size, so that economies-of-scale will be available in interbanking activities. Consequently, we can no longer use the concept of net margins (M_i and M_j in (7) and (8)), but we have to compare gross revenues, funding costs and administrative costs.

First we calculate the short-term net revenue (R_i) for each category (i) of assets:

$$R_i = \underbrace{L_i A_i N_i}_{\text{gross revenues}} + \underbrace{(p_i - a_i) N_i}_{\text{fee income - running costs}} \qquad (16)$$

Then we estimate the short-term variable costs (C_j) for each category (j) of liabilities:

$$C_j = \underbrace{D_j A_j N_j}_{\text{funding costs}} + \underbrace{(a_j - p_j) N_j}_{\text{running costs - fee income}} \qquad (17)$$

Furthermore, neither the amount (N_i) of asset accounts in (16) nor the amount (N_j) of liability accounts in (17) may be chosen separately. Total assets must be matched by total liabilities. This implies that:

$$\Sigma_i A_i N_i \quad = \quad \Sigma_j A_j N_j \qquad (18)$$

Finally, we calculate the Aggregated Net Margin (ANM) as the difference between net revenues (R_i) and the short-term variable costs (C_j):

$$ANM \quad = \quad \Sigma_i R_i \ - \ \Sigma_j C_j \qquad (19)$$

Consider a bank with the purpose to maximize its ANM for a given set of market prices for assets (L_i) and liabilities (D_j). Such a bank will have to choose asset accounts (N_i) and liability accounts (N_j) in such a way that will maximize (19) subject to (12), (13), (16), (17) and (18).

This model may be further expanded in order to consider risks for unexpected credit losses (see e.g. Santomero 1984, pp 587-591). One approach is to introduce for such a risky asset *i* a risk premium γ_i (in percent). This implies that the estimated lending rate L_i has to be adjusted upwards in correspondence to the expected credit losses. Such a construction implies that the uncertain revenue R_i in (16) will be replaced by a risk-adjusted one R_i' such that:

$$R_i' = (L_i - \gamma_i)\, A_i\, N_i + (p_i - a_i)\, N_i \qquad (20)$$

The level of this premium will depend on the estimated distribution of outcomes.

These balance sheet models treat asset and liabilities as being independent except for the requirement that total assets have to be matched by total liabilities. However, there is a need to extend these formulations further in order to include interdependencies that are called <u>economies of scope</u>. These economies comes from joint production. They imply that av wider product assortment will result in that revenues may be improved or costs may be saved. The reasons may be that (Berger et al. 1987, p. 503-4):

a) fixed costs may be distributed over a wider product mix,

b) information about customers may be used for several products,

c) risks may be reduced by diversification and by matching maturities on assets and liabilities, and

d) customer costs may be reduced by concentrating financial services to one institution.

Consequently, the willingness to pay for services may be somewhat greater if performed jointly.

These activities may be included in the above analysis with different consequences. A <u>wider product mix</u> (a) means the activation of demand capacities for certain new classes of accounts (i or j). An interesting observation is that in a bank or in a financial institution the cost for expanding certain and often non-existing demand capacities seems to depend on the existing capacities. This implies that there is a capacity expansion cost that is not additative.

Therefore, there may be a cost advantage for such an expansion (as computers, branches etc may be used simultaneously for a wide product assortment). Then the cost for capacity expansion may be given as a non-separable function $c(W_i, W_j)$ of the demand capacities. For the formulation of such a non-separable function for joint production, see e.g. Adar, Agmon, & Orgler 1975. The cost advantage of a simultaneous expansion will imply that $c(W_i, W_j) <$ $< c(W_i, 0) + c(0, W_j)$. Consequently, a strategy to offer a wider product mix may lead to investment costs that are smaller than if the corresponding services were produced and distributed separately.

Several theoretical studies on multi-product economics are based upon the assumption that the main part of the economics of scope originates from a reduction in fixed costs rather than from lower variable costs for production and distribution. Panzar & Willig (1981, p. 270) assume that running costs are separable what concerns production, while they are focusing on cases for which the capital cost is "strictly subadditative". According to them, this quality will be the only reason for economies of scope. (Strictly subadditativity stands for the case when a certain capital input may be used for production of several outputs. Then capital is at least partly a public good). MacDonald & Slivinski (1987, p. 942) assume that there is a fixed cost F per firm (bank) independent of the size of production.

When information about customers (b) may be used jointly between products, this implies that there will be a discount in the administrative costs (see Berger et al. 1987, p. 507). However, there seems to be no indications available that these discounts should concern running costs. Several studies stress that the reduction will concern fixed set-up costs (see e.g. Panzar & Willig 1981, p. 270). If so, this will be a second reason for the capacity expansion function $c(W_i, W_j)$ to be non-convex.

Risks (c) may be handled in different ways. One is to introduce new classes (i,j) of optional contracts with the single purpose to reduce risk. A second one concerns the use of deposit insurance (see e.g. Diamond & Dybig 1983). A third one is to introduce claims on capital adequacy as a constraint, which give an upper bound on the risky assets $(\Sigma_i \mu_i A_i N_i)$:

$$\sum_{i \in \Delta} \mu_i A_i N_i \leq \sum_{j \in \Gamma} A_j N_j \tag{21}$$

A fourth alternative is to introduce claims on leverage as a constraint, which give an upper bound on liabilities:

$$\eta \sum_{j \notin \Gamma} A_j N_j \leq \sum_{j \in \Gamma} A_j N_j \tag{22}$$

Here Δ stands for the set of risky assets, μ_i denotes the percentage of asset i that is treated as being risky, Γ stands for the set of liability classes treated as capital, and η stands for the leverage factor.

In combination, these two constraints will induce economies of scope from a joint expansion of lending and borrowing. The reason is that such a combined expansion will not require a proportional expansion of equity.

Lower customer costs (d) through a wider product mix may have a direct effect on demand capacity. A larger willingness to pay for the bank products will imply the upper limits on demand (12+13) to increase. The structural formulations will then remain unchanged.

Consequently the optimal control of the capacity expansion under economies of scope will be to find simultaneously the set of accounts (N_i, N_j) and the set of expansion strategies (W_i, W_j) that will maximize the Aggregated Net Margin:

$$ANM = \Sigma_i R_i - \Sigma_j C_j - c(W_i, W_j) =$$

$$= \Sigma_i (L_i A_i N_i + (p_i - a_i) N_i) - \Sigma_j (D_j A_j N_j + (a_j - p_j) N_j) - c(W_i, W_j) \quad (23)$$

subject to demand capacities (12) & (13), an asset & liability balance (18), a constraint on capital adequacy (21), and a leverage constraint (22). The Kuhn-Tucker optimality conditions hold as necessary requirements and will determine the marginal costs of capacity as $\partial_i = \partial c(W_i, W_j)/\partial W_i$ and $\partial_j = \partial c(W_i, W_j)/\partial W_j$.

Even if these conditions will only guarantee a local optimum they may be used for pricing and cost control. As such they are presented in Table 2 as principles for Standard Banking Allocation problems of type B (SBA:B) .

Table 2: SBA:B Principles for Controling Revenues and Costs

Asset Accounts (i)		Equation
a) the marginal revenue from lending =	$[L_i A_i + p_i] =$	(23)
b) the running cost of lending +	$[a_i] +$	(23)
c) the shadow price of funding +	$[\rho A_i] +$	(18)
d) the marginal cost of additional demand +	$[\partial_i] +$	(12)
e) the risk premium for capital adequacy	$[\beta \mu_i A_i]$	(21)
Liability Accounts (j)		
a) the shadow price of funding -	$[\rho A_j] -$	(18)
b) the marginal cost of borrowing =	$[D_j A_j + a_j - p_j] =$	(23)
c) the marginal cost of additional demand -	$[\partial_j] +$	(13)
d) the cost of leverage	$[\eta \lambda A_j]$	(22)

Here the funding cost ρ is given as the shadow price of constraint (18). The shadow price β of the capital adequacy constraint (21), and the shadow price λ of the leverage constraint (22) will both become risk premia. The liability accounts considered here are those for non-equity only. The column "Equation" indicates the equation that generates the corresponding revenue, cost or shadow price.

Then, rearrange the terms in Table 2 and divide them by size of account $(A_i$ or $A_j)$. The results are given for asset i in (24) and for liability j in (25):

$$L_i - \rho - (a_i - p_i)/A_i = \partial_i/A_i + \mu_i \beta \quad (24)$$

$$[\text{NIM}] = \begin{bmatrix}\text{Capacity Costs} \\ \text{per Account}\end{bmatrix} + \begin{bmatrix}\text{Cost of Capital} \\ \text{Adequacy}\end{bmatrix}$$

$$\rho - D_j - (a_j - p_j)/A_j = \partial_j / A_j + \eta\lambda \qquad (25)$$

$$[\text{NIM}] = [\text{Capacity Costs per Account}] + [\text{Marginal Cost for Maintaining Leverage}] \qquad j \notin \Gamma$$

Consequently, the introduction of a constraint for adequate capital (21) will imply a wider NIM for the asset side. And claims on leverage (22) will have the same effect on the liability side. Observe that a constraint on capital adequacy will widen the NIM just in the same way as if a risk adjusted revenue (20) had been introduced. The two formulations will be equivalent as soon as $\gamma_i = \beta\mu_i$.

4. Practical Implications

The preceding section gave principles of how to handle two Standard Banking Allocation problems - SBA:A and SBA:B. They both concerned the short-term operation in a bank. The first one (SBA:A) gave a method to calculate the short-term net interest margins (NIM) for loan and deposit accounts. By rearranging equation (9) into: $m_i = L_i + p_i/A_i - r - a_i/A_i$, the NIM should be determined for each class i of assets as:

NIM = LENDING RATE + FEE RATE - MARKET RATE - RUNNING COST

In the same equation (10) may be rearranged as $m_j = r + p_j/A_j - D_j - a_j/A_j$. Then each class of liabilities may be given as:

NIM = MARKET RATE + FEE RATE - DEPOSIT RATE - RUNNING COST

Then capacity constraints were introduced. Equations (14) and (15) stipulate that the assets and liabilities that are considered have to take such a volume that their NIM will be equal to the marginal capacity cost per account:

NIM = CAPACITY COST PER ACCOUNT

The second one SBA:B was a further development of SBA:A in order to include interdependencies in terms of balance sheet constraints as well as consequences from economies of scope. The balance sheet constraints resulted in a "shadow price" (ρ) on funding that replaced the market rate (r) in calculating the NIM. The economies of scope have such an effect on the asset side, that the NIM should cover not only the marginal cost of capacity, but also the cost for capital adequacy. And on the liability side, equations (25) and (26) certify that the NIM will cover the marginal capacity cost as well as the costs for maintaining a stable leverage. That means:

NIM FROM LENDING = CAPACITY COST PER ACCOUNT + MARGINAL COST FOR CAPITAL ADEQUACY

NIM FROM BORROWING = CAPACITY COST PER ACCOUNT + MARGINAL COST FOR FINANCIAL LEVERAGE

Consequently, the NIM must not only cover the cost of demand capacity, but also a capital convergency factor for assets and a leverage factor for liabilities.

References

Adar, Z., Agmon, T. & Orgler, Y. E.: "Output Mix and Jointness in Production In the Banking Firm", J. of Money, Credit, and Banking, 1975.

Baltensperger, E. & Milde, H.: Theorie des Bankverhaltens, Springer-Verlag, Berlin & Heidelberg 1987.

Bergendahl, G.: "The Management of Assets and Liabilities in Banks: Principles and Applications", Revue de la Banque, No 6, Brussels, 1989.

Berger, A. N., Hanweck, G. A. & Humphrey, D. B.: "Competitive Viability in Banking", Journal of Monetary Economics 20, 1987 (pp 501-20).

Berger, A. N. & Humphrey D. B.: The Dominance of Inefficiencies over Scale and Product Mix Economies in Banking, Working Paper, Board of Governors of the Federal Reserve System, Washington D.C., May 1990.

Diamond, D. W. & Dybvig P.H.: "Bank Runs, Deposit Insurance, and Liquidity", Journal of Political Economy, Vol. 91, No. 3, 1983.

Friedman, B. M.: Financial Intermediation in the United States, in Handbook for Banking Strategy (edit. R. C. Aspinwall & R. A. Eisenbeis), Wiley, New York, 1985.

Holm, K. & Thorburn, D.: Kostnadskalkylering i tre banker ("Cost Calculation in Three Banks"), The Stockholm School of Economics, Stockholm 1989.

Horngren, C. T.: Introduction to Management Accounting, Prentice-Hall, London 1981.

Hörngren, L.: Kostnadsutveckling och konkurrens i banksektorn ("Cost Changes and Competition inside the Banking Sector"), SOU 1989:16, Ministry of Finance, Stockholm 1989.

Humphrey, D. B.: "Cost and Scale Economies in Bank Intermediation" in Handbook for Banking Strategy (edit. Aspinwall, R C & Eisenbeis, R A), Wiley 1985.

Lawrence, C. & Shay, R. P.:"Technology and Financial Intermediation in Multiproduct Banking Firms. An Econometric Study of U.S. Banks 1972-1982", in Technological Innovation, Regulation, and the Monetary Economy (edit. Lawrence C & Shay R P), Cambridge, Mass. 1986

MacDonald, G. M. & Slivinski, A.: "The Simple Analytics of Competitive Equilibrium with Multiproduct Firms", The American Economic Review, December 1987.

Panzar, J. C. & Willig, R. D.: "Economies of Scope", American Economic Review, May 1981.

Revell, J. R. S.: Costs and Margins in Banking: an International Survey, OECD, Paris 1980.

Santomero, A M: "Modeling the Banking Firm", Journal of Money, Credit, and Banking 16, No 4, 1984 (pp 576-602).

Stiglitz, J. E. & Weiss, A.: "Incentive Effects of Terminations: Applications to the Credit and Labor Markets", American Economic Review, Vol. 73, No 3, December 1983.

Turvey, R.: Economic Analysis and Public Enterprises, George Allen & Unwin, London 1971.

A DECOMPOSITION OF RANDOM NET PRESENT VALUES

Elisa Luciano – Lorenzo Peccati
Ist. Mat. Fin. - Univers. - P. Arbarello 8 - 10122 Torino

Some recent papers (PECCATI (1989) and the references therein) have put forward a method for distinguishing the contributions (i) of each source of financing and (ii) of each time period to the net present value (from now on NPV) of a non-random financial project.

The method applies both to point input – point output investments (from now on PIPO) and to other financial projects. Its aim is to offer useful insights for financial decisions[1].

Our purpose is to extend the approach to the appraisal of random financial projects, with the possibility of learning from experience through the use of standard Bayesian inference[2].

The plan of the paper is as follows: in section 1 the model is set up. Section 2 solves some technical problems, while section 3 focuses on Bayesian information processing. Section 4 presents some examples. Section 5 summarizes and suggests further extensions.

1 THE MODEL

Let a financial project be characterized by the random cash flows $\{f_s\}$ with maturity at the times $s = 0, 1, \ldots, N$ respectively.

Suppose first that this project is entirely equity financed, and that the (random) opportunity costs of equity are R_s, $s = 1, 2, \ldots, N$ for the corresponding time periods. Let us group the rates of return R_s in an N-dimensional (random) vector R.

Finally, let us denote with $F(t, \tau)$ the compound amount at time τ of 1\$ paid at time t:

$$F(t,\tau) \stackrel{d}{=} \prod_{u=t+1}^{\tau} (1 + R_u) \quad \tau > t$$

with the assumption $F(t, \tau) \equiv 1$ when $\tau \leq t$.

With these notations, the NPV of the investment, $G(R)$, is:

$$G(R) = \frac{\sum_{s=0}^{N} f_s}{F(0, s)}$$

Given that G is a function of the interest rates used for discounting, let us assume that at least one N-dimensional random vector I exists (with components I_s, $s = 1, \ldots, N$), which solves the equation $G(I) = 0$. Any such vector I generalizes the concept of internal rate of return. We shall say that it characterizes an internal financial law (from now on IFL) for the project. Uniqueness of this vector, of course, is not guaranteed: on the contrary, more than one IFL is generally feasible for each project.

[1]See LUCIANO (1989), PECCATI (1989) and the references therein.

[2]The paper extends a previous research of the same authors, in which the learning process was not allowed. See LUCIANO – PECCATI (1990).

No matter what IFL has been chosen, let us define the outstanding capitals sequence w_s ($s = 1, \ldots, N$) by the following recurrence relation:

$$w_s = w_{s-1}(1 + I_s) - f_s,$$

with the initial condition $w_0 = -f_0$.

These outstanding capitals are random variables, one of which at least is degenerate[3]: w_N. It can be easily demonstrated in fact that $w_N = 0$.

Suppose now that the investment under consideration is partially financed with debt.

Let δ_s be the (random) cost of debt from $s-1$ to s, D_{s-1} the corresponding amount of external financing. These quantities are connected by the following recurrence relation:

$$D_s = D_{s-1}(1 + \delta_s) - \alpha_s \quad s \geq 1$$

where α_s is the instalment paid at time s.

Suppose that the debts are non-random, *i.e.*, that the randomness on δ_s is absorbed by α_s.

Define also α_0 as $-D_0$ and note that that D_N must be zero.

If we denote with θ_s the leverage ratio at time s, *i.e.*

$$\theta_s = \frac{D_s}{w_s}$$

the NPV of the investment under scrutiny when there are both equity and debt financing, $\Gamma(R)$, can be written as[4]:

$$\Gamma(R) = \sum_{s=1}^{N} \mu_s(R^s)$$

where:

$$\mu_s \stackrel{d}{=} w_{s-1} \frac{[(1 - \theta_{s-1})(I_s - R_s) + \theta_{s-1}(I_s - \delta_s)]}{F(0,s)}$$

is the addendum due to the period between s-1 and s. This addendum depends on the rates of interest $R_1, R_2, \ldots, R_s$ only, which are collected in the s-dimensional vector R^s.

The splitting up of the NPV $\Gamma(R)$ into the N addenda μ_s represents an inter-period decomposition, while the division of each μ_s into the two addenda:

$$w_{s-1}(1 - \theta_{s-1}) \frac{I_s - R_s}{F(0,s)} \, ; \quad w_{s-1}\theta_{s-1} \frac{I_s - \delta_s}{F(0,s)}$$

due to equity and debt respectively, represents a natural intra-period decomposition.

When the distribution functions of f_s, δ_s, R_s are given for each s, and the IFL has been chosen, the distribution function for the addenda of $\Gamma(R)$ is well defined too. In spite of this, however, it is not very easy to explicit it analytically.

The next section suggests a choice criterium for the IFL which makes it possible to find some properties of the random variables μ_s, for instance the analytical expression of their moments.

2 THE CHOICE OF AN IFL

As stated above, the IFL of a project is generally not unique. At the same time, it is a turning point of the NPV splitting up. It follows that the choice of the IFL is extremely important.

As concerns this choice, it must be stressed that the existence of more than one IFL is not a defect of the method. Since the decomposition is intended as an evaluation method for managers,

---

[3] This can be done combining the recurrence relation for w_s and the definition of IFL.

[4] See LUCIANO (1989).

on the contrary, having several IFL means that the method is flexible enough for being useful in different contexts. This flexibility would be undesirable if the splitting up were intended as a financial report for people outside the firm, not for its managers.

2.1 A STANDARD CHOICE

A method for choosing the IFL of a financial project – standard in the sense that it is suggested by standard bond evaluation – is the following.

Consider the cash-flows f_s, and suppose that their expected value $\mathrm{E}(f_s)$ is well-defined. Choose as an IFL the exponential one with interest rate i^*, where i^* satisfies the equation:

$$\sum_{s=0}^{N} \mathrm{E}(f_s)(1+i^*)^{-s} = 0.$$

This IFL produces non-random outstanding capitals w_s, provided that $w_0 = -f_0$ is non-random and that the following recurrence relation is used:

$$w_s = w_{s-1}(1+i^*) - \mathrm{E}(f_s).$$

When substituting in the splitting up of the NPV we suggest that these outstanding capitals be used, together with the "true" IFL, that is to say together with the (random) interest rates I_s which solve:

$$w_s = w_{s-1}(1+I_s) - f_s$$

These ones can be thought of as the sum of i^* and of a random spread h_s:

$$I_s = i^* + h_s$$

By so doing, we obtain a splitting up in which the outstanding capitals are non-random, while the interest rates (I_s and in case δ_s and R_s) are uncertain. This causes each addendum μ_s to be charged with the uncertainty of the corresponding time span (uncertainty coming from f_s).

3 BAYESIAN INFORMATION PROCESSING: A SKETCH

It is well known that a financial tool "equivalent" to NPV is the Net Final Value (NFV form now on):

$$V[R] = \sum_{s=0}^{N} f_s F(s, N)$$

Obviously the NFV admits an inter-period decomposition quite analogous to the one we have seen for the NPV. Let $\phi_s(r^s)$ be the addendum due to the period from $s-1$ to s. Of course it will depend on the rates of interest $R_{s+1}, R_{s+2}, \ldots, R_N$ which are collected in the (random) $(N-s)$-vector r^s.

The analytical expression for $\phi_s(r^s)$ is the following:

$$\phi_s(r^s) = w_{s-1}[(1-\theta_{s-1})(I_s - R_s) + \theta_{s-1}(I_s - \delta_s)]F(s, N)$$

as it is easy to prove on the basis of the identity $F(0,N) \equiv F(0,s).F(s,N)$.

Suppose that at time s we evaluate an investment which began at 0 and will last till N. If $s > 0$ (at least) a part of the history of the investment is no more uncertain, so that the evaluation of its NFV, which we shall denote by $W(R, s)$, may incorporate this further knowledge. The ways in which this information can affect the evaluation of the NFV are two:

(1) substitution of some random quantities concerning the periods from 0 to s with their observed values;

(2) modification of the opinions concerning the future of the investment (from s to N)[5].

We assume, according to the standard choice of the IFL, that the outstanding capitals and the financing source proportions θ_s and $(1-\theta_s)$ are certain. In this case the substitution *sub* (1) affects the values of I_s, δ_s, R_s, while $F(s,N)$ generally remains uncertain. Point (2) allows however for a revision about its probability distribution.

Consider in fact the (random) $(3N+1)$-vector $[f,\alpha,R]$ collecting the cash-flows of the investment and of the debt and, in its last block of components, the opportunity costs of capital. Denote by $G_0(.)$ its distribution function, used at 0 to evaluate $W(R,0)$ and its N inter-period and infra-period addenda.

At s each one of the three blocks in $[f,\alpha,R]$ can be splitted into two parts (′ and ″). In the first part $[f',\alpha',R']$ are considered the already observed variables, while in the second $[f'',\alpha'',R'']$ the future ones – those concerning the periods from s to N – enter.

Through the use of Bayes's Theorem it is possible to get the "revised" distribution function $G_s(.)$ for the future part $[f'',\alpha'',R'']$ and to use it to re-evaluate the inter-period and intra-period decomposition elements from the $(s+1)$-th period onward as well as the coefficients $F(s,N)$ multiplying the addenda concerning the first s periods.

This will lead to revised assessments and to the opportunity in a control system to introduce adaptive controls via ordinary feed-back loops.

4 EXAMPLES

Given the general setting described in the previous sections, let us consider now two models, for which both the standard IFL choice and the Bayesian mechanism of information processing prove to be extremely useful.

In model A the cash-flows f_s, $s \geq 1$, are random, while both the opportunity costs R_s, $s \geq 1$, and the costs of debt δ_s, ≥ 1, are non-random.

In model B the financial project is PIPO with random final value f_N and certain costs R_s and δ_s, both for $s \geq 1$.

MODEL A

When the cash flows f_s, $s \geq 1$, are the only random components of the financial project, no matter what their distribution functions are, but provided that they have at least the first two moments, we can easily determine the first two moments of μ_s.

First of all we compute the expected value of the spreads h_s – as defined in section 2.1. above – through the recurrence relation for w_s:

$$\mathrm{E}(h_s) = [w_s - w_{s-1}(1+i^*) + \mathrm{E}(f_s)]/w_{s-1}$$

Then, noting that this expected value is always zero, and having defined $m_s(R^s) = \mathrm{E}(\mu_s(R^s))$, we obtain the following expected NPV decomposition:

$$m_s(R^s) = w_{s-1}[(1-\theta_{s-1})(i^* - R_s) + \theta_{s-1}(i^* - \delta_s)]/F(0,s),$$

where the opportunity compound amount factor is non-random: $F(0,s)$.

[5]For a systematic use of Bayesian reasoning in this kind of problems see, for instance, ZAMBRUNO (1983), PECCATI (1983), SCARSINI (1985).

Analogously, having calculated c_{rs}, the covariance between the spreads h_s and h_r, and having defined m and M, respectively as $\min(r,s)$ and $\max(r,s)$, we get the following expression for the covariance between the addenda μ_r and μ_s:

$$\operatorname{cov}[\mu_r(R^r), \mu_s(R^s)] = c_{rs} \frac{w_{r-1} w_{s-1}}{F^2(0,m)F(m+1,M)}$$

MODEL B

As it is well known, a PIPO financial project entails:

(i) an initial non-random outflow C, so that $f_0 = -C$;

(ii) no cash-flow on the way, *i.e.* $f_s = 0$, $s = 1, 2, \ldots, N-1$;

(iii) a final inflow which, no matter what IFL has been chosen, can be described by:

$$f_N = C \prod_{s=1}^{N} (1 + I_s)$$

In particular, if we denote with $X(N)$ the (random) value of the project at maturity, and if we maintain the notation C for its initial (non-random) value, the standard IFL choice gives rise to:

$$i^* = \left\{ \frac{\mathrm{E}[X(N)]}{C} \right\}^{1/N} - 1$$

to which the non-random outstanding capitals:

$$w_s = C(1 + i^*)^s$$

correspond.

If both the opportunity and debt costs of this investment are non-random, we can use the formulas of model A. Since now all of the cash-flows f_s on the way are null, we get:

(i) h_s null with probability one, $s = 1, \ldots, N-1$;

(ii) μ_s non-random when $s = 1, \ldots, N-1$:

$$m_s(R^s) = C(1+i^*)^{s-1}[(1-\theta_{s-1})(i^* - R_s) + \theta_{s-1}(i^* - \delta_s)]/F(0,s)$$

The only random component of the NPV is the last one, μ_N, whose first two moments are given by:

$$m_N(R^N) = C(1+i^*)^{N-1}[(1-\theta_{N-1})(i^* - R_N) + \theta_{N-1}(i^* - \delta_N)]/F(0,N)$$

and

$$\operatorname{var}(\mu_N(R^N)) = \operatorname{var}(f_N)/F^2(0,N)$$

Obviously, the exact form of these expressions depends on the probability distribution of $X(N)$.

Suppose for instance that the dynamics of $X(N)$ is decribed by a linear stochastic differential equation:

$$\mathrm{d}X(t) = \left[K(t)X(t) + k(t)]\mathrm{d}t + \sum_{i=1}^{j} [C_i(t)X(t) + c_i(t)] \right] \mathrm{d}w_i(t)$$

where $\mathrm{d}w_i(t)$ are independent white noises, K, k, C_i, c_i are scalar functions, measurable and bounded on $[0, N]$.

As usual, let C be the initial non-random amount invested in the asset X.

As it is well known, if $C_i(t)$ is not null for every i and t, we have:

$$X(N) = \psi(N)\left\{C + \int_0^N \psi^{-1}(t)\left[k(t) - \sum_{i=1}^{j} C_i(t)c_i(t)\right]\mathrm{d}t + \right.$$
$$\left. + \sum_{i=1}^{j} \int_0^N \psi^{-1}(t)c_i(t)\mathrm{d}w_i(t)\right\}$$

with:

$$\psi(s) = \exp\left\{\int_0^s \left[K(t) - \sum_i C_i^2(t)/2\right]\mathrm{d}t + \sum_i \int_0^s C_i(t)\mathrm{d}w_i(t)\right\}$$

As a consequence the standard choice for the IFL corresponds to:

$$i^* = \left\{e^{\int_0^N K(u)\mathrm{d}u} \cdot \left[1 + \int_0^N e^{-\int_0^t K(u)\mathrm{d}u} k(t)/C\mathrm{d}t\right]\right\}^{1/N} - 1$$

with outstanding capitals

$$w_s = C\left\{e^{\int_0^N K(u)\mathrm{d}u} \cdot \left[1 + \int_0^t e^{-\int_0^t K(u)\mathrm{d}u} k(t)/C\mathrm{d}t\right]\right\}^{s/N}$$

The corresponding expected values of μ_N are not difficult to determine.
In the geometric Brownian motion case for instance:

$$\mathrm{d}X(t) = \mu X(t)\mathrm{d}t + \sigma X(t)\mathrm{d}w(t)$$

we have:

$$i^* = \exp(\mu) - 1; \quad w_s = C\exp(\mu s)$$

and also:

$$m_s(R^s) = Ce^{\mu(s-1)} + \frac{(1-\theta_{s-1})(e^\mu - 1 - R_s) + \theta_{s-1}(e^\mu - 1 - \delta_s)}{F(0,s)}$$

5 SUMMARY AND EXTENSIONS

This paper provides an intra-period, inter-period decomposition of the NPV of random financial project, with some insights on its integration with the Bayesian inference approach. The paper studies both general financial projects and PIPO investments. In addition, it provides some elementary examples.

The splitting up suggested in the paper is thought of as a tool for decision-making. As a consequence, first of all it should be enriched with optimization techniques. A comparison with the optimal choices under certainty could be done referring to PECCATI (1989).

Obviously, Bayesian information processing deserves further analysis too.

REFERENCES

LUCIANO, E. (1989): 'A new perspective on Dynamic Portfolio Policies', *Rivista di Matematica per le Scienze Economiche e Sociali*, **12**, Fasc. 1, pp. 91-106.

LUCIANO, E. – PECCATI, L. (1990): 'VAN e risultati di periodo in condizioni d'incertezza', in AA.VV. *Scritti in omaggio a Luciano Daboni*, LINT, Trieste.

PECCATI, L., 'Multiperiod analysis of a levered portfolio', *Rivista di Matematica per le Scienze Economiche e Sociali*, **12**, Fasc. 1, pp. 157-166.

PECCATI, L. (1983), 'Sull'uso del procedimento inferenziale Bayesiano in un classico problema di matematica finanziaria', *Quaderni dell'Istituto di Matematica Finanziaria dell'Università di Parma*, Serie II, n. 13.

SCARSINI, M. (1985): 'Sull'accumulo di un capitale in condizioni di incertezza', *Rivista di Matematica per le Scienze Economiche e Sociali*, **8**, Fasc. 2, pp. 153-163.

ZAMBRUNO, G. M. (1982): 'La valutazione dinamica della forza di interesse', *Atti del VI Convegno AMASES*, Marina di Campo, Isola d'Elba.

DYNAMIC PORTFOLIO MANAGEMENT WITH A DISCRETE-TIME STOCHASTIC MAXIMUM PRINCIPLE *

Elio Canestrelli and Carla Nardelli
Department of Applied Mathematics and Computer Science
University of Venice
Dorsoduro 3825/E
Venice - Italy

1. INTRODUCTION

The purpose of this paper is to present the optimality conditions obtained by the maximum principle in its constrained discrete-time stochastic version and to discuss the results ensuing from their application to the dynamic portfolio management problem.

In the literature concerning this kind of problems, the dynamic programming method has been preferred and used for their solution. Referring to this method, Bertsekas [2] discusses an optimal control problem for a discrete dynamic system over a finite horizon, where the portfolio is formed by n risk-return securities, and by a riskless security. Here, the same problem is tackled using the maximum principle, first considering portfolios made up only by risk securities and then introducing also a riskless security.

Many works regarding the stochastic version of the maximum principle can be found in the literature: it is worth-while to refer to Florentine [10], Sworder [25] and Kushner [15], [16], in which the necessary conditions highly resemble the ones developed by Pontryagin for the deterministic problem.

In particular in [15], [16], Kushner developed necessary conditions for optimality, in which the costate system giving the Lagrange stochastic multiplier coincides with the one of the deterministic problem; moreover the (deterministic) hamiltonian is substituted by its

---

* Research financially supported by C.N.R. (Italian National Council of Researches) contrib. n. 89.05098 CT10.

expected value conditional on the σ-algebra induced by the observable process.

More generally, Ahmed [1] considers a system controlled by the following continuous Itô stochastic differential equation:

$$dx(t) = f(t,x(t),u(t))\ dt + g(t,x(t))\ dw.$$

After proving the theorem concerning the optimality conditions of the couple (x^*,u^*), he discusses the particular case in which the diffusion matrix g is null. Then he shows that under such hypothesis the theorem reduces to the maximum principle with fixed final time and free final conditions, provided that the system starts from a fixed state x_0 with probability one and the state variables are unconstrained.

The discrete-time stochastic case, with unconstrained state and control variables, was discussed by Kushner and Schweppe [17]. They resume the maximum principle necessary conditions, which derivation is analogous to the one presented by Chang [9] and by Katz [14] for the deterministic case.

As far as the deterministic case is concerned in 1966, both Halkin [12] and Holtzman [13] gave a mathematical proof of a discrete version of the maximum principle for systems described by non-linear difference equations. The stochastic version of this result is simple and easy to obtain, following the procedure given by Kushner. He states the fundamental axioms essentially concerning σ - algebras and probability distribution properties, as well as the measurability characteristic of the control spaces, and then he derives the stochastic maximum principle. His argument is strictly based on Cannon, Cullum and Pollak [6]. In 1970, the latter authors proved the equivalence of a discrete-time optimal control problem with a mathematical programming maximum problem. On the same line, in 1977, Ortega and Leake gave a new version of such principle for the discrete case, in which constraints involving both the state and the control variables were included [22].

In the following, in order to obtain a discrete-time stochastic version with constraints on state and control variables, we use the analytical formulation of the problem developed by Canestrelli, which is conveniently modified to take into account what has been demonstrated in [15] and [17] (see [4] for the general case and [3] for the linear case). Moreover, this last version is used to solve the problem of the dynamic portfolio management.

2. FORMULATION OF THE PROBLEM AND NECESSARY CONDITIONS

Let us consider the following optimization problem:

$$\text{MIN} \sum_{k=0}^{N-1} E_k\{ L_k[\underline{x}(k),\underline{u}(k)] \} + E_N\{L_N[\underline{x}(N)]\} \tag{2.1}$$

$$\underline{x}(k+1) = \underline{x}(k) + f(\underline{x}(k),\underline{u}(k),k) \tag{2.2}$$

$$\underline{x}(0) = \underline{x}_0 \tag{2.3}$$

$$\underline{u}(k) \in U(k) \tag{2.4}$$

$$g(\underline{x}(k),\underline{u}(k),k) = 0 \tag{2.5}$$

$\forall k = 0,1,\ldots,N-1$

where $\underline{x}(k)$ is an m-dimensional random variable taking on the certain value $\underline{x}_k \in \mathbb{R}^m$ at time k and representing the state vector; $\underline{u}(k) \in \mathbb{R}^n$ is the control vector; $E_k\{L_k[\underline{x}(k),\underline{u}(k),k]\}$, the expected value of L_k, is a function with continuous derivatives with respect to $\underline{x}(k)$ and $\underline{u}(k)$ in $\mathbb{R}^m\times \mathbb{R}^n$; $f(\underline{x}(k),\underline{u}(k),k)$ is a function with continuous derivatives with respect to $\underline{x}(k)$ and $\underline{u}(k)$ in $\mathbb{R}^m\times \mathbb{R}^n$; $U(k) \subseteq \mathbb{R}^n$ is a set with interior points; the set $X(k)=\{(\underline{x},\underline{u}) \mid \underline{x} \in \mathbb{R}^m, \underline{u} \in \mathbb{R}^n, g(\underline{x},\underline{u},k)=0\}$ is convex; $g(\underline{x}(k),\underline{u}(k),k) = 0$ is the set of r constraints.

If we denote with $\underline{x}^*(k)$, $\underline{u}^*(k)$ an optimal solution of the problem **(2.1),...,(2.5)**, for k=0,...,N-1, at such a point the gradients of the constraints (2.5) are linearly independent; the m+1-dimensional vector $[E_k\{L_k(\underline{x},\underline{u})\},f(\underline{x},\underline{u})']$ is directionally convex in $X(k)$ with respect to $\underline{x}$. Namely, $\underline{x} \in \mathbb{R}$, $\underline{u}'$ and $\underline{u}''$ being fixed so that $(\underline{x},\underline{u}'),(\underline{x},\underline{u}'') \in X(k)$, there must exist for each $\alpha \in [0,1]$ an $\underline{u}(\alpha)$ such that $(\underline{x},\underline{u}(\alpha)) \in X(k)$ and, with probability one, the following relations must hold

$$\alpha\, E\{L_k(\underline{x},\underline{u}')\} + (1-\alpha)\, E\{L_k(\underline{x},\underline{u}'')\} \geq E\{L_k(\underline{x},\underline{u}(\alpha))\}$$

$$\alpha\, f(\underline{x},\underline{u}',k) + (1-\alpha)\, f(\underline{x},\underline{u}'',k) = f(\underline{x},\underline{u}(\alpha),k).$$

After introducing the N+1 costate vectors $\underline{y}(k) \in \mathbb{R}^m$, (k=0,...,N), representing the dual vectors of the $\underline{x}(k)$, and the N Kuhn-Tucker multipliers $\underline{\mu}(k) \in \mathbb{R}^r$ (k=0,...,N-1), we define the following (hamiltonian) function:

$$H(\underline{x}(k),\underline{u}(k),\underline{y}(k+1),\underline{\mu}(k),k) = \{ L_k(\underline{x}(k),\underline{u}(k)) -$$
$$- \underline{y}(k+1)\, f(\underline{x}(k),\underline{u}(k),k) - \underline{\mu}(k)'\, \underline{g}(\underline{x}(k),\underline{u}(k),k) \} \tag{2.6}$$

Following what has been exposed in the deterministic case in [4], one has to minimize the expected value of **(2.6)** with respect to $\underline{u}(k)$ and at the same time a maximize it with respect to $\underline{\mu}(k)$.

In particular, if the problem is linear in the state and in the control variables, the constraints (2.2)...(2.5) become:

$$\underline{x}(k+1) = \underline{x}(k) + A(k)\,\underline{x}(k) + B(k)\,\underline{u}(k) + \underline{p}(k) \tag{2.7}$$

$$G(k)\,\underline{x}(k) + F(k)\,\underline{u}(k) + \underline{q}(k) = \underline{0} \qquad \forall\ k=0,..,N-1 \tag{2.8}$$

where: $\underline{p}(k) \in \mathbb{R}^m$; $\underline{q}(k) \in \mathbb{R}^r$; $A(k) \in \mathbb{R}^{m\times m}$; $B(k) \in \mathbb{R}^{m\times n}$; $G(k) \in \mathbb{R}^{r\times m}$; $F(k) \in \mathbb{R}^{r\times n}$.

The hamiltonian function (2.6) becomes:

$$H(\underline{x}(k),\underline{u}(k),\underline{y}(k+1),\underline{\mu}(k),k) = L_k(\underline{x}(k),\underline{u}(k)) - \underline{y}(k+1)'\,[A(k)\,\underline{x}(k) + B(k)\,\underline{u}(k) + \underline{p}(k)] - \underline{\mu}(k)'\,[G(k)\,\underline{x}(k) + F(k)\,\underline{u}(k) + \underline{q}(k)]. \tag{2.9}$$

In order to find the saddle points $(\underline{x}(k)^*,\underline{\mu}(k)^*)$ of the Hamiltonian, we have to investigate the solutions of the following four sub-problems, which constitute necessary, but not sufficient conditions:

$$\begin{cases} \min\limits_{\underline{u}(k)}\ E_k\{L_k(\underline{x}(k),\underline{u}(k)) - \underline{y}(k+1)'B(k)\underline{u}(k)\} \\ G(k) + F(k)\,\underline{u}(k) + \underline{q}(k) = 0 \end{cases}$$

$$\begin{cases} \underline{x}(k+1) = \underline{x}(k) + A(k)\underline{x}(k) + B(k)\underline{u}(k) + \underline{p}(k) \\ \underline{x}(0) = \underline{x}_0 \end{cases}$$

$$\begin{cases} \max\limits_{\underline{\mu}(k)}\ \{ -\underline{\mu}(k)'\,[G(k)\,\underline{x}(k) + \underline{q}(k)] \} \\ \underline{\mu}(k)'\,F(k) = \dfrac{\partial\, E_k\{L_k(\underline{x}(k),\underline{u}(k)) - \underline{y}(k+1)'\,B(k)\,\underline{u}(k)\}}{\partial\, \underline{u}(k)} \end{cases}$$

$$\begin{cases} \underline{y}(k) = \underline{y}(k+1) + A(k)\,\underline{y}(k+1) - \dfrac{\partial\, L_k(\underline{x}(k),\underline{u}(k))}{\partial\, \underline{x}_k} + G(k)\,\underline{\mu}(k) \\ \underline{y}(N) = -\dfrac{\partial\, L_N(\underline{x}(N))}{\partial\, \underline{x}_N} \end{cases}$$

3. DYNAMIC PORTFOLIO MANAGEMENT

Now we shall expose the special problems of constrained dynamic optimization which are related to the portfolio selection and management in a finite time interval [0,N] (for a thorough definition of the problem see [2], [21], [23]).

We follow the Markowitz' decisional criterion [18],[19], trying to develop the dynamic aspect, which is not present in the mean-variance analysis. Although the Markowitz contribution have been criticized frequently and modified [27], [26], [24], [7], [8], [11], we hold that it is still valid, both for its applicability and its comparative simplicity.

Therefore, let us formulate our problem of linear control of a discrete dynamic system on a finite horizon N. It consists in determining an admissible control rule $\{u_0,\ldots,u_{N-1}\} \subseteq U$ minimizing the cost function (functional objective)

$$E\ \{\ L_N(x_N)\ +\sum_{0}^{N-1} L_k(x_k,u_k)\ \}$$

where L_i, $i= 0,..,N$, are functions dependent on the state variables and on the first N-1 control variables.

Furthermore, we assume that the investor is risk-averse and that his objective is to minimize the final variance (risk) of his investment.

Once fixed a future date N, the time interval [0,N] is partitioned into N equal periods and the investor modifies the expected "weights" of his portfolio at the end of each of them, until the final selling.

He makes use of the so-called rebalancing strategy, in which his portfolio is periodically reconsidered so that the weights of the securities, chosen from the beginning of each period, are modified.

According to the initial proposal in [28] and subsequently in [2] and [20], returns are supposed to be serially uncorrelated.

We have to solve the following optimization problem without constraints $\underline{u}(k)\geq\underline{0}$ on control variables, where the dynamic equation is linear in state and control variables:

$$\text{MIN}\quad \text{Var}[x(N)] = E\ \{(x(N)\ -\ \bar{x}_N)^2\}$$

$$x(k+1) = x(k) + \underline{u}(k)'\ [\ \underline{R}(k)\ -\ \underline{1}\ ]$$

$$x(0) = x_0$$

where: x(k) is the random variable representing the risk capital in the period [k-1,k] and taking on the certain value x_k at time k (state variable); $\bar{x}_N$ is the final capital expected value, that is a parameter a priori fixed by the investor; $\underline{u}(k) \in \mathbb{R}^n$ is a vector the n components of which represent the amounts invested in the n risk securities during the k-th period (decision or control variable); $u_{n+1}(k) \in \mathbb{R}$ is the capital amount invested in the riskless security (additional decision variable); $\underline{R}(k)$ is an n-dimensional vector, the components of which are n random variables representing the risk returns of the n risk securities in the k-th period; $R_{n+1}(k)$ is the return of the riskless security in the k-th period.

Let us note that the variance of the final capital x(N) can be expressed as a quadratic function of the decision variables $\underline{u}(N-1)$ relative to the period [N-1,N]. In fact, during that time interval the available wealth at the decisional instant N-1 is the certain value $x_{N-1} \in \mathbb{R}$ which must be subdivided among the n investments present on the market. Therefore the optimal decision $\underline{u}^*(N-1)$ results to be a vector of $\mathbb{R}^n$ with components depending on x_{N-1}. Such a value has been got by the random variable x(N-1) in the periods preceding the instant N-1, because it is dependent on the probability distributions of returns in the period [N-2,N-1].

Then, using the variance-covariance matrices of the asset returns, we obtain an objective function expressed through the control variables only, as follows

$$[x(N)-\bar{x}_N]^2 = [x(N)-\bar{x}_N][x(N)-\bar{x}_N] = \underline{u}'(N-1)\; M_{N-1}\underline{u}(N-1) \tag{3.1}$$

if the variables $\underline{u}(N-1)$ satisfy the two constraints:

$$\begin{aligned} &\underline{u}(N-1)'\; \underline{R}(N-1) = x(N) \\ &\underline{u}(N-1)'\; \underline{r}(N-1) = \bar{x}_N \end{aligned} \tag{3.2}$$

where: $\underline{r}(k) = E\{\underline{R}(k)\} \in \mathbb{R}^n$ is the vector of the n expected values of the random variables $R_i(k)$ in the k-th period; $r_{n+1}(k) = E\{\, R_{n+1}(k)\} = R_{n+1}(k) \in \mathbb{R}$ is the certain value of the return of the (n+1)-th security and it will be denoted by ρ_k; M_k is the matrix in which the element in (i,j) represents the random variable

$[R_i(k)-r_i(k)]\;[R_j(k)-r_j(k)]$.

Therefore, considering the expected values of **(3.1)** with respect to the probability distributions of the last period returns and imposing constraints analogous to the preceding **(3.2)** for all the control variables, the problem becomes:

$$\begin{aligned} &\underset{\underline{u}_k}{\text{MIN}}\;\; \underline{u}'(N-1)\; V_{N-1}\; \underline{u}(N-1) \\ &\underline{u}'(k)\; \underline{1} = x_k \\ &\underline{u}'(k)\; \underline{r}(k) = \xi_{k+1} \qquad \forall\; k=0,1,\dots,N-1 \\ &x(0) = x_0 \end{aligned} \tag{3.3}$$

where $\xi_k \in \mathbb{R}$, k=0,...,N-1, is a parameter dependent on $\bar{x}_N=\xi_N$; V_k is the matrix such that $E\{\, M_k\} = V_k$, namely it represent the variance and covariance of the returns.

The first constraint (the same budget constraint as in the static case), means that the whole capital, available at the beginning of the k-th period, and only it, is used for the investment in the same period. Even if the capital x(k) is expressed by a random variable dependent on the previous period returns, its value, at time k, is supposed to be completely known (it is denoted with x_k).

On the other hand, the second constraint represents the expected value of the portfolio return, fixed on a parametrical level ξ_{k+1}.

Finally, the last equation shows that at the initial time k=0 the decision maker knows his capital x_0 with certainty.

4. SOLUTION OF THE PROBLEM

4.1 The case without any riskless security

Let us apply the formulation presented in section 2 to the problem (3.3). We have to solve N optimization problems with respect to the control variables $\underline{u}(k)$ and N problems with respect to the dual variables $\underline{\mu}(k)$. We must also determine the N state variables x(k) by means of the finite difference equations with fixed initial condition, and N costate variables y(k) by means of the dual finite difference equations with known final condition.

In the case in which both the functions $L_k(x(k),\underline{u}(k))$ for every $k = 0,1,\ldots,N-2$, and the final function $L_N(x(N))$, are constantly equal to zero, whereas $L_{N-1}(x(N-1),\underline{u}(N-1)) = \underline{u}(N-1)' \, M_{N-1} \, \underline{u}(N-1)$, the four blocks presented in section 2 become:

$$\begin{cases} \underset{\underline{u}(k)}{\text{MIN}} \quad E_k\{ L_k(x(k),\underline{u}(k)) - y(k+1)\, \underline{R}(k)'\, \underline{u}(k) \} \\ \underline{u}(k)'\, \underline{1} = x_k \\ \underline{u}(k)'\, \underline{r}(k) = \xi_{k+1} \end{cases} \tag{4.1}$$

$$\begin{cases} x(k+1) = \underline{R}(k)'\, \underline{u}(k) \\ x(0) = x_0 \end{cases} \tag{4.2}$$

$$\begin{cases} \underset{\underline{\mu}(k)}{\text{MAX}} \quad [x_k,\ \xi_{k+1}]\, \underline{\mu}(k) \\ [\underline{1},\underline{r}(k)]\, \underline{\mu}(k) = \dfrac{\partial\, E_k\{L_k(x(k),\underline{u}(k)) - y(k+1)\, \underline{R}(k)'\underline{u}(k)\}}{\partial\, \underline{u}(k)} \end{cases} \tag{4.3}$$

$$\begin{cases} y(k) = -\mu_1(k) \\ y(N) = 0 \end{cases} \qquad \forall\, k = 0,\dots,N-1 \tag{4.4}$$

Let us proceed to the solution of these problems, beginning from the terminal interval, since in that period the objective function at the minimum point does not depend on y, being y(N)=0, and in general we shall obtain for the j-th period [5]:

$$\underline{u}^*(j) = \frac{(aV^{-1}\underline{r}-bV^{-1}\underline{1})_j\ \xi_{j+1} + (cV^{-1}\underline{1}-bV^{-1}\underline{r})_j\ x_j}{a_j\, c_j - b_j^2} \tag{4.5}$$

$$\mu_1^*(j) = 2\,\frac{c_j\, x_j - b_j\, \xi_{j+1}}{a_j\, c_j - b_j^2}\ \frac{2\, c_{j+1}}{a_{j+1} c_{j+1} - b_{j+1}^2} \cdots \frac{2\, c_{N-1}}{a_{N-1} c_{N-1} - b_{N-1}^2} \tag{4.6}$$

$$\mu_2^*(j) = 2\,\frac{a_j\, \xi_{j+1} - b_j\, x_j}{a_j\, c_j - b_j^2}\ \frac{2\, c_{j+1}}{a_{j+1} c_{j+1} - b_{j+1}^2} \cdots \frac{2\, c_{N-1}}{a_{N-1} c_{N-1} - b_{N-1}^2} \tag{4.7}$$

$$y^*(j) = -\mu_1^*(j) \tag{4.8}$$

$$\xi(N-j) = \frac{b_{N-j}}{c_{N-j}}\ \frac{b_{N-j+1}}{c_{N-j+1}} \cdots \frac{b_{N-1}}{c_{N-1}}\ \bar{x}_N\ . \tag{4.9}$$

where:

$$a_j = \underline{1}'\, V_j^{-1}\, \underline{1}\ ;\quad b_j = \underline{1}'\, V_j^{-1}\, \underline{r}_j\ ;\quad c_j = \underline{r}_j'\, V_j^{-1}\, \underline{r}_j\ .$$

We recall that it is possible to determine uniquely the optimal decision variables sequence under the assumption that all the matrices V_j are not singular and that all the vectors $\underline{r}_j$ are not constant.

A sequence of optimal control rules is determined identical to the one found by the dynamic programming method (see Bertsekas [2], Mossin [20], whereas for the static case see Szegö [27]). In the same time a sequence of optimal multipliers $\underline{\mu}^*(j)$ is determined. Two other sequences {x(N),...,x(1)} and {y(N-1),..,y(0)} are evaluated, the former of which allows to evaluate, with probability one, all the random variables x(j) having a known initial condition, whereas the latter all the costates y(j) having a known final condition.

We note that the optimal solution **(4.5)** coincides exactly with the one found in the static case in the period [j-1,j] (see [27]) and it represent what Markowitz defines as critical line in parametrical form, when the parameter ξ_{j+1} varies in the set of real numbers and it is connected at $\bar{x}_N$ by the equality **(4.9)** (see following section 4.2)

4.2 The case with a riskless security

By applying the maximum principle, with the suitable modifications of dimensions, to the case in which a riskless security is present on the market, we obtain the following necessary conditions (which also become sufficient under the assumptions on the variance-covariance matrices):

$$\begin{cases} \underset{\underline{\tilde{u}}(k)}{\text{MIN}} \; E_k\{ L_k(x(k),\underline{\tilde{u}}(k))-y(k+1)\underline{\tilde{R}}(k)'\underline{\tilde{u}}(k)\} \\ \underline{\tilde{u}}(k)'\underline{\tilde{I}} = x_k \\ \underline{\tilde{u}}(k)'\underline{\tilde{r}}(k) = \xi_{k+1} \end{cases}$$

$$\begin{cases} x(k+1) = \underline{\tilde{R}}(k)' \; \underline{\tilde{u}}(k) \\ x(0) = x_0 \end{cases}$$

$$\begin{cases} \underset{\underline{\mu}(k)}{\text{MAX}} \; [x_k, \; \xi_{k+1}] \; \underline{\mu}(k) \\ [\underline{\tilde{I}}, \; \underline{\tilde{r}}(k)] \; \underline{\mu}(k) = \dfrac{\partial \; E_k\{L_k(x(k),\underline{\tilde{u}}(k))-y(k+1) \; \underline{\tilde{R}}(k)'\underline{\tilde{u}}(k)\}}{\partial \; \underline{\tilde{u}}(k)} \end{cases}$$

$$\begin{cases} y(k) = -\mu_1(k) \\ y(N) = 0 \end{cases} \qquad \forall \; k = 0,\ldots,N-1$$

Such conditions lead to a sequence of optimal control vectors which is the same as the one found following the dynamic programming method:

$$\underline{u}^*(x_j,j) = \frac{(V^{-1}\underline{r}-\rho V^{-1}\underline{1})_j \; \xi_{j+1} + \rho(\rho \; V^{-1}\underline{1}-\rho V^{-1}\underline{r})_j \; x_j}{a_j \; \rho_j^2 \; - 2 \; b_j \; \rho_j \; + c_j} \tag{4.10}$$

with respect to the amounts to be invested in risky securities, while for what concerns the riskless security one has

$$u^*_{n+1}(x_j,j) = \frac{(a_j \; \rho_j - b_j) \; \xi_{j+1} + (c_j - b_j \; \rho_j) \; x_j}{a_j \; \rho_j^2 - 2 \; b_j \; \rho_j \; + \; c_j} \tag{4.11}$$

The parameters ξ_{j+1} result to be related with the following equality

$$\xi_{j+1} = \frac{1}{\rho_{j+1}} \; \cdots \; \frac{1}{\rho_{N-1}} \; \bar{x}_N \tag{4.12}$$

4.3 Some remarks

A consideration to be made on the relation **(4.12)** concerns the expected value of the capital in the j-th period. It happens as if the investor, having attained the objective ξ_{j+1}, should consider to reinvest all the capital, realized until that moment, only in the riskless security during all the successive periods.

Such an investment policy is called partially myopic, to distinguish it from the so-called myopic policy, in which the investor behaves as if the examined period were the last one and he ignored to have the opportunity for successively reinvesting his capital.

The characterization of those policies depends on a property of the utility function (see [20], [2]). The same consideration can be made also with respect to the relation **(4.9)** in the case of non-existence of a riskless security. After solving the problem to determine the optimal amounts in the j-th period, the so built portfolio **(4.5)** can be considered as a unique security to be added to the n securities already existing. Such a "security" has a known return (and riskless, by construction) just equal to the fixed value ξ_{j+1}.

This way, the investor who has to decide at time j-1 how to invest his initial capital x_{j-1} in the n risk securities to achieve the objective ξ_j, has to fix this latter so as to reach the objective ξ_{j+1}. In order to achieve that, he may envisage to invest all his capital x_j in this new security that, being riskless, surely allows him to preserve his objective ξ_{j+1} unaltered. For what said above, we can readily note that the role played by the riskless security of the previous case is now played by the "portfolio security", whose rate of return is: $\rho_j = c(j) / b(j)$.

Recalling how the coefficients b_j and c_j have been defined, we have

$$\rho_j = \frac{\underline{r}'(j) \;\; V_j^{-1} \, \underline{r}(j)}{\underline{r}'(j) \;\; V_j^{-1} \, \underline{1}} \qquad \textbf{(4.13)}$$

that is, ρ_j results to be a weighted mean of the expected returns (where the weights are given by the expected returns of n risk securities). Then we may conclude that

$$\xi_j = \frac{b(j)}{c(j)} \, \xi_{j+1} \qquad \forall \; j = 1,\dots,N-1 \; . \qquad \textbf{(4.14)}$$

A last important remark concerns a difference between the static case and the dynamic one. In the first one, it is proved [26] that the problem of the portfolio, though it is multiobjective, can be reduced easily to a problem of optimization with respect to the control variables $\underline{u}$ only.

This way, a perfect equivalence of behaviour, (and so of optimal solutions) is created between the maximization of the expected return, at a parity of risk, and the minimization of the variance, at a parity of mathematical expectation of return.

That does not hold in the dynamic case, where the problem is the optimization with respect to both state and control variables in each of the N sub-periods. As a matter of fact, if we consider the expected value of the optimal objective function in the period j,

$$E_j\left(\frac{a(j)\ \xi_{j+1}^2 - 2\ b(j)\ \xi_{j+1}\ x_j + c(j)\ x_j^2}{a(j)\ c(j) - b(j)^2}\right) =$$

$$= \frac{c(j)}{a(j)\ c(j) - b(j)^2}\ \underline{u}(j-1)\ V_{j-1}\ \underline{u}(j-1) +$$

$$+ \frac{a(j)\ \xi_{j+1}^2 - 2\ b(j)\ \xi_{j+1}\ x_j + c(j)\ x_j^2}{a(j)\ c(j) - b(j)^2},$$

it can be shown [21] that it is minimized both by the control vector in **(4.5)**, with respect to the first addendum and by the state variables **(4.9)**, with respect to the second one.

4.4 An exemple

We consider N=2 years, n=2 risk securities, x_0= 1000 unit of the initial capital, $\bar{x}_2$= 1190 unit of the final capital expected value; in the first and second period let the two variance-covariance matrix be

$$V_0 = \begin{bmatrix} 0.04 & 0.03 \\ 0.03 & 0.05 \end{bmatrix} \qquad V_1 = \begin{bmatrix} 0.04 & 0.02 \\ 0.02 & 0.03 \end{bmatrix}$$

and let the two vectors of risk returns be

$\underline{r}(0)$=[1.08 , 1.12] $\quad\underline{r}(1)$=[1.10 , 1.09].

In the second period, from **(4.5)**,...,**(4.9)** we obtain a(1)=37.5, b(1)=41, c(1)=44.83, $a(1)c(1)-b(1)^2$=0.125, and the optimal solution $\underline{u}^*(1)$= [119000-109 x_1, 110 x_1-119000].

Then the expected value of the capital at the end of the first period is $\xi_1 = \bar{x}_1 = b(1)/c(1)\ \bar{x}_2$= 1088.33 so that, in the first period, by the same formulas, we obtain a(0)=27.2727, b(0)=29.8181, c(0)=32.6545, $a(0)c(0)-b(0)^2$= =1.4546 and the optimal solution $\underline{u}^*(0)$= =[791.75, 208.25].

One can conclude that the optimal decision in the first period is to invest 791.75 in the first security (with rate of expected return 0.08 and variance 0.04, both less than the ones of the second security) and to invest 208.25 in the second security (with rate of expected return 0.12 and variance 0.05).

In the last period, the optimal decision $\underline{u}^*(1)$ depends on the capital x_1 available at the beginning of the second year.

REFERENCES

[1] N.U.Ahmed, *Optimal Control of Stochastic Sistems* in *Probabilistic Analysis and related topics*, Bharucha-Reids (eds.), Academic Press, 1979.

[2] D.P.Bertsekas, *Dynamic programming and stochastic control*, Academic Press, 1976.

[3] E.Canestrelli, *Soluzione numerica di problemi di controllo ottimo nel discreto a vincoli lineari*, Atti del IX Convegno A.M.A.S.E.S. 1985.

[4] E.Canestrelli, *Sulla ricerca di soluzioni ottimali per una classe di problemi di controllo ottimo nel discreto*, Atti del IV Convegno A.M.A.S.E.S. 1981.

[5] E.Canestrelli, C.Nardelli, *Sulla gestione dinamica del portafoglio*, Atti del XIII Convegno AMASES, Verona 1989, Pitagora Editore, Bologna, 1990.

[6] M.D.Canon, C.D.Cullum, E.Polak, *Theory of Optimal Control and Mathemathical Programming*, McGraw-Hill, New York, 1970.

[7] E.Castagnoli, *La selezione del portafoglio*, Università Bocconi, Milano, 1988.

[8] E.Castagnoli, *Sull'uso di valore medio e varianza nei problemi di scelta*, Istituto di Matematica Finanziaria di Torino, serie III, n.16, 1979.

[9] S.L.Chang, *Dynamic Programming and Pontryagin's maximum principle*, Proceedings of the Dynamic Programming Workshop 1961, Joint Automatic Control Conference,169-189, AIEE Publication, New York.

[10] J.J.Florentine, *Optimal Control of continuous time Markow stochastic systems*, Journal of Electr. Control, vol. 10 (1961), pp. 473-88.

[11] P.Gigante, *Analisi media-varianza in teoria del portafoglio e della riassicurazione proporzionale*, Tesi di Dottorato in matematica applicata ai problemi economici, Universitá di Trieste, 1987.

[12] H.Halkin, *A maximun principle of the Pontryagin type for systems described by nonlinear difference equations*, SIAM Journal Control, vol.4 (1966), pp. 90-111.

[13] J.M.Holtzman, *On the maximun principle for nonlinear discrete time systems*, IEEE Trans. Automatic Control, vol. 4 (1966), pp.528-47.

[14] S.Katz, *A discrete version of Pontryagin's maximum principle*, Journal of Electronic and Control, vol. 11, 1962, pp. 179-184.

[15] H.J.Kushner, *Necessary conditions for discrete parameter stochastic optimization problems*, Proc. 6th Berkeley Symp. Math., Statist. Probability.

[16] H.J.Kushner, *On the stochastic maximum principle; fixed time of control*, J. Math. Anal. Appl., vol.11, (1965), pp.78-92.

[17] H.J.Kushner, F.C.Schweppe, *A Maximum Principle for Stochastic Control Systems*, Journal of Mathematical Analysis and Applications, vol. 8, pp. 287-302, 1964.

[18] H.Markowitz, *Portfolio Selection: efficient diversification of investments*, Wiley, New York, 1959.

[19] H.Markowitz, *Portfolio Selection*, Journal of Finance, (1952).

[20] J.Mossin, *Optimal multiperiod portfolio policies*, J. of Business, 41 (1968), pp.215-229.

[21] C.Nardelli, *Selezione e gestione dinamica di un portafoglio di azioni e opzioni finanziarie*, Tesi di Laurea in Matematica, Universitá di Padova, 1989.

[22] J.A.Ortega, R.S.Leake, *Discrete Maximum Principle with state constrained control*, SIAM Journal on Control and Optimization, vol. 15, n. 6, (1977).

[23] K.V.Smith, *Portfolio Management*, Holt, Rinehart and Winston (eds.), (1971).

[24] U.M.Sulpasso, *La selezione del portafoglio*, ETAS Libri, Milano, 1974.

[25] D.D.Sworder, *On the Stochastic Maximum Principle*, Journal Math. Anal. Appl., 24 (1968), pp. 627-640.

[26] G.P.Szëgo, *Sulla selezione ottima del portafoglio*, CEDAM, Padova, 1970.

[27] G.P.Szëgo, *Portfolio Theory with Application to Bank Asset Management*, Academic Press, 1980.

[28] J.Tobin, *The Theory of Portfolio Selection*, in F. H. Hahn, F. P. R. Brechling, *The Theory of Interest Rates*, Mc Millan, New York, 1966.

FACTOR IMMUNIZATION

G.H.M.J.Kremer
dept. of Finance
Erasmus University Rotterdam
Burg. Oudlaan 50
3062 PA Rotterdam
The Netherlands

1 Introduction

Immunization is becoming increasingly popular. The idea of adjusting a portfolio of assets in order to reflect the structure of the liabilities of an investor is very appealing to most institutional investors. But hardly any attention is given to the underlying ideas. The principles of bond pricing and the factors that determine the bond prices are central in immunization. One very popular model, Macaulay's duration matching, uses a very simple structure. The assumptions made in this model are usually banned to footnotes. The model is defended by pointing out the results, compared to more sophisticated models. Good results are defined by deviation from the expected, or desired results. But, as will be pointed out, it is very hard to define the desired result.

In this paper attention will be given to the links between the different immunization models. The factor time will be given more than the usual attention, for it is this factor that is mostly the source of trouble in analyzing the results of an immunization strategy. An alternative model will be presented, not to make it operational but to point out the wealth of choices one is confronted with using immunization models.

2 Discount function and term structure of interest rates

In bond pricing the traditional view is that the price of a bond in a world without transaction costs and taxes is determined by the term structure of interest rates. For each cash flow generated by the bond the corresponding interest rate is taken to calculate the present value of the cash flow. Then the present values of the cash flows are summed in order to calculate the bond price. In calculating the present value of a cash flow the spot interest rate is used to derive the discount for the relevant period. Mind however, this is no explanation of the price of the bond, it is simply the price of the bond given the prices of the other bonds in the market. Using the term structure of interest rates is simply applying the measure of the market to a given bond. In the same vein, modelling the volatility of the term structure means modelling the volatility of bond prices with the exclusion of arbitrage-possibilities in the market.

A derived market is created when the term structure is measured, the market for discounts. A discount can be interpreted as the prive of a zero-coupon bond with a face value of 1 and a time to maturity equal to the period associated with the discount. There is a direct link between the term structure of interest rates and the discounts for the periods defined by the market cash flows. In modelling bond prices both can be used. In this paper the term structure is not explicitly used. It is assumed that the discounts are functions of a number of factors and (sometimes implicitly) of time to cash flow. If "time" is used, it is meant as "time to cash flow". Changes in the discounts are induced by changes in the factors and the passage of time. (Passage of time is defined as the decreasing of time to cash flow and as such negative.) Because of the linear relation between bond prices and the discounts it is also assumed that the bond prices are functions of the factors (a bond is assumed to be a portfolio of zero-coupon bonds).

The problem in specifying an immunization model is centered on the specification of the discounts. This specification is what differentiates the models, but it is also the hardest part for the practitioner.

3 Immunization

Immunization is the elimination of portfolio value fluctuations due to fluctuations in the factors. The factors influence the discounts, so it seems that the risk of bond portfolio fluctuations is induced by term structure risk (the alternative representation of the discounts). This explains the definition of immunization by Fisher and Weil:

> "A portfolio of investments is immunized for a holding period if its value at the end of the holding period, regardless of the course of rates during the holding period, must be at least as large as it would have been had the interest rate function be constant throughout the holding period. If the realized return on an investment in bonds is sure to be at least as large as the appropriately computed yield to the horizon, then that investment is immunized."

The effect of the passage of time is usually not meant to be eliminated, as can be concluded from the quotation. This is a potential source of trouble, not in calculating the immunized portfolio but in analyzing the immunization results. If there is no clear understanding about the price change induced by the passage of time it is impossible to calculate the immunization result (checking wether the price change is zero).

4 The model

The model to be presented can be derived in two ways. Firstly, discrete changes in the factors can be assumed. This results in discrete changes in the discounts. This approach is deterministic in nature and of course closely related to the one-period model. An investment horizon is taken and the goal of the immunization is defined on this horizon. The second approach is using stochastic processes. This makes an investment horizon in first instance superfluous. Immunization means the hedging of a portfolio as is done in option pricing. The effect that remains is the time-dependent change in the portfolio value. Only the first approach will be presented in this paper but the second approach can easily be derived using the technique presented here. In fact, without resorting to stochastic processes some simplifications are made in order to preserve clearity. These simplifications result in a model that is closely related to the stochastic processes case.

In this paper the following notation is used.

$\underline{p}$ = vector of P bond prices

$\underline{w}$ = vector of T discounts (the discount function)

C = matrix of cash flows on T moments for the P bonds

$\underline{f}$ = vector of K factors

Assume the discount for period t is a function of the factors and of time.

$$w_t = w(\underline{f},t)$$

so

$$dw_t = \sum_{j=1}^{K} \frac{\partial w_t}{\partial f_j} df_j + \frac{\partial w_t}{\partial t} dt$$

In matrix notation

$$d\underline{w} = \nabla d\underline{f} + \Gamma dt$$

with $\nabla = \left(\frac{\partial w_t}{\partial f_j} \right)_{TxK}$ and $\Gamma = \left(\frac{\partial w_t}{\partial t} \right)_{Tx1}$

These discount changes can de used to calculate the changes in the price vector. The price of a bond is given by

$$p_k = \sum_{t=1}^{T_k} CF_{kt} w_t$$

with CF_{kt} = cash flow period t for bond k

T_k = period of last cash flow

For the market this can be expressed as

$$\underline{p} = C\underline{w}$$

The price changes are given by

$$d\underline{p} = Cd\underline{w} = C\nabla d\underline{f} + C\Gamma dt$$

Now assume the investor has a portfolio of assets and liabilities. The portfolio is described by two vectors, one for the assets, $\underline{x}_A$, and one for the liabilities, $\underline{x}_L$. For the sake of clearity the liabilities are assumed to be bonds, but any other cash flow can be used. The excess cash flow is given by the vector

$$\underline{e}' = \underline{x}_A{}'C - \underline{x}_L{}'C$$

The present value of the portfolio is given by

$$V = \underline{e}'\underline{w}$$

The change of the present value of the portfolio due to the change in the factors and the passage of time is

$$\begin{aligned} dV &= [\underline{x}_A{}'C - \underline{x}_L{}'C]d\underline{w} = \\ &= [\underline{x}_A{}'C - \underline{x}_L{}'C][\nabla d\underline{f} + \Gamma dt] \\ &= \underbrace{[\underline{x}_A{}'C - \underline{x}_L{}'C]\nabla d\underline{f}}_{\text{term 1}} + \underbrace{[\underline{x}_A{}'C - \underline{x}_L{}'C]\Gamma dt}_{\text{term 2}} \end{aligned}$$

Term 1 gives the value change due to change in the factors, Term 2 gives the value change due to the passage of time. Mind, $dt<0$!

Some preliminary remarks can be made.

1) In case of cash flow matching $V = 0$. For the excess cash flow it is clear that

$$\underline{x}_A{}'C = \underline{x}_L{}'C \quad \text{so}$$

$$\underline{e} = \underline{0} \quad \Rightarrow \quad dV = 0$$

This means that in case of cash flow matching the portfolio is perfectly immunized.

2) If non-negative forward rates are assumed, the discount function is downward sloping ($w_t < w_\tau \quad \forall_{t,\tau} \ : t > \tau$)

This results in

$$\frac{\partial w_i}{\partial t} < 0 \qquad \text{for all } i$$

Now if $\underline{e} \geq \underline{0}$ (that is the excess cash flow is non-negative) then $\underline{e}'\Gamma \leq 0$. With the passage of time the portfolio will increase in present value or it will stay the same (if the excess cash flow is zero).

3) On the outset it was noted that two approaches are possible, the deterministic approach and the stochastic approach. It is clear that in using the factors and time seperately the above model is deterministic in nature. The changes in the factors are assumed to be infinitesimal small; this is not realistic (but the error made is usually small. The effect for discrete factor changes can be investigated. Given the fact that a discount is a function of the factors and of time and if weassume the discount function ios twice differentiable then a Taylor-expansion can be applied up to the second derivative. Higher terms are collected in the residual term. Then the model becomes

$$\Delta w_t = \sum_{j=1}^{K} \frac{\partial w_t}{\partial f_j} \Delta f_j + \frac{\partial w_t}{\partial t} \Delta t + ½ \sum_{i=1}^{K} \sum_{j=1}^{K} \frac{\partial^2 w_t}{\partial f_i \partial f_j} \Delta f_i \Delta f_j +$$

$$+ \sum_{i=1}^{K} \frac{\partial^2 w_t}{\partial f_i \partial t} \Delta f_i \Delta t + ½ \frac{\partial^2 w_t}{\partial t^2} \Delta t^2 + R$$

with R the residual term. The first two right hand side terms are the discrete analogons of the sensitivities to a change in the factors and a change in time respectively. The other terms express the fundamental misspecification of the result of changes in factors and time due to the use of first derivatives only. A very interesting aspect can be noted. An investor wishes to set the cross-effects of the changes in the factors to zero, for the result can have a positive or a negative effect on his portfolio. But whereas $\Delta f_i \Delta f_j$ can be positive or negative, $\Delta f_i{}^2$ is always non-negative. Maximizing the sensitivity of the portfolio for these effects will result in an increase in portfolio value. In this paper we will use dp instead of Δp, for working with the higher derivatives would only obscure the point to be made in this paper.

5 Two existing models

Two well-known duration models will be described in factor model terms, Macaulay's duration and the Fisher/Weil duration. It will be shown that these two models can be derived from the factormodel. However, it should be noted that Macaulay's duration and the Fisher/Weil duration are not proper factormodels.

The discount function is in both models related to the term structure of interest rates. Changes take place in the term structure itself.

5.1 Macaulay's duration

In Macaulay's duration it is assumed that the term structure is flat. This results in the same yield for each bond in the market. The only change in the term structure is a parallel shift. This means a yield shift that is the same for each bond.

The discount is defined as

$$w_t = (1+y)^{-t}$$

so

$$\frac{\partial w_t}{\partial y} = -t(1+y)^{-t-1} \quad \Rightarrow \quad \nabla = \frac{1}{1+y} \begin{pmatrix} -t_1 & & \emptyset \\ & \ddots & \\ \emptyset & & -t_T \end{pmatrix} \underline{w}$$

and

$$dV = [\underline{x}_A{}'C - \underline{x}_L{}'C]\nabla dy = \frac{1}{1+y} [\underline{x}_A{}'C - \underline{x}_L{}'C] \begin{pmatrix} -t_1 & & \emptyset \\ & \ddots & \\ \emptyset & & -t_T \end{pmatrix} \underline{w}dy$$

$$= \frac{1}{1+y} \left(\underline{x}_A{}'C \begin{pmatrix} -t_1 & & \emptyset \\ & \ddots & \\ \emptyset & & -t_T \end{pmatrix} \underline{w} - \underline{x}_L{}'C \begin{pmatrix} -t_1 & & \emptyset \\ & \ddots & \\ \emptyset & & -t_T \end{pmatrix} \underline{w} \right) dy$$

Macaulay's duration is defined as

$$D = -\frac{1}{p} \sum \frac{t * \text{cash flow}_t}{(1+y)^t} \quad \Rightarrow \quad \frac{dp}{dy} = -pD \frac{1}{(1+y)}$$

Now if D_A, D_L, p_A and p_L are the duration of all assets and liabilities and the price of assets and liabilities it is clear that

$$pD = (1+y)\ \underline{x}'C \begin{pmatrix} -t_1 & . & \emptyset \\ & . & \\ \emptyset & . & -t_T \end{pmatrix} \underline{w}$$

Immunizing means that the product of price and duration of the assets has to be equal to the product of price and duration of the liabilities. If the value of the portfolio is equal to zero, prices of assets and liabilities are equal and $p_A D_A = p_L D_L \Rightarrow D_A = D_L$.

The change in value of the portfolio due to the passage of time is

$$\frac{\partial w_t}{\partial t} = -\ln(1+y)\ w_t \qquad \text{Term 2 becomes}$$

$$-\ln(1+y)[\underline{x}_A{}'C - \underline{x}_L{}'C]\underline{w} =$$

$$-\ln(1+y)\ V < 0$$

$$\text{if} \quad V > 0$$

Because $dt < 0$ the value of the portfolio will increase. If $V < 0$ the value of the portfolio will decrease (become more negative). This is to be expected, for the yield curve is assumed to be flat. Ignoring the discrete nature of the change in the yield can be demonstrated by presenting the Taylor expansion :

$$\Delta p_i = \sum_{j=1}^{\infty} \frac{(\Delta y)^j}{j!} p^{(j)}(y_0)$$

The first derivative is related to duration, the second is related to convexity and so on. Practitioners are becoming aware of the possibilities offered by convexity after years of experience with duration only.

5.2 Fisher/Weil

The Fisher/Weil duration can be derived for T different factors. But this results in conditions that can be very difficult to satisfy, so these factors are assumed perfectly correlated with a multiplicative factor. This will result in a multiplicative shift in the term structure. In this paper the Fisher/Weil duration will be derived firstly by using T factors and then narrowing the model down to the multiplicative factor.

The specification of the discounts is in spotrates for the cash flow periods.

$w_t = (1+r_t)^{-t}$ with r_t the spot rate for t

Now there are T factors

$$\frac{\partial w_t}{\partial r_\tau} = 0 \quad \forall\, t \neq \tau \qquad \text{and} \qquad \frac{\partial w_t}{\partial r_t} = -t(1+r_t)^{-t-1}$$

and so
$$\nabla = \begin{pmatrix} -t_1(1+r_1)^{-1}w_1 & . & \emptyset \\ & . & \\ \emptyset & & \cdot\; -t_T(1+r_T)^{-1}w_T \end{pmatrix}$$

Term 1 becomes

$$[\underline{x}_A'C - \underline{x}_L'C]\nabla d\underline{r} =$$

$$\underline{x}_A'C\begin{pmatrix} -t_1(1+r_1)^{-1}w_1 & . & \emptyset \\ & . & \\ \emptyset & & \cdot\; -t_T(1+r_T)^{-1}w_T \end{pmatrix}d\underline{r}$$

$$-\ \underline{x}_L'C\begin{pmatrix} -t_1(1+r_1)^{-1}w_1 & . & \emptyset \\ & . & \\ \emptyset & & \cdot\; -t_T(1+r_T)^{-1}w_T \end{pmatrix}d\underline{r}$$

But to immunize against each possible change in $d\underline{r}$

$$[\underline{x}_A'C - \underline{x}_L'C] = \underline{0}$$

This is too restrictive so the following assumption is made

$$(1+r_i) = (1+r_i^*)f$$

with r_i^* fixed. Now the vector of factors is reduced to a single factor with

$$d\underline{r} = \underline{r}^* df\ , \qquad \underline{r}^* = (\ ..\ (1+r_i^*)\ ..)'$$

$[\underline{x}_A'C - \underline{x}_L'C]\underline{r}^*$ is a scalar wich is set equal to zero. This results in equalising the Fisher/Weil durations of assets and liabilities.

For the time-sensitivity an approximation can be made in order to get idea about the magnitude of the possible changes in the portfolio value due to the passage of time. For the derivation see appendix A. The effect found can be either positive or negative, dependent on the structure of cash in- and outflows and the term structure. Special care should be given while analyzing the results of immunization using Fisher/Weil durations.

6 Conclusions

In this paper a factor model is used to derive immunization conditions for portfolios of assets and liabilities. It is shown that the factor model approach encompasses the Macaulay's duration and the Fisher/Weil duration. But the model can use more than one factor, and as such it can be used for hybrid forms of cash flow/duration matching. It must be born in mind that addition of factors can severely limit the usefulness of these models for an investor that wants to be totally immunized has to immunize against each factor seperately. For each factor an additional restriction is imposed on the immunizing portfolio. The trade-of between factors and useability of the model is not an easy decision to make, factor analysis may prove useful in order to determine how many factors are relevant and should be included in the model.

It is shown that time is an important factor, not in determining the immunizing portfolio, but in analyzing the results. It must be kept in mind that the effect of time is included in the specification of the discount function.

APPENDIX A DERIVATION OF TIME SENSITIVITY FOR FISHER/WEIL

$$\frac{\partial w_t}{\partial t} = -\ln(1+r_t)w_t$$

so

$$\frac{\partial V}{\partial t} = -\,[\,\underline{x}_A'C - \underline{x}_L'C\,]\begin{pmatrix} \ln(1+r_1) & . & \emptyset \\ & . & \\ \emptyset & & \cdot\ \ln(1+r_T) \end{pmatrix}$$

If $\underline{x}_A'C - \underline{x}_L'C > \underline{0}'$ the value of the portfolio increases with the passage of time. But suppose $V = 0$.

$$[\,\underline{x}_A'C - \underline{x}_L'C\,]\underline{w} = 0 \quad => \quad \underline{E}'\underline{w} = 0$$

$$tr(\,\underline{E}'\underline{w}\,) = 0 \quad => \quad tr(\,\underline{wE}'\,) = 0$$

define : $\underline{wE}' \equiv Q \quad , \; Q = (q_{ij})_{TxT}$

$$\text{and} \quad S \equiv \begin{pmatrix} \ln(1+r_1) & . & \emptyset \\ & . & \\ \emptyset & & \cdot\ \ln(1+r_T) \end{pmatrix} = \begin{pmatrix} s_1 & . & \emptyset \\ & . & \\ \emptyset & & \cdot\ s_T \end{pmatrix}$$

$$\frac{\partial V}{\partial t} = tr(\,\underline{E}'\Gamma\,) = -\,tr(\,\underline{E}'S\underline{w}\,) = -\,tr(\,\underline{w}\,\underline{E}'S\,) = -\,tr(\,QS\,)$$

1) because $tr(\,\underline{wE}'\,) = 0 \quad => \quad \sum_{i=1}^{T} q_{ii} = 0$

def. $A = \{\, i \mid q_{ii} \geq 0 \,\}$ and $B = \{\, i \mid q_{ii} < 0 \,\}$

then $\quad \sum_A q_{ii} + \sum_B q_{ii} = 0 \quad => \quad \sum_A q_{ii} = -\sum_B q_{ii}$

$$2) \qquad QS = \begin{pmatrix} q_{11} & . & . & q_{1T} \\ . & & & . \\ q_{T1} & . & . & q_{TT} \end{pmatrix}\begin{pmatrix} s_1 & . & \emptyset \\ & . & \\ \emptyset & & \cdot\ s_T \end{pmatrix} =$$

$$\begin{pmatrix} q_{11}\,s_1 & . & q_{1n}\,s_T \\ . & & . \\ q_{n1}\,s_1 & . & q_{nn}\,s_T \end{pmatrix}$$

and so $tr(QS) = \sum_{i=1}^{T} q_{ii}\,s_i = \sum_A q_{ii}\,s_i + \sum_B q_{ii}\,s_i$

define $s_{max} = \max_i(s_i)$ and $s_{min} = \min_i(s_i)$

then $$-(s_{min} - s_{max}) \sum_A q_{ii} s_i \leq \frac{\partial V}{\partial t} \leq (s_{min} - s_{max}) \sum_A q_{ii} s_i$$

and because $$(s_{min} - s_{max}) = \ln\left(\frac{1 + r_{min}}{1 + r_{max}}\right)$$

Literature

Cox,J.C., J.E. Ingersoll Jr. en S.A. Ross (1985), A Theory of the Term Structure of Interest Rates, Econometrica 53, p385-407

Fisher, L. and R. Weil, 'Coping with the Risk of Interest Rate Fluctuations: Returns to Bondholders from Naive and Optimal Strategies', Journal of Business, oct. 1971, pag. 408-431

Nelson en Schaefer (1983), The Dynamics of the Term Structure and Alternative Immunization Strategies, In G.O. Bierwag, G.G. Kaufman and A. Toevs (eds.), Innovations in Bond Portfolio Management: Duration Analysis and Immunization. Greenwich: JAI Press, p61-102

APPLICABILITY AND FUTURE OF MODERN PORTFOLIO THEORY

Jan van der Meulen
Erasmus University Rotterdam, Department of Finance
P.O. Box 1738, NL-3000 DR The Netherlands

Education and research regarding the CAPM has not become simpler since the publication of Roll's critique. In this paper the 'classical' equilibrium investment methodology is criticised in the light of empirical results regarding changing market conditions. A new approach seems necessary and suggestions are made in order to retain the applicability of modern portfolio theory[1] as a valuable field of research.

INTRODUCTION

In this paper we investigate the possibilities of applying performance measurement, i.e. measuring the risk-return 'quality' of an investment portfolio, within the context of *modern portfolio theory*[2]. The analysis hereafter emphasizes the fact that financial markets are characterized by structural instability regarding prices, risks and returns as opposed to a situation of a partial equilibrium which characterizes the CAPM. The paper contains two paragraphs. The first paragraph discusses the CAPM in its orthodox equilibrium setting while in the second paragraph the most important results of the author's empirical research into the degree of market instability are presented.

1. THE CAPM

The roots of the Capital Asset Pricing Model (CAPM) can be traced back tò William Sharpe's 1964 article. In its essential form the model can be described by the following equilibrium relation also known as the Security Market Line (SML),

$$E(r_i) = r_f + \beta_i \, [E(r_m) - r_f] \qquad (1)$$

where

$E(r_i)$, $E(r_m)$ = expected one-period return for asset i and the market portfolio m respectively,

r_f = risk free rate assuming limitless lending and borrowing,

β_i = measure of systematic risk, calculated as the covariance of the return for i and m, divided by m's variance of returns, also called the *beta* of asset i.

---

1 In the dissertation which forms the basis of this paper we discuss this subject more extensively (cp.Van der Meulen, 1989).

2 Even in Markowitz (1987) an exact definition of modern portfolio theory is missing. In this paper both the *normative* portfolio theory (à la Markowitz), and the *positive* Capital Asset Pricing Model (CAPM) will both be regarded as members of the Modern Portfolio Theory family.

This model and its empirical counterpart, the so-called *market model*[3] or MM, has dominated scientific investment research for the last 25 years. From as early as 1965 a continuous flow of empirical papers has been published, wherein the hypothesis regarding the existence of the CAPM has not been rejected. Of course this does not mean that the linear CAPM relation was found to exist in reality, it merely means that there was insufficient ground for the rejection of its existence. In the next paragraph we hope to illustrate that such grounds for rejection do in fact exist especially if one is interested in the practical applicability of the model.

1.1 CAPM critique

The CAPM can be considered a *static equilibrium model.* Within this type of models there is hardly any room for market imperfections like transaction costs, liquid assets, or a margin between the lending and the borrowing rate. Despite this methodological truism a number of imperfections have been dealt with in literature, of which probably the most well-known is Black's 'zero-beta CAPM' (Black, 1972). Almost exclusively these 'extended CAPMs' deal with one imperfection only thus excluding the existing reality of interdependent imperfections from our models.
Fama (1970, p. 400) suggested that empirical research on the SML implies a *joint hypothesis*, because testing the linear SML presupposes market price efficiency [as well as the existence of a mean variance (MV) efficient market portfolio]. In his critique of the empirical test procedures developed in literature Roll (1977, 1980) expands on the consequences of this joint hypothesis. Roll states that because it is impossible to track down the MV efficient market portfolio, the exact position of the SML is indeterminate. From Roll (1980) we cite "The error in position (*JM*: of the SML) is the result of two problems, neither of which is related to statistical variation: First, a non-optimized market index has been employed, an index whose expected return .. differs from that .. of the optimized index appropriate for the true risk-free asset. Second, the true risk-free asset has a return .. that is different from the return on the nominal "riskless" asset ... The net result is *measured* performance .. that differs from *true* performance .." (p. 6, italics by *JM*). In short, the model cannot be tested.
Apart from Roll's critique the *static equilibrium character* of the model can be seen as an obstacle for practical implementation of the CAPM. To illustrate this I consider it useful to look carefully at the 'generally accepted' specification of the 'CAPM-world'.
The set of assumptions that underlie the CAPM shows us the rather dull world of a static (i.e. unchanging) equilibrium. In this world there is a *given* set of financial assets and a *given* set of preferences for all market participants. Uncertainty -a 'common' phenomenon in the real world- is non-existent. Instead financial models transform the concept of certainty to its distributional equivalent, thereby introducing the concept of *risk*. At the beginning of the period for which the model is designed market participants assume so-called 'buy-and-hold' positions. These positions are not liquidated until the end of the predefined period which for that reason is defined as the 'buy-and-hold-period'. Trading during the buy-and-hold-period is thus undefined. As a matter of fact all 'trade' takes place during the model's moment of 'creation' and all (ex-post) performance is measured immediately after the model's 'judgement' day, i.e. at the end of the

3 The market model tries not, unlike the CAPM, to establish the linear relation between return and beta. It presupposes its existence without underlying theory. The market model states that a linear relation exists between the return on a financial asset and the return on a representative market index. The market model has the following form: $r_{i,t} = a_i + b_i r_{It} + e_{it}$ where, $r_{i,t}$, r_{It} = return for period t on asset i and index I respectively, a_i, b_i = 'alpha' and 'beta', i.e. the regression parameters and e_{it} = residual term.

buy-and-hold-period. Also the existence of prices other than those that were known at the beginning of the buy-and-hold period is undefined. Based upon all relevant and known information the ex-ante risk of a change in value of the investor's portfolio is calculated resulting in a given set of prices for all investors at the beginning of the period. Not until the portfolio's liquidation moment, i.e. immediately after the end of the buy-and-hold-period, the drawing from the relevant probability distribution becomes public knowledge and instantaneously an ex-post set of prices is set for which every investor is assumed to liquidate his portfolio. So, in the CAPM-world the existence of dynamics and or changing circumstances[4] is denied. Performance measurement, if at all possible given Roll's critique, has no meaning in such a world. Every investor earns an ex post return which is in accordance with his ex ante expectations. Therefore there is no 'bad' or 'good' performance. Strictly speaking there is only *performance*. guaranteed as it were by the static nature of the CAPM world.
Of course the static character of the model implies that empirical CAPM research is only useful if for a long period (in principle for an infinite period length), the so-called *parameter stability*[5] applies. Insufficient research or even no research at all into the nature of this type of stability, for example in the case of empirical performance measurement research, can lead to insufficiently qualified conclusions. In the case of measuring the performance of investment portfolios in a portfolio theoretic framework one should therefore take into account whether market conditions concerning risk and return have remained stable from the moment the investment decision was made until the moment of portfolio evaluation. In a changing market environment during the period of evaluation not doing so will result in a technically correct but in terms of operational value utterly useless performance measurement. Consequently there is a danger that in case of market instability performance measurement is constantly outdated or 'out of sample'.

2. INSTABILITY

The importance of instability research as such, as well as the importance that researchers attached to the subject up till the recent past has been evaluated by Hayes en Upton (1986) in the following way: "....one of the most troublesome difficulties has been the possibility of instability in the parameters (*JM*: of the CAPM and the MM)...The early indications of parameter nonstationarity were..`sealed and largely ignored`. Due to a lack of suitable techniques, the standard approach has been to assume parameter stationarity over the interval under consideration. More recently, however, a number of studies have demonstrated the existence of instability and brought the topic into focus once again" (p. 307). Kryzanowski en To (1987) state the following on the subject of instability: "Both E and V (*JM*: Expected returns and Variance of returns) must be stationary in order to validate the use of time series returns in empirically testing (or applying) asset pricing models such as the CAPM. In other words, the intertemporal stationarity of one or the other (i.e. E or V) is not sufficient for such testing, since *both* E and V must be intertemporally stationary" (p. 123). From this quote it is clear that instability is redefined from *parameter* stability to *distributional* stability, because the combination of E and V can be identified as the first two moments of a probability distribution of asset returns, i.e. the mean vector (E) and the covariance matrix (V) of asset returns. We will define these first two distributional moments as the *risk structure of financial assets*. For empirical purposes we will follow the generally accepted custom to calculate these risk structures for a specific time interval from historic market data of asset categories.

4 In the words of Joan Robinson (1953-54) "It is impossible for a system to get into a position of equilibrium for the very nature of equilibrium is that the system is already in it and has been in it for a certain length of past time" (p. 84).

5 Parameter stability as used in the literature is mainly understood in terms of the stability of 'alpha' and 'beta', the parameters of the market model or of comparable parameters.

As a consequence of Roll's critique we will hereafter take our leave from the CAPM world, including its assumed existence of a unique market portfolio and its equilibrium price per unit of systematic risk. Instead we will analyse instability in the original Markowitz portfolio theoretic tradition, thereby defining portfolio return in the usual way and the standard deviation of asset returns as the measure of (total) portfolio risk . Since 1980 Jobson and Korkie published a number of articles on portfolio performance in a Markowitz context. In Jobson en Korkie (1980) the authors developed a probability distribution for the composition of MV efficient portfolios. Such a distribution is of particular importance for the measurement of portfolio performance, because it provides insight in the sensitivity of MV efficient portfolios *in terms of risk and return* as well as *in terms of portfolio composition.* Seen in this way performance measurement receives its proper distributional quality. Portfolio ranking evolves from a ranking based on unidimensional measures to a ranking based on distributional or *statistical equivalence.*
In the same context Kandel en Stambaugh (1987) proceed from the Markowitz framework and analyse the consequences of Roll's critique with respect to (positive) modern portfolio theory. Kandel and Stambaugh look for the class of portfolios (i.e. *'quasi'-market portfolios*) that bear a specific relation (i.e. a level of correlation of 0.9) with a given market index which serves as a benchmark. This class of portfolios is then analysed on its quality in terms of MV efficiency. To accomplish this the authors position all portfolios that have the same correlation with the benchmark portfolio in a mean-variance framework.
Two illustrations from Kandel and Stambaugh (1987) are reproduced in Figure 1. In Figures 1a and 1b '•' is defined as the *benchmark*-portfolio. The shaded region is the region where portfolios (x) are positioned that have a level of correlation with • (the benchmark) of $\rho(\bullet,x) = 0.999$ and $\rho(\bullet,x) = 0.45$ respectively (N.B. the solid lines represent the opportunity set including the efficient frontier).

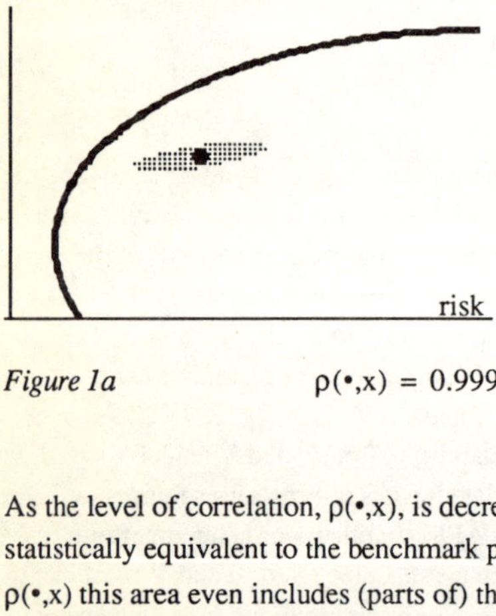

Figure 1a $\rho(\bullet,x) = 0.999$

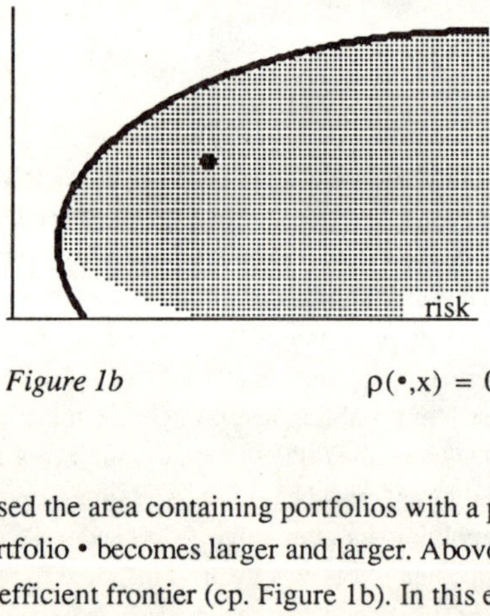

Figure 1b $\rho(\bullet,x) = 0.45$

As the level of correlation, $\rho(\bullet,x)$, is decreased the area containing portfolios with a performance that is statistically equivalent to the benchmark portfolio • becomes larger and larger. Above a certain level of $\rho(\bullet,x)$ this area even includes (parts of) the efficient frontier (cp. Figure 1b). In this example a multitude of portfolios which differ in terms of risk and return as well as in terms of portfolio composition receive an equivalent (in fact equal) performance judgement.

Three important insights can be deduced from our short selection of relevant literature:
1) *MV-efficiency*. Where instability prevails it should be (and in fact is) possible to discriminate between portfolios with statistically equivalent returns and statistically different total risk. The same should apply for portfolios with statistically equivalent risk and statistically different returns. The traditional criterion of MV efficiency is herewith broadened to a criterion in terms of *statistical equivalence*.

efficiency is herewith broadened to a criterion in terms of *statistical equivalence.*
2) *Iso-performance.* A portfolio which is highly correlated with a benchmark portfolio should receive a performance evaluation equivalent to the evaluation of the benchmark portfolio (cp. Kandel en Stambaugh, 1987). An alternative definition of this criterion is in terms of statistical equivalence of risk structures. A portfolio that can be qualified as MV efficient, given an efficient frontier calculated from a specific risk structure R', should have the same ('iso'-) performance as a second also MV efficient benchmark portfolio which in terms of risk and return may be compared with R' but is calculated with risk structure R, given the fact that R and R' are statistically equivalent. Hereafter we will use iso-performance based on this last definition.

The investor who is confronted with the existence of capital markets instability can in general not be held responsible for this instability. His investment decisions can only be evaluated given his original , i.e. ex ante expectations. For empirical purposes these expectations as mentioned earlier are to be calculated as the risk structure that includes the most recent information. This leads us to the third important aspect concerning instability:
3) *Predictive stability.* On applying any ex post performance measurement technique one should refrain from measuring performance whenever an unexpected change in the risk structure has taken place. Concretely put, performance measurement cannot be applied whenever the period of evaluation is longer than the period for which the investor perceives *predictive stability* in terms of risk structures (cp. paragraph 2.1).

In the next paragraph the results of a recently concluded research project on instability will be presented thereby giving special attention to the three aspects mentioned above.

2.1 Empirical research on the stability of risk structures

In this paragraph the existence of (in)stability is tested, given the definition of risk structures we arrived at earlier. We define stability as the statistical equivalence of risk structures against a benchmark or reference risk structure. In short we will analyse for which values of k and j relation (2) holds,

(2) $$\text{risk structure}_{t-k} \approx \text{reference risk structure}_t \approx \text{risk structure}_{t+j}$$

In (2) the operator '≈' stands for statistical equivalence. Furthermore the indices t-k and t+j indicate the time interval for which risk structures are calculated as compared to the time interval t for the reference risk structure. In our research we used real monthly returns for 17 different asset categories, among which there are dutch and other (foreign) stocks as well as real estate, interest bearing categories and gold. The different risk structures were calculated for 121 consecutively overlapping 72-month time intervals from january 1972 up to and including december 1987[6].
As a test of stability we used a multivariate test designed by Anderson (1959) which for reasons of brevity will not be explained here. This test exists in two versions which we will define as models 1 and 2. In model 1 the complete risk structure, i.e. the first two distributional moments, is analysed whereas in model

6 Of course this procedure where overlapping risk structures are tested on their statistical equivalence implies auto correlation. On the other hand there is the advantage that this procedure creates a maximum amount of information regarding the existence of (in)stability.

2 only the second distributional moment is part of the analysis.
In Figure 2 we present our test results according to model 1. On the horizontal as well as on the vertical axis the test results for our 121 overlapping risk structures are depicted.

First we look at the diagonal, i.e. line DD. This diagonal can at best be interpreted as the position over time of the consecutive reference risk structures. At the upper left part we find the reference risk structure per january 1978 while the reference risk structure per december 1987 is found at the bottom right part.

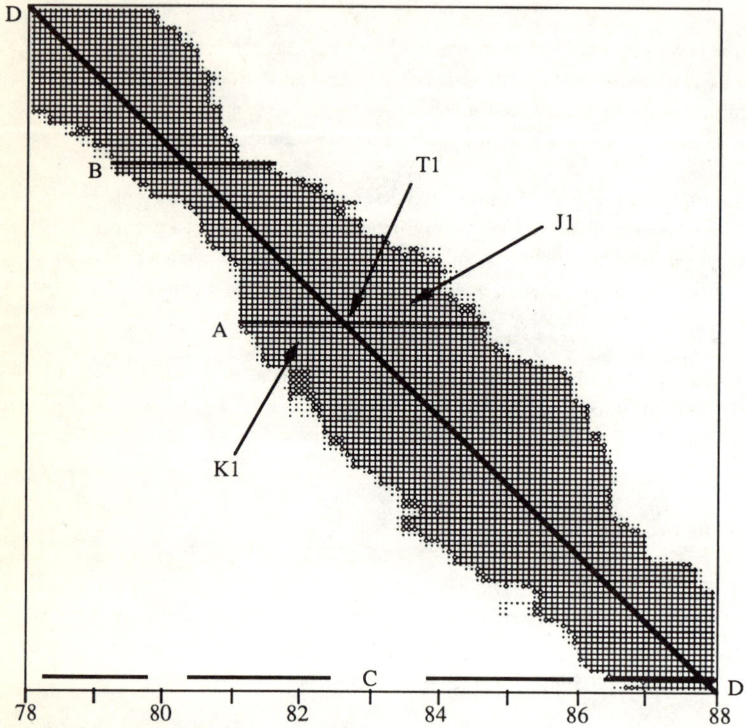

Figure 2 Significance of risk structures[7]

Subsequently we look at the horizontal line A. This line represents *all* risk structures that show statistical equivalence with the *selected* reference risk structure (i.e. with the diagonal point, in this case representing

[7] The different patterns in Figure 2 correspond to the chosen level of significance. These significance levels (a) are 5%, 1% en .1%, based upon a cumulative normal distribution, as follows:

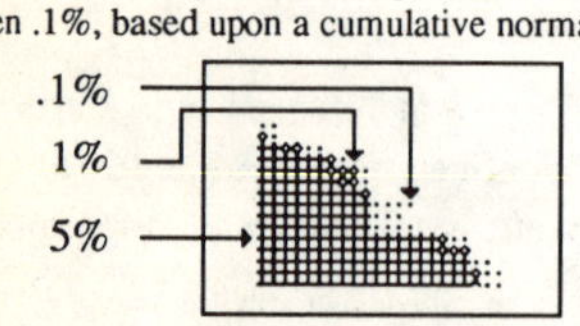

The meaning of these percentages is as follows: As the value of a decreases the 'area' of statistical equivalence is enlarged *at a cost* because at the same time the potential error (1 - a) increases.

the risk structure per august 1982). The parts of this line representing risk stuctures before and after the reference risk structure (T1) are denoted by K1 and J1 respectively. In the case of line A all risk structures from january 1981 up to and including the risk structure for september 1984 show statistical equivalence with risk structure T1. We will define this period as the *horizontal stability* of reference risk structure T1. In this case the values of k and j in (2) are equal to 17 and 25 months respectively. Evidently all risk structures before january 1980 and after november 1984 show no equivalence with risk structure T1.
From Figure 2 it is clear that the values of k and j are not equal through time. When we look at line B we see that the parts of the line before and after the selected reference risk structure are equal to 12 and 16 months respectively.

Besides horizontal stability we can also define a vertical measure of (in)stability. In the same sense as before a vertical line connects all *different* distributions in which a *specific* risk structure can be placed. The shorter this vertical line, the more unique distributional qualities are attached to the corresponding risk structures. From Figure 2 we see that an absolutely unique risk structure has not been found.
Though Figure 2 is based on test results according to model 1 of our test we also analysed our data according to model 2. We expected that this test version would show a much larger degree of stability. This expectation was mainly based on the results of comparable empirical research on parameter stability performed by others and resulted for fairly long periods in the acceptance of the stability hypothesis. Our results contradict these findings. In Table 1 our results for variable j in (2) are summarised. Given reference risk structure$_t$ variable j informs us on the length of the period after t for which equivalence with t holds. We will define this period as the *predictive stability* for reference risk structure$_t$. From Table 1 we conclude that our hypothesis regarding the differences between models 1 and 2 is not supported. The predictive stability given model 2 appears on average to be less than 10% larger as compared to the results for model 1 which certainly does not seem to be spectacular.

	model 1)	**model 2)**
minimum	10	11
maximum	32	32
average	21.32	23.04
standard deviation	5.31	5.67

Table 1 Comparison of predictive (horizontal) stability (in months) for models 1 and 2

Instability as it appears is more the rule than the exception. Risk structures are constantly changing over time. In fact we can say that capital markets are characterised by instability. From Table 1 we derive a *minimum* predictive stability of almost one year and an average predictive stability of almost two years. Given the fact that for example large institutional investors draw up a plan of action regarding their investments for the next fiscal year this result offers ample practical possibilities. After all the investment plan can be drawn up for the next fiscal year given the fact that statistically this period can be relied upon in terms of predictability. In principle asset selection policy can remain unchanged during this year, although it is of course useful to make policy adjustments based on changes in the risk structure as time progresses forwards in order to avoid the necessity of structural portfolio revision for the next fiscal year.
Assuming for the moment that we might draw conclusions from the development of horizontal stability over time, Figure 2 shows that horizontal stability seems to be developing in a general way along sometimes

more or less clearly visible or demonstrable patterns. Without proof we can illustrate this by pointing at the period in which the appreciation of the american dollar became apparent (i.e. the period from 1981 until the moment of depreciation during 1986) and in the same period at the boom of share prices. This period can be designated as a period with a relative *constant* horizontal stability and a gradually *developing* set of consecutive risk structures.

Another conclusion is that Figure 2 only shows statistically significant equivalence for consecutive risk structures. In other words; the process of changing risk structures has *no cyclical nature*. The diagonal structure in Figure 2 can be considered the general picture and only incidentally another image appears. This conclusion is we feel very important because it implies that the *history* of a risk structure does not repeat itself[8]. Risk structures appear to develop gradually *without* cyclical patterns.

The fact that cyclical patterns cannot be traced in the development of risk structures over time means that a relatively distant history does not play any part in the actual return generating process of portfolios. This empirical conclusion is on the one hand proof against the existence of a long term random walk behavior of returns but on the other hand also proof against the existence of any economic benefit for technical or chart analysis. As is well known this 'theory' assumes that price patterns of a possibly distant past have relevance for the (future) development of actual prices.

The results of our stability tests presented in this paragraph indicate clearly that the hypothesis of long term stability of risk structures cannot be accepted. In the next paragraph we shall see how investors can try to use this phenomenon to their advantage.

2.2 Iso-performance

The problem of asset selection in an environment that is dominated by instable capital markets is surely not an easy one to solve. A bad ex post performance of a portfolio selected by an investor on sound portfolio theoretic grounds might be the result of changing market conditions (cp. our criterion of predictive stability) and is therefore not the responsibility of that investor. As we have shown the theoretical assumption of stability contrasts sharply with empirical real world findings. The condition of constantly changing risk structures might therefore result in a lack of confidence in the applicability of portfolio theory. For, changing market conditions may result in a changed or different risk structure and may lead to the selection of an MV efficient portfolio that differs from a portfolio selected before the market changes became apparent. The concept of iso performance deals with this problem in that it departs from the fact that instability on capital markets prevails. Iso performance evaluates as equivalent not one but a whole range of portfolios belonging to the same distribution of portfolios. This range of iso-MV efficient portfolios *might* contain the ex ante portfolio that was originally selected by the investor. In that case a formerly negative performance judgement is turned into a postive judgement on the basis of iso efficiency.

Iso-performance is thus defined as *equivalence* in statistical terms for MV efficient portfolios that *differ* in terms of composition. Consequently the *iso-performance area* is defined as the range of equivalent portfolios. Within this area the portfolio manager is free to vary his portfolio with no change in performance quality.

Efficient frontiers calculated from risk structures that are statistically equivalent form the basis of iso performance portfolios. These efficient frontiers offer the possibility of creating a set of equivalent but different portfolios given some specific risk (or return) level. Analysis of this set of different portfolios

8 As an illustration we have drawn a set of lines at the bottom of Figure 2 (see the lines 'C') representing a hypothetical situation where a cyclical pattern *does* exist.

provides information about the permitted degree of flexibility regarding the composition of MV efficient portfolios.

As an illustration we selected from Figure 2 seven different reference risk structures evenly spread over the test period. Based upon the results of model 1 we then created seven series of risk structures that show equivalence with our selected reference risk structures. We will call these our *iso performance groups*. From these seven series of equivalent risk structures seven series of equivalent efficient frontiers were calculated.

In Table 2 we present for three levels of risk the range of permissable portfolios for three out of the seven iso performance groups (numbers 1, 4 and 7, corresponding with iso performance groups at the beginning, in the middle and at the end of our test period).

Per iso-performance group Table 2 presents the minimum, the average and the maximum weights for MV efficient portfolios for six asset categories. Around the average portfolio composition the iso performance area for asset categories is bounded downwards by the minimum weights and upwards by the maximum weights. The *degree of flexibility* implied by this area is expressed by the *range* of possible MV efficient portfolio weights. (N.B. In terms of performance measurement this means that only those portfolios that can be found beneath the lower bound of the iso performance area will show a negative performance as compared to the market.)

category:	**Guilders**			**Forex**			**Gold**			**Bonds**			**Real Estate**			**Stocks**		
iso-group:	1	4	7	1	4	7	1	4	7	1	4	7	1	4	7	1	4	7
low risk:																		
Minimum	3	-	-	42	5	11	-	32	62	8	-	4	-	-	-	-	2	2
Average	13	2	-	51	16	17	2	68	71	27	1	7	-	2	-	7	11	5
Maximum	47	4	-	60	30	26	7	88	75	39	7	10	1	20	-	20	41	7
Range	44	4	-	18	25	15	7	56	13	31	7	6	1	20	-	20	39	5
middle high risk:																		
Minimum	8	-	-	7	1	-	2	-	18	14	-	18	-	-	-	-	2	13
Average	17	1	-	27	39	13	27	26	31	27	6	34	-	6	-	2	22	22
Maximum	34	5	-	61	67	37	61	81	44	37	19	49	1	50	-	6	44	35
Range	26	5	-	54	66	37	59	81	26	23	19	31	1	50	-	6	42	22
high risk:																		
Minimum	6	-	-	4	-	-	23	-	-	8	-	11	-	-	-	-	-	66
Average	13	-	-	18	46	4	47	10	-	21	1	21	-	7	-	1	36	75
Maximum	25	6	-	34	100	12	79	87	1	28	8	34	1	100	-	4	81	90
Range	19	6	-	30	100	12	56	87	1	20	8	23	1	100	-	4	81	24

Table 2 Iso-performance portfolio weights in percentages

A closer inspection of Table 2 firstly reveals that the degree of flexibility (the range of MV efficient weights) is positively related to the total risk level. Secondly the results in Table 2 show clearly that portfolio composition varies with the development of risk structures over time. In general the results show that in low risk portfolios foreign exchange investments are gradually replaced over time by gold. In portfolios with middle high risk levels we can add to these changes the position of stocks, which position is even more important when considering high risk portfolios.

The selection of results presented here incidentally shows an extreme (as well as a changing) degree of flexibility and also a strongly changing average portfolio composition over time. These strong changes are understandable given the fact that between each of the three selected iso performance groups a period of five years has elapsed during which period obviously a lot of changes in the environment can occur. Closer analysis of the development of iso performance groups over time reveals that an investor who wishes to escape from the harmful consequences of the phenomenon of instability has ample possibilities to do so. Especially when applying a strategy of regular portfolio revision he can relatively easy as well as continuously realise market related performance without the necessity of investing heavily in know how. Our final conclusion may therefore be that accepting the existence of the phenomenon of market instability does not imply the lack of applicability of portfolio theory. By acknowledging the distributional character of MV efficient portfolios the normative Markowitz model enters a new dimension in which there is room for an investor's subjective considerations regarding the composition of MV efficient portfolios.

Literature

Anderson, T.W., An Introduction to Multivariate Analysis, Wiley, New York, 1959.

Black, F., Capital Market Equilibrium with Restricted Borrowing, Journal of Business, 45, 1972, pp. 444-455.

Fama, E.F., Efficient Capital Markets: A Review of Theory and Empirical Work, Journal of Finance, 25, 1970, pp. 383-417.

Hayes, P.A. and D.E. Upton, A Shifting Regimes Approach to the Stationarity of the Market Model Parameters of Individual Securities, Journal of Financial and Quantitative Analysis, 21, 1986, pp. 307-321.

Jobson, J.D. and B. Korkie, Estimation for Markowitz Efficient Portfolios, Journal of the American Statistical Association, 75, 1980, pp. 544-552.

Kandel, S. and R.F. Stambaugh, On Correlations and Inferences About Mean-Variance Efficiency, Journal of Financial Economics, 18, 1987, pp. 61-90.

Kryzanowski, L. and M.C. To, The E-V Stationarity of Secure Returns, Some Empirical Evidence, Journal of Banking and Finance, 11, 1987, pp. 117-135.

Markowitz, H.M., Portfolio Selection, Journal of Finance, 7, 1952, pp. 77-91.

Markowitz, H.M., Mean-Variance Analysis in Portfolio Choice and Capital Markets, Basil Blackwell Inc., New York, NY, USA, 1987.

Meulen, J. Van der, The Missing Link, in: Hallerbach, W.G., F.C.J. Bemelman, J.W.R. Schuit and P.J. Van Mierlo (eds.), 'Finance and Investments, 10, State of the Art 1987', Rotterdam, 1987, pp. 73-94.

Meulen, J. Van der, Portefeuilleperformance en Instabiliteit, Dissertation EUR, Rotterdam, 1989.

Robinson, J., The Production Function and the Theory of Capital, Review of Economic Studies, 21, 1953-54, pp. 81-106.

Roll, R., A Critique of the Asset Pricing Theory's Tests, Part I: On Past and Potential Testability of the Theory, Journal of Financial Economics 4, 1977, pp. 129-176.

Roll, R., Performance Evaluation and Benchmark Errors (I), Journal of Portfolio Management, Summer 1980, pp. 5-12.

Sharpe, W.F., Capital Asset Prices: A Theory of Market Equilibrium Under Conditions Of Risk, Journal of Finance, Vol. XIX, 1964, pp. 425-442.

PRESENT VALUE MODELS AND MULTI-FACTOR RISK ANALYSIS

Winfried G. Hallerbach*)
Dept. of Finance, Erasmus University Rotterdam
POB 1738, NL-3000 DR Rotterdam, The Netherlands

1. INTRODUCTION

The adequate representation of risk is a predominant problem in investment analysis. In this light, multi-factor models form a field of increasing theoretical challenge and practical application. Conceptually, a multi-factor model of security returns entails the simplified representation of the changing economic environment in which these returns are generated, by reducing the dimensionality of the interrelationships therein. Implicitely, some function $g_t(.)$ is introduced that links a set of N security returns in period t to a set of, say, K common underlying stochastic state variables or factors (with $K < N$). In general, with a suitable linearization of $g_t(.)$ and an assumed intertemporal stationarity, this return generating process (RGP) can be expressed as:

$$r_{i,t} = a_i + \sum_{j\in K} b_{ij}\delta_{j,t} + e_{i,t} \qquad , i\in N \tag{1}$$

where $r_{i,t}$ = the total return of security i in period t;
a_i = a constant intercept term;
$\delta_{j,t}$ = the value of factor j in period t;
b_{ij} = the sensitivity of security i for factor j;
$e_{i,t}$ = the non-factor related return of security i in period t.

It can be assumed that the residual return component $e_{i,t}$ is truly idiosyncratic, implying that the residual returns are mutually independent as well as independent of the common factors, and implying that the set of common factors is exhaustive. With these assumptions, the dimensionality of the economic environment is reduced from ½N(N-1) relationships between the security returns to *(i)* the ½K(K-1) relationships between the factors and *(ii)* the N·K relations between the securities and the factors, as measured by the response coefficients $\{b_{ij}\}_{i,j}$. Note that we do not

----
*) I would like to thank Willem-Max van den Bergh for stimulating discussions, and Richard Flavell, Jaap Spronk and an anonymous referee for critical remarks. Of course, all remaining errors are mine.

assume that the factors are mutually independent.

In a fairly (informationally) efficient market, the expectations with respect to the K factors will be incorporated in the security prices. Only unanticipated factor movements will result in price changes as these movements will cause investors to revise their expectations. In that case, the intercept term a_i will represent the expected return on security i.

The sensitivity coefficients $(b_{ij})_{i,j}$ represent the link between the fluctuations of the factors and the security returns. In a large, well-diversified portfolio, the fluctuations of the idiosyncratic return components tend to compensate each other (as a result of the law of large numbers, the variance of the idiosyncratic portfolio return approaches zero in this naive diversification process). Consequently, the fluctuations of the portfolio's return can be attributed to the fluctuations of the factors in a degree that depends on the size of the sensitivity coefficients. In this view, the factor sensitivities are the relevant measures for investment risk.

In comparison with the familiar Mean-Variance-framework, multi-factor models yield a multi-farious risk concept with an intuitive appeal. If the identity of the return generating factors would be known, the factor sensitivities of various investment categories from the opportunity set could be estimated from eq. (1). These factor sensitivities in turn can be inputs for the process of risk management. The main advantage is that the risk characteristics of various investment categories can be analyzed in a unified framework.

Unfortunately, the identity and number of the relevant factors is not known. Chen, Roll & Ross [1986] have *ex cathedra* specified some set of factor candidates and tested whether these can be considered as pervasive economic factors by performing regression analysis. However, a general theoretical framework in which factor models can be developed and in which their properties can be examined, is absent.

In this paper, we will focus on a methodology for deriving multi-factor models of security returns. The theoretical basis is the Present Value (PV) or Discounted Cash Flow framework, indeed a classic tool in finance. In PV-models, it is assumed that the current price (present value) of a security is equal to the appropriately discounted value of all future expected cash flows accruing to the investor. The basic idea is to develop an adequate price function for securities in which state variables act as arguments. With the help of a closed form version of this price function, first a relationship between the securities' returns and changes in the state variables ($g_i(.)$) is modelled. Then, relations between these arguments and economic factors are specified. The advantage of this approach lies in our opinion in the fact that the resulting expressions of the elasticities or sensitivities for the factors can be examined, providing insight in the nature of the relations between returns and factor movements and in their expected intertemporal stationarity. In the form of 'Dividend Discount Models', PV-models are often used to derive the required or expected return on securities. Instead of then relying on other models to derive risk measures of these securities, we show how the risks, accompanying this expected return, can be identified and measured. Using the PV-framework for deriving the price function, we closely join in with the analysis in which duration and (hyper-) convexity characterictics of bonds are used to relate bond returns to changes in interest rates (cf. Fabozzi & Fabozzi [1989]).

In this paper, we limit ourselves to common stock returns. In section 2, we discuss some PV-models for stock prices and develop a simple closed-form PV-formula for mixed scenarios of dividend growth. In section 3, we provide a start to develop a multi-factor model from this price function. Section 4 summarizes the paper and contains directions for future research.

2. PRESENT VALUE MODELS FOR COMMON STOCK PRICES

For default free straight bonds, changes in the term structure of interest rates are the 'only' sources of risk. Common stocks, however, have an additional risk component, stemming from changes in the investors' expectations of the risky future dividends. Risk averse investors will require compensation for this cash flow risk. In the following, we'll use a risk adjusted discount rate (RADR), where both the risk free interest rate and the risk premium are assumed to be constant. (Under an alternative approach, certainty equivalents of the dividends are discounted against the risk free rate.)

The current (i.e. at t=0) theoretical stock price can be expressed as:

$$P_0 = \sum_{t=1}^{\infty} \frac{E(D_t)}{(1+k_t)^t} = \sum_{t=1}^{\infty} \frac{E(D_t)}{(1+k)^t} \qquad (2)$$

where $E(D_t)$ = the current expectation for the dividend at time t;
k = $r + \pi$ = the RADR;
r = the risk free interest rate, reflecting time preference;
π = the risk premium, reflecting the risk of the dividend stream.

For theoretical analyses, this PV-model must be simplified. As cash flow growth is the most outstanding feature separating bonds and common stocks, we'll concentrate on specifying growth patterns of the expected dividend stream over time.

The most simple closed-form PV-formula results if it is assumed that expected dividends grow at a constant rate g:

$$P_0 = \sum_{t=1}^{\infty} \frac{D_0(1+g)^t}{(1+k)^t} = \frac{D_0(1+g)}{k - g} = \frac{E(D_1)}{k - g} \qquad \text{for } k > g \tag{3}$$

where D_0 = the dividend received at time t=0.
While the derivation of this formula is often attributed to Williams [1938] and is even widely identified as the Gordon & Shapiro [1956]-formula, its origin may go back as early as Makeham [1869].

Depending on the magnitude (and uncertainty) of the growth rate implied by the projected dividend stream, we can say that common stock can be situated in a continuum where at one side the common stock predominantly possesses the characteristics of a straight, default risk free bond and where at the other side its characteristics of earnings growth potential dominate. The nature of interest rate risk of a bond-like stock mirrors the nature of a bond's interest rate risk; this risk can mainly be attributed to the denominator of the PV-formula. When the common stock is issued by a corporation that can be characterized as a 'growth engine', the expected growth rate and the uncertainty with respect to that growth will dominate (the numerator of the PV-formula).

These growth stocks offer a problem. If the dividend growth rate is larger than the discount rate, eq. (2) represents a diverging geometric series, yielding an infinitely large stock price. Yet we can observe stocks that have (had) a growth rate in excess of the discount rate. A solution to this 'growth paradox' (Durand [1957]) is to let decrease the expected growth rate after some time to a 'normal' level. From all the proposed, more or less mechanical or arbitrary, dividend growth models, the 3-phase growth model, developed by Molodovsky, May & Chottiner [1965], is the most appealing and widely used (see Bierman & Hass [1971] and Bierman, Downes & Hass [1972] for a further overview). The model assumes a period of above normal growth, a transition phase in which the growth rate gradually declines to the 'normal' level, and finally a steady growth state in which the normal growth rate is maintained in perpetuity. A problem with this 3-phase model is that there exists no simple closed-form expressions for the theoretical stock price for this realistic dividend growth pattern.

Ideally, we are looking for a PV-model formulation that gives enough flexibility to incorporate a realistic pattern of dividend growth rates without at the same time becoming untractable. A suchlike model must offer the possibility to incorporate investment analyst's dividend forecasts over the next, say, 3 to 5 years as well as the possibility to specify a transition phase in which the growth rates gradually decline/ incline until some 'steady state' economy-wide growth rate is reached. The restriction for a suchlike formulation would be the description of the growth rate curve by means of only a limited number of parameters, so that a simple closed-form expression for the PV-formula can be derived.

Below, we propose a simplified flexible growth model. In the derivation, we'll use a constant risk adjusted discount rate. We assume that the investment analyst has forecasted dividends over the next T_1 periods. From then on, it is expected that the dividend growth rate gradually declines/inclines until at time T_2 the rate of growth in the economy is reached. Dividend growth will continue from T_2 in perpetuity at that 'normal' rate g.

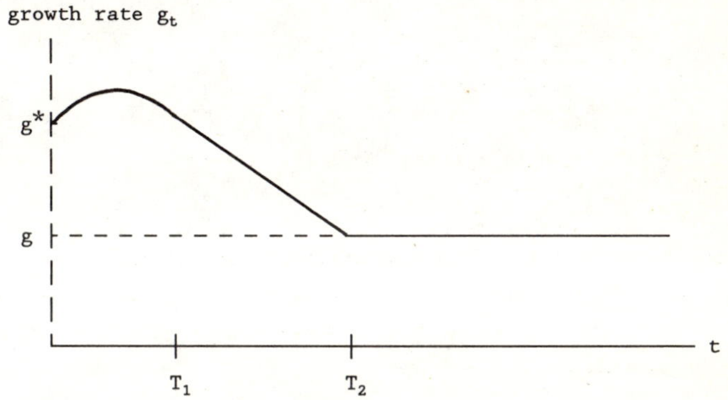

Exhibit 1: The curve of projected dividend forward growth rates g_t.
g^* = above normal growth rate; g = normal growth rate.

The forward growth rates (i.e. the growth rates per period) as depicted in Exhibit 1, are defined by

$$D_t/D_{t-1} = 1 + g_t \tag{4}$$

We assume that the specific dividend forecasts or growth rates are known for the above normal growth period $[0,T_2]$. The basic idea, now, is to use one single forward growth rate as a *spanning point* for all other growth rates during the period of above normal growth $[1,T_2]$. This reference rate can be specified exogenously, or estimated from the forward growth rates $\{g_t\}_{t=1,\dots,T1}$, implied by the dividend forecasts. Next, any abnormal growth rate g_t can be decomposed in the normal growth rate g and the effects of excess growth g^*-g. For period 1 we have:

$$D_1/D_0 = 1 + g_1 = (1 + g)\left[1 + \frac{g^*-g}{1+g} \right]^{d_1} \tag{5}$$

where d_t = the relative excess growth multiplier for period t.
Using, for example, the first growth rate as the reference rate for above normal growth ($g^* = g_1$), it follows that $d_1=1$.

In general, the total dividend growth over the first t periods ($t \le T_2$) can be expressed as:

$$D_t/D_0 = (1 + g)^t \left[1 + \frac{g^*-g}{1+g} \right]^{d_1+\ldots+d_t}$$

$$\approx (1 + g)^t + \sum_{i=1}^{t} d_i (g^*-g)(1+g)^{t-1} \tag{6}$$

where we used the first term of a binomial expansion to get rid of the exponent. As $(g^*-g)(1+g)$ will be small, we expect this to be a reasonable approximation[1]. By successive repetition of the process, the relative excess growth multipliers $\{d_t\}_{t=1,..,T2}$ can be computed.

Recapitulating, we can express the expected dividend stream as:

$t=1$: $D_1 = D_0 \left[(1+g) + d_1(g^*-g)\right]$

$t=2$: $D_2 = D_0 \left[(1+g)^2 + (d_1+d_2)(g^*-g)(1+g)\right]$

.

.

$t=T_2$: $D_{T2} = D_0 \left[(1+g)^{T_2} + (d_1+\ldots+d_{T2})(g^*-g)(1+g)^{T_2-1}\right]$

.

$t=T_2+i$: $D_{T2+i} = D_0 \; (1+g)^i \left[(1+g)^{T_2} + (d_1+\ldots+d_{T2})(g^*-g)(1+g)^{T_2-1}\right]$

.

.

---

1) The forward growth rates, as defined by eq. (4), then satisfy $D_t/D_{t-1} = (1+g_t) = (1+g)[1+(g^*-g)/(1+g)]^{d_t} \approx (1+g)[1+d_t(g^*-g)/(1+g)]$.

From this, we see that in each period $t<T_2$ an excess growth dividend component $d_t(g^*-g)(1+g)^{t-1}D_0$ is introduced, whereafter this component grows at rate g in perpetuity. From time T_2, the forward growth rate is constant and equals g.

Note that in each period an extra component is added to the dividend stream. This extra dividend is a function of the excess growth rate (g^*-g) and grows at the normal rate g. The extra dividend components can be discounted at the stock's required return k, yielding an expression for the transformed first dividend D'_1:

$$D'_1 = D_0(1+g)\left[1 + \frac{g^*-g}{1+g}\left\{d_1 + \frac{d_2}{1+k} + \frac{d_3}{(1+k)^2} + \ldots + \frac{d_{T2}}{(1+k)^{T_2-1}}\right\}\right] \qquad (7)$$

This transformed dividend stream grows in perpetuity at the normal rate g and is equivalent to the original dividend stream. As an approximation to eq. (7), we ignore the discounting of the relative excess growth multipliers over the period $[1,T_2]$. The expression between braces in eq. (7) then simplifies to:

$$\Gamma = \sum_{i=1}^{T_2} d_i \qquad (8)$$

where Γ = the unweighted sum of the relative excess growth multipliers.

The PV-formula for the stock price finally becomes:

$$P_0 = \sum_{t=1}^{\infty} \frac{D_0\,\{1 + \Gamma(g^*-g)/(1+g)\}\,(1+g)^t}{(1+k)^t}$$

$$= \frac{D_0\,\{\,(1+g) + \Gamma(g^*-g)\,\}}{k-g} \qquad \text{for } k > g \qquad (9)$$

Eq. (9) is a simple expression, but can at the same time embrace a flexible dividend growth pattern[2]. It shows that the stock price can be decomposed in the PV

---

2) Fuller & Hsia [1984] introduced a simplified PV-formula that approximates a standard three-phase discount model and that bears resemblence with our formula (9). As they do not allow for specific dividend forecasts, their 'H-model' can more or less be seen as a special case of our valuation model. However, as Fuller & Hsia do not present the derivation of their model, we cannot decide on this issue. Moreover, the variable we call Γ equals in their model the number of H periods from now through halfway the transition period in the three-phase model; in our formulation of the model, Γ would then equal H-½ (see eq. (8)).

of steady state growth opportunities and the PV of abnormal growth opportunities. As we used some approximations during the derivation, the formula will not yield exact results. More important, however, is that the formula can serve as a tool to investigate the expected price effects of changes in firm specific excess dividend growth more or less isolated from price effects due to changes in economy wide growth. In section 3, we will elaborate this point.

3. TOWARDS A MULTI-FACTOR MODEL OF COMMON STOCK RETURNS

Inspired by the bond analysis, a profound attention is paid in the literature to estimate 'equity duration', as a measure for the sensitivity of common stocks to interest rate changes. An appropriately defined equity duration is the basis for an adequate analysis and control of interest rate risk. Observing institutional investors (like pension funds) in many countries extending their bond portfolios with increasing investments in stocks, incorporating an equity duration measure into the calculation of portfolio duration would be a further step towards the effective management of their assets. After discussing interest rate sensitivity of common stocks, we derive in section 3.2 a more general theoretical multi-factor model from the PV-formula (9).

3.1 Measuring the interest rate sensitivity of common stocks

Aside from empirical approaches to estimate the interest rate sensitivity of stock returns (cf. Stone [1974], Haugen, Stroyny & Wichern [1978], Chance [1982] and Leibowitz [1986]), we have theoretical analyses that start from a PV-model of the stock price. In the majority of the work in this field, equity duration is defined as the negative of the elasticity of the theoretical stock price with respect to a change in the risk adjusted discount rate k. Starting from the constant growth model eq. (3), this elasticity can be computed as (cf. Durand [1957, p.358] and Boquist, Racette & Schlarbaum [1975, p.1363]):

$$\frac{dP_0/P_0}{dk/(1+k)} = -\frac{1+k}{k-g} = -\frac{P_0}{D_0} - 1 \qquad (10)$$

According to the latter equality (Williams & Pfeifer [1982]), the equity duration equals one plus the reciprocal of the dividend yield[3].

Haugen & Wichern [1974] consider a two-stage growth scenario, but their formulas become so complex that they can only be evaluated numerically. This stresses the importance of simple closed-form formulas for stock prices under mixed growth scenarios. Haugen & Wichern also analyze the sensitivity of the derived interest rate elasticity to changes in the model parameters r, g and the risk premium π (Casabona, Fabozzi & Francis [1984], considering the constant growth case, do this for r, g and the certainty equivalent factor). This analysis is important in the light of the expected intertemporal stationarity of the interest rate sensitivity. From eq. (10) it follows that the interest rate sensitivity is cet. par. positively related to the dividend growth rate, but changes inversely with interest rates and the risk premium.

Although interest rate changes may explain a significant portion of stock return variability (cf. Haugen [1970] and Lanstein & Sharpe [1978]), there will exist more factors that influence stock returns. Hence, the importance of a general theoretical framework in which the sensitivities of common stock returns with respect to various factors can be analyzed, will be clear.

3.2 A multi-factor model of common stock returns

In this section, we will derive a multi-factor model of common stock returns, based on a PV-model. We will extend the analysis of Casabona, Fabozzi & Francis [1984] by considering more factors than 'the' interest rate alone. Instead, we join in with the analyses of Estep, Hanson & Johnson [1983], Estep et al. [1984] and Leibowitz et al. [1989] and extend their results.

Leibowitz et al. [1989] develop a measure of the total sensitivity of stock returns to interest rate movements, that recognizes the important role of inflation: the inflation rate forms the link between changes in the discount rate and the growth rate of profits (Jahnke [1975], Joehnk & Petty [1980] and Estep, Hanson & Johnson [1983] also touch upon this issue). Insofar changes in the (nominal) interest rate are induced by changes in inflation expectations, the resulting changes in the discount rate and the growth rate can compensate each other. Apart from the multiple effect of inflation on stock returns, Estep, Hanson & Johnson [1983] and Estep et al. [1984] believe that a systematic component of return variability (risk) comes from the effect of economy-wide influences on earnings (dividend) growth expectations. They model this relationship by combining the elasticity of the stock price with respect to changes in the growth rate and the sensitivities of the growth rate with

---

[3] In case of continuous compounding, we get $(dP_0/P_0)/dk = -1/(k-g) = -P_0/E(D_1)$. The equity duration then equals the reciprocal of the expected dividend yield.

respect to these economy-wide factors.

We will develop the multi-factor model in three stages. First, the semi-elasticities of the stock price with respect to the arguments of the price function (9) are determined. Then, the relationship between the price function's arguments and a set of general state variables is modelled. Combining the results finally yields a multi-factor model.

We will assume a constant risk premium π, and an expected growth pattern of dividends that can be related to short term excess growth and long term economy-wide growth. Furthermore, assuming a flat term structure of nominal interest rates r, we will confine ourselves to measuring the elasticity with respect to parallel shifts in a flat term structure of interest rates. (As stocks have an infinite maturity, their returns will be predominantly affected by changes in the interest rate level and not by changes in the shape of the term structure of interest rates; cf. Cooper [1977].)

The total differential of the logarithm of the theoretical stock price $P=P_0$ represents the stock return:

$$d\ln(P) = \frac{\partial \ln(P)}{\partial r}\, dr + \frac{\partial \ln(P)}{\partial \pi}\, d\pi + \frac{\partial \ln(P)}{\partial (g^*-g)}\, d(g^*-g) + \\ + \frac{\partial \ln(P)}{\partial g}\, dg + \frac{\partial \ln(P)}{\partial \Gamma}\, d\Gamma \tag{11}$$

where the terms $\partial\ln(P)/\partial x = (\partial P/P)/\partial x$ represent the semi-elasticities of the theoretical stock price with respect to x. We neglect the interdependence between Γ, g and g^*, and included Γ as an argument in the price function. In particular, we consider the firm- (or industry-) specific excess growth rate (g^*-g) as independent of g. The excess growth multiplier Γ can then be interpreted as some measure (duration) for the period that this difference in growth will last (see eq. (8)).

From eq. (9) it follows that (note that $k = r + \pi$):

$$\frac{\partial \ln(P)}{\partial r} = \frac{\partial \ln(P)}{\partial \pi} = - \frac{1}{k - g} < 0 \tag{12}$$

The nominal interest rate r is directly related to the nominal yield in the bond market. As an increase of r raises the opportunity cost of holding stocks, investments in bonds will become more profitable. Stock prices will cet. par. decline, thus raising their expected returns in line with the expected returns on competitive securities. Likewise:

$$\frac{\partial \ln(P)}{\partial g} = \frac{1}{k - g} > 0 \tag{13}$$

$$\frac{\partial \ln(P)}{\partial (g^* - g)} = \frac{\Gamma D_0/P}{k - g} = \frac{y\Gamma}{k - g} \gtrless 0 \tag{14}$$

where $y \equiv D_0/P$ = the current dividend yield of the stock; and

$$\frac{\partial \ln(P)}{\partial \Gamma} = \frac{y(g^* - g)}{k - g} \gtrless 0 \tag{15}$$

Note that all semi-elasticities are functions of $(k-g)^{-1}$, which equals the negative of the continuous compounded equity duration, or the reciprocal of the expected dividend yield $P_0/E(D_1)$ (see footnote 3).

Next, we analyze the relations with the factors. The relationship between nominal interest rates and inflation expectations has been subject to extensive empirical analysis (see for example Fama [1975], Gultekin [1983] and Fama & Gibbons [1984]). According to the Fisher-hypothesis, the nominal interest rate consists of two (independent) components: the real interest rate and expected inflation. Assuming a flat term structure of inflation expectations, we have:

$$r = r_r + i \tag{16}$$

where r_r = the real interest rate;
i = expected inflation.

As noted before, the factor inflation has a special feature: it does not only affect the discount rate, but can also affect the expected dividend growth rates. Unanticipated inflation will cause investors to revise their inflation expectations. Depending on the degree in which the firm can increase the (expected) growth rate of its profits in line with (expected) inflation, the increased growth rates may (partially) offset the effect of the increased discount rate. The total effect of an unanticipated inflation shock on stock returns is thus ambiguous.

To gain a better understanding of the expected effects of inflation on the growth rate of the firm's profits (dividends), we decompose the characteristics of the firm into two categories: operating and financial characteristics. Both types of characteristics have an influence on the firm's cash flows and, hence, profitability. On the operating side, changes in cash outflows can assumed to be related to changes in the prices of specific inputs. The relative change in a producers' price index

(PPI) can serve as a proxy for these price changes. The PPI thus serves as a benchmark for the cost of doing business. In this view, changes in the cash inflows depend on the degree in which the firm is able to pass on the price changes of the specific inputs to the consumers. Changes in the general price level (consumer price index, CPI) will be the consumers' benchmark for evaluating the increased prices of the firm's products. As a result, we hypothesize that a firm can easier maintain some degree of operating profitability when CPI-changes exceed PPI-changes. Of course, the sensitivities of both cash inflows and outflows for specific price changes cannot be merely considered as technical coefficients; they will, more or less, depend on the general degree of competitiveness of the firm's markets and the firm's relative position therein.

On the financing side of the firm, we expect that changes in the CPI will serve as a benchmark for the suppliers of the firm's capital. In contrast to the firm, these investors are faced with changes in the price of a general consumption basket, and they will require compensation for these general price changes.

The gap between specific and general price changes will in part determine the profitability of the related activities. On a longer term, we may expect that the firm can raise its profitability to compensate the general inflation effect to a certain extent. In a whole, we propose that the expected growth rate of the firm's earnings or dividends is positively related to changes in the general price level (CPI) and negatively related to the difference between specific and general price level changes. The degree in which these price changes result in changes of the expected dividend growth rate can be measured by means of 'flow-through' parameters (this term is introduced by Estep, Hanson & Johnson [1983] with respect to general price level changes).

Aside from inflationary effects, the expected growth rate will be influenced by the real interest rate. An increase in the real rate may increase the cost of doing business. Furthermore, as consumption may decline in favour of savings, firms may find it hard to pass on these higher costs to their customers. This lowers the firms' profitability.

From the above discussion, we assume that the economy-wide growth rate g depends on the general inflation rate and the real interest rate. This assumption is in line with Leibowitz et al. [1989]. In addition, we assume that company or industry specific effects dominate in the excess growth rate (g^*-g) and we expect it to be related to both specific and general price level changes. These relations can be expressed as:

$$g = g_0 + \theta_1 i - \theta_2 r_r \qquad (17)$$

$$g^{*}-g = \theta_3 i - \theta_4 i_p \tag{18}$$

where g_0 = a constant growth parameter;

θ_1 = the general inflation flow-through parameter for the economy-wide growth rate;

θ_2 = the sensitivity of the economy-wide growth rate for real interest rates;

θ_3 = the general inflation flow-through parameter for the excess growth rate;

θ_4 = the specific inflation flow-through parameter for the excess growth rate.

The risk premium π is supposed to offer compensation for the risks, attached to the uncertain growth of the future dividend stream. As the risk premium depends on both the investors' risk perceptions and the investors' risk attitudes, it is very difficult (if not impossible) to specify some relationship between π and economic factors. However, we can hypothesize that an unanticipated change in a factor not only causes investors to revise their expectations with respect to future values of that factor: an unanticipated shock can also increase investors' uncertainty with respect to these future values. The result of the latter effect would be an increase in the risk premium. This leaves us with the assumption that the risk premium is a (positive) function of the previously discussed factors:

$$\pi = \pi(r_r, i, i_p, \ldots.) \tag{19}$$

Computing the total differentials of eqs. (16) through (19), substituting the results in eq. (11), and collecting terms yields:

$$d\ln(P) = -\eta_{r_r} dr_r - \eta_i di - \eta_{i_p} di_p + \eta_\Gamma d\Gamma \tag{20}$$

with semi-elasticities or sensitivities:

$$\eta_{r_r} = \frac{1 + \theta_2 + \partial\pi/\partial r_r}{k - g} \tag{21}$$

$$\eta_i = \frac{1 + \partial\pi/\partial i - \theta_1 - \theta_4 y\Gamma}{k - g} \tag{22}$$

$$\eta_{i_p} = \frac{\theta_4 y\Gamma + \partial\pi/\partial i_p}{k - g} \tag{23}$$

$$\eta_\Gamma = \frac{y(g^{*}-g) - \partial\pi/\partial\Gamma}{k - g} \tag{24}$$

From eq. (21), we can hypothesize that the total effect of an increase in the real interest rate on stock returns will be negative. From eq. (23), we could expect stock returns to be negatively related to changes in specific (producer) prices, cet. par. From the effect of the risk premium in eq. (24), it is difficult to predict the effect of an increase in the excess growth multiplier. When, as a result of improved market conditions, the period of excess growth is extended, this positive effect can be overshadowed by an increase in perceived risks and increased risk premium. However, even when risk premium effects are neglected, it will be hard to draw conclusions with respect to the signs of the general inflation rate sensitivity in eq. (22). The total inflation flow-through in excess and normal growth rates may be larger or smaller than one.

In connection with this last point, it will be relevant whether a change in the nominal rate of interest can be attributed to a change in the real interest rate or to a change in inflation expectations (Leibowitz et al. [1989] also stress this point). Considering eqs. (21) and (22), the sensitivities for these factors can differ very much. This may be particularly relevant for empirical investigations on the basis of nominal interest rates.

Another interesting point for empirical research is the intertemporal stationarity of factor sensitivities. From the presented equations, it follows that the theoretical sensitivities cannot be considered as constants. For example, as all factor sensitivities have the term $(k-g)^{-1}$ in common, we would expect the factor sensitivities to depend negatively on the levels of the nominal interest rates and the risk premium, and positively with the steady-state growth rate. It may thus be overly optimistic to omit the time subscripts of the sensitivities b_{ij} in eq. (1)!

4. CONCLUSIONS

In this paper, we showed how multi-factor models of security returns can be derived from Present Value models. In a multi-factor model, fluctuations in security returns are attributed to fluctuations in economic factors. As factor models give rise to a multi-farious risk concept, they can serve an important role in risk management. The advantage of using an underlying theoretical model is that the expressions for the sensitivities can be examined, providing insight in the nature of the relations between returns and factor movements as well as in the expected intertemporal stationarity of the sensitivity coefficients. As an additional feature, information from fundamental analysis can be incorporated in the model to enhance the statistical estimation and periodic revision of the sensitivity estimates.

The presented model is simple and serves to illustrate the general methodology. Extending the present basic model (by specifying additional factors that affect the growth rates) may improve the understanding of the relations between security returns and the structure of the economic environment in which these returns are generated. Some candidates are factors relating to the prices of specific inputs, like raw materials, energy &c. In addition to the excess growth rate (g^*-g), we can try to link the excess growth multiplier to factors like the firm's competitive position in the market. Given a more complete model, it would be worthwile to combine the theoretical analysis with an empirical analysis, in order to test some features of the underlying PV-model.

REFERENCES:

Bierman, H. & J. Hass, 1971, Normative Stock Price Models, *Journal of Financial and Quantitative Analysis* September, pp. 1135-1144

Bierman, H., D.H. Downes & J.E. Hass, 1972, Closed-Form Stock Price Models, *Journal of Financial and Quantitative Analysis* June, vol. 7/3, pp. 1797-1808

Boquist, J.A., G.A. Racette & G.G. Schlarbaum, 1975, Duration and Risk Assessment for Bonds and Common Stocks, *The Journal of Finance* Dec., vol. 30/5, pp. 1360-1365

Casabona, P.A., F.J. Fabozzi & J.C. Francis, 1984, How to Apply Duration to Equity Analysis, *The Journal of Portfolio Management* Winter, pp. 52-58

Chance, D.M., 1982, Interest Sensitivity and Dividend Yields, *The Journal of Portfolio Management* Winter, pp. 69-75

Chen, N.-F., R. Roll & S.A. Ross, 1986, Economic Forces and the Stock Market, *Journal of Business* 59, pp. 383-403

Cooper, I., 1977, Asset Values, Interest Changes, and Duration, *The Journal of Financial and Quantitative Analysis* Dec, vol.12/5, pp. 701-723

Durand, D., 1957, Growth Stocks and the Petersburg Paradox, *The Journal of Finance* Sept., vol. 12, pp. 348-363

Estep, T., M. Clayman, C. Johnson & K. McMahon, 1984, *The Evolution of a New Approach to Investment Risk*, Salomon Bros Inc., May

Estep, T., N. Hanson & C. Johnson, 1983, Sources of Value and Risk in Common Stocks, *The Journal of Portfolio Management* Summer, pp.5-13

Fabozzi, F.J. & T.D. Fabozzi, 1989, *Bond Markets, Analysis and Strategies*, Prentice Hall, Englewood Cliffs N.J.

Fama, E.F., 1975, Short-Term Interest Rates as Predictors of Inflation, *The American Economic Review* June, vol.65/3, pp. 269-282

Fama, E.F. & M.R. Gibbons, 1984, A Comparison of Inflation Forecasts, *Journal of Monetary Economics* vol.13, pp. 327-348

Fuller, R.J. & C.C. Hsia, 1984, A Simplified Common Stock Valuation Model, *Financial Analysts Journal* Sept/Oct, pp. 49-56

Gordon, M.J. & E. Shapiro, 1956, Capital Equipment Analysis: The Required Rate of Profit, *Management Science* 3 Oct., pp. 102-110

Gultekin, N.B., 1983, Stock Market Returns and Inflation Forecasts, *The Journal of Finance* June, vol.38/3, pp. 663-673

Haugen, R.A., 1970, Expected Growth, Required Return and the Variability of Stock Prices, *Journal of Financial and Quantitative Analysis* 5, pp. 297-307

Haugen, R.A. & D.W. Wichern, 1974, The Elasticity of Financial Assets, *The Journal of Finance* Sept., vol.3/4, pp. 1229-1240

Haugen, R.A., A.L. Stroyny & D.W. Wichern, 1978, Rate Regulation, Capital Structure, and the Sharing of Interest Rate Risk in the Electric Utility Industry, *The Journal of Finance* June, vol.33/3, pp. 707-721

Jahnke, W.W, 1975, What's Behind Stock Prices?, *Financial Analysts Journal* Sept/Oct, pp. 69-76

Joehnk, M.D. & J.W. Petty, 1980, The Interest Sensitivity of Common Stock Prices, *The Journal of Portfolio Management* Winter, pp. 19-25

Lanstein, R. & W.F. Sharpe, 1978, Duration and Security Risk, *The Journal of Financial and Quantitative Analysis* Nov., vol. 13/4, pp. 653-668

Leibowitz, M.L., 1986, Total Portfolio Duration: A New Perspective on Asset Allocation, *Financial Analysts Journal* Sept/Oct, pp. 18-29, 77

Leibowitz, M.L., E.H. Sorensen, R.D. Arnott & H.N. Hanson, 1989, A Total Differential Approach to Equity Duration, *Financial Analysts Journal* Sept/Oct, pp. 30-37

Makeham, W.M., 1869, On the Theory of Annuities Certain, *Journal of Institute of Actuaries, and Insurance Magazine* 14, pp. 189-199

Molodovsky, N., C. May & S. Chottiner, 1965, Common Stock Valuation, *Financial Analysts Journal* March/April, vol.21, pp. 104-123

Stone, B.K., 1974, Systematic Interest Rate Risk in a Two-Index Model of Returns, *The Journal of Financial and Quantitative Analysis* Nov, vol.12/4, pp. 709-721

Williams, A.O. & P.E. Pfeifer, 1982, Estimating Security Price Risk Using Duration and Price Elasticity, *The Journal of Finance* May, vol. 37/2, pp. 399-411

Williams, J.B., 1938, *The Theory of Investment Value*, Harvard University Press, Cambridge Mass.

INTEREST RATES AND POLICY REACTIONS: SOME INTERNATIONAL EVIDENCE[1]

Matti Virén
University of Turku, Department of Economics
SF-20500 Turku, Finland

I Introduction

We are used to thinking that nowadays interest rates are determined by "market forces" in almost all countries and that the existing capital market imperfections are of minor importance. This shows up not only in the determination of interest rates but also in the demand for and supply of assets and liabilities. Moreover, one might now assume that capital is almost perfectly mobile between countries. This, in turn, means that interest rates in various countries are very much interrelated (i.e. the interest rate parity holds) and that financing of domestic investment is not effectively constrained by domestic financial market conditions.

This paper follows a somewhat different interpretation of the current institutional framework. However, we do not argue for (or, indeed, against) capital market imperfections but instead merely emphasize the importance of monetary policy in general and of central banks' interest rate policy in particular. This policy view can be seen as some sort of alternative to the more traditional "market force" interpretation of the data. For instance, we might here refer to the standard Fisher parity interpretations of the interest rate data. In this connection we are mainly interested in the question as to whether we are able to derive a policy reaction function which would help us to explain the behaviour of central banks' discount rates and possibly also short-run interest rates in various countries and which could also explain some puzzling results in terms of international capital mobility. To be a bit more explicit, we analyze the finding that countries' investment rates are highly correlated with their national saving rates. This finding was originally made by Feldstein and Horioka (1980) and it has now been confirmed by many subsequent studies using both cross-section and time-series regressions over different sets of countries and time periods (see e.g. Dooley, Frankel and Mathieson

[1] I am indebted to Carolina Sierimo and Marja-Liisa Halko for computational help and the Yrjö Jahnsson Foundation for financial support. The participants of the 8th Meeting of the Euro Working Group on Financial Modelling provided useful comments on an earlier version of this paper. The current version of the paper is based on a paper (co-authored by Erkki Koskela) entitled "Monetary Policy Reaction Functions and Saving Investment Correlations: Some Cross-Country Evidence".

(1988) for a survey of the literature). But there is currently very little agreement on explanations for this apparent empirical regularity. Three broad sets of explanations for these high correlations have emerged: low international capital mobility, private sector behaviour and government targeting of the current account.

Despite evidence to be contrary, international capital mobility may, for various reasons – such as information constraints, exchange risk with risk aversion, exchange controls etc – be very low. This was the original explanation proposed by Feldstein and Horioka (1980) and reaffirmed by e.g. Feldstein and Bacchetta (1989). The first interpretation has been challenged by a number of people. On the one hand it has been argued that even if capital mobility were perfect, national saving and investment would be correlated because they both react to some common shocks, such as business cycle shocks, productivity shocks and/or population growth (see e.g. Obstfeld (1986)). But there are problems with this interpretation, too. It has been argued by Summers (1988) and by Feldstein and Bacchetta (1989) that evidence does not support the "spurious factor" explanation for the close association of national savings and investment rates. On the other hand, it has been argued that the close association between national savings and investment rates may in fact be due to the possibility that governments have used fiscal and monetary policy to target the current account.

According to the government targeting of the current account interpretation capital is not actually immobile, but only appears to be so because countries pursue policies which ultimately bring savings and investments into balance. Recently, Summers (1988) has interpreted saving-investment correlations as being due to fiscal policy reactions; according to the "maintained external balance" hypothesis, fiscal policy – measured by the budget deficit – reacts to the saving-investment gap. The budget deficit is not, however, a good summary measure of fiscal policy; it is not entirely under the control of the government in that it is likely to be affected by growth and other factors. Moreover, it is not totally clear how this kind of evidence should be interpreted (see e.g. Feldstein & Bacchetta (1989)).

Somewhat surprisingly, the possibility that monetary policy reactions to target the current account might explain saving-investment correlations has not been studied, with the exception of some preliminary research by Artis and Bayomi (1989). Clearly, however, this possibility deserves a more thorough analysis, which is what this paper seeks to provide.

We start by postulating a simple linear dynamic reaction function for the short-term interest rate, which includes some potential external and internal targets of monetary policy – current account, domestic inflation and output growth – as explanatory variables. But there is no reason to suppose that the reaction function would be linear; there may be some nonlinearities owing to the possibility that monetary authorities react asymmetrically to the (internal and/or external) target variables, depending on whether the actual values of the variables are below or above the target values. These possible nonlinearities are analyzed using the so-called threshold models (see Tong (1983) for an overview of the earlier literature).[2] The state of the current account is an obvious threshold variable, to which monetary authorities may react asymmetrically depending on whether there is a current account deficit or surplus. We also scrutinize the possibility that the domestic inflation rate might have this threshold property. The empirical analysis makes use of quarterly data from four countries: Germany, Italy, Japan and the United States. The sample period varies somewhat from country to country, the longest period being 1960Q3—1989Q2. A brief background and the empirical results are presented in section 2, and some concluding remarks follow in section 3.

2 Background and Empirical Results

2.1 On the Specification of a Monetary Policy Reaction Function

Start by assuming that the monetary authorities behave as if they maximize a "welfare function" subject to an implicit perceived (econometric) model of the economy. This process is assumed to yield a reaction function relating the policy instrument to a set of internal or external policy targets. In order to describe this process we can use the following simple quadratic loss function as a point of departure:

$$W_t = \alpha(\hat{X}_t - X^*)^2 + \beta(\hat{Y}^t - Y^*)^2 + \Gamma(\hat{R}_t - R^*)^2, \tag{1}$$

[2] Recently, Black (1983) has also estimated monetary policy reaction functions for ten industrial countries by applying another kind of threshold regression technique suggested originally by Dagenais (1975). The idea is that the dependent variable is equal to some linear function of observable variables plus a disturbance if a change in the value of the dependent variable exceeds some critical value. Otherwise, the dependent variable is unchanged. A justification for this technique is that policy variables often undergo discrete changes and then remain fixed for a time until another discrete change occurs.

where $\hat{X}_t$ and $\hat{Y}_t$ are the expected values of the policy target variables X and Y, X* and Y* being the constant target values. R is the policy instrument, which may also appear on the right hand side of (1). Now, the policy maker minimizes the expected value of (1) subject to a set of constraints with respect to X, Z and R. In general the constraints are of the following type:

$$\hat{X}_t = f^*(\hat{R}_t) + g^*(Z_t), \tag{2}$$

and similarly for Y (and for other possible target values), where $f(R_t)$ and $g(Z_t)$ are (linear) functions of $\hat{R}_t$ as well as of expected and known values of all predetermined variables given by the vector Z_t. Minimizing (1) subject to these constraints yields the optimum setting for $\hat{R}_t$. (In the simplest case, it is a linear function in terms of $\hat{X}_t$ and $\hat{Y}_t$.) Solving the final reaction function still requires a forecasting rule for the policy maker so that the expected values of X and Y can be generated (see e.g. Abrams, Froyen and Waud (1983) for details of some alternative solutions).

The loss function presented above could of course be extended by allowing some rate of change terms (say $R_t - R_{t-1}$) to affect W_t. This would only make the resulting reaction function genuinely dynamic. In practice, the econometric reaction function specifications are almost always dynamic although it is by no means clear what is the source of dynamics. The problem is that one can arrive at the same dynamic specification from many alternative assumptions concerning the intertemporal nature of the welfare (or loss) function, the forecasting rule or the formation of the policy targets. Thus, the reduced form estimating equation which is typically used in empirical applications is of the form:

$$\Delta R_t = a(L)X_t + b(L)Y_t + \varepsilon_t, \tag{3}$$

where a(L) and b(L) denote some lag polynomials and ε a stochastic error term (see e.g. Joyce (1986) for a survey of the derivation and estimation of reaction functions and Seehan (1985) and Gregory and Reynauld (1985) for some recent applications).

In our application the set of target variables consists of three variables: the rate of inflation, p_t, the rate of change of industrial production, y_t, and the current account (surplus), ca_t. The policy instrument is the interest rate, r_t. Now, the linear estimating specification simply reads:

$$\Delta r_t = b_0 + b_1 p_t + b_2 p_{t-1} + b_3 y_t + b_4 y_{t-1} + b_5 ca_t + b_6 ca_{t-1} + \mu_t, \tag{4}$$

where μ is the error term. In the subsequent empirical application the interest rate variable is either the three-month treasury bill rate (RS) or the central bank's discount rate (RD). Otherwise, it may suffice to note that the data are derived from the OECD Main Economic Indicators tape and that both the industrial production and the current account variables are seasonally adjusted. To get some idea of the data we present the graphs of time series for the discount rate and the current account in Figure 1.

This equation states that the authorities behave so as to raise or lower the interest rate depending upon the recent behaviour of the three target variables, namely inflation, output growth and the size of the current account relative to GDP. Obviously, higher inflation and higher output growth would be expected to lead to tighter money, ceteris paribus. A current account deficit would also lead to tighter money, if the authorities wanted to encourage foreign borrowing to finance the deficit or if they simply adopted an expenditure-reducing policy for external reasons. Under these circumstances the expected signs on these targets would be: $b_1 + b_2 > O$, $b_3 + b_4 > O$ and $b_5 + b_6 < 0$.

There are some issues associated with the policy reaction function specification (3) which should be discussed before the estimation. The first is the possible endogeneity of the policy variable; if the chosen interest rate is not fully under the control of the monetary authorities, then the estimated coefficients may reflect endogenous behaviour rather than policy reactions. From the point of view of controllability, the official discount rate would seem to be a natural dependent variable. What makes it a bit problematic, however, is the fact that a considerable portion of the observations are just zeroes so that the OLS estimates are not appropriate. Moreover, it is, after all, a somewhat moot point as to what should be used as the dependent variable; to the extent that open market operations constitute the main monetary policy instrument, it might be appropriate to use the treasury bill rate as the dependent variable. A detailed investigation of this issue lies beyond the scope of this paper. In order to check the robustness of results, in what follows we have estimated reaction functions using both the discount rate and the treasury bill rate as the dependent variable in (4).

Here we should point that equation (4) also includes a constant term although this term cannot be easily rationalized (and, in fact, typically this term turns out to be completely insignificant). A constant term is included here simply to make it easier to compare the OLS estimation results with some alternative (nonlinear) estimation results which are discussed somewhat later.

Figure 1
The discount rate (——) and the current account (----), %

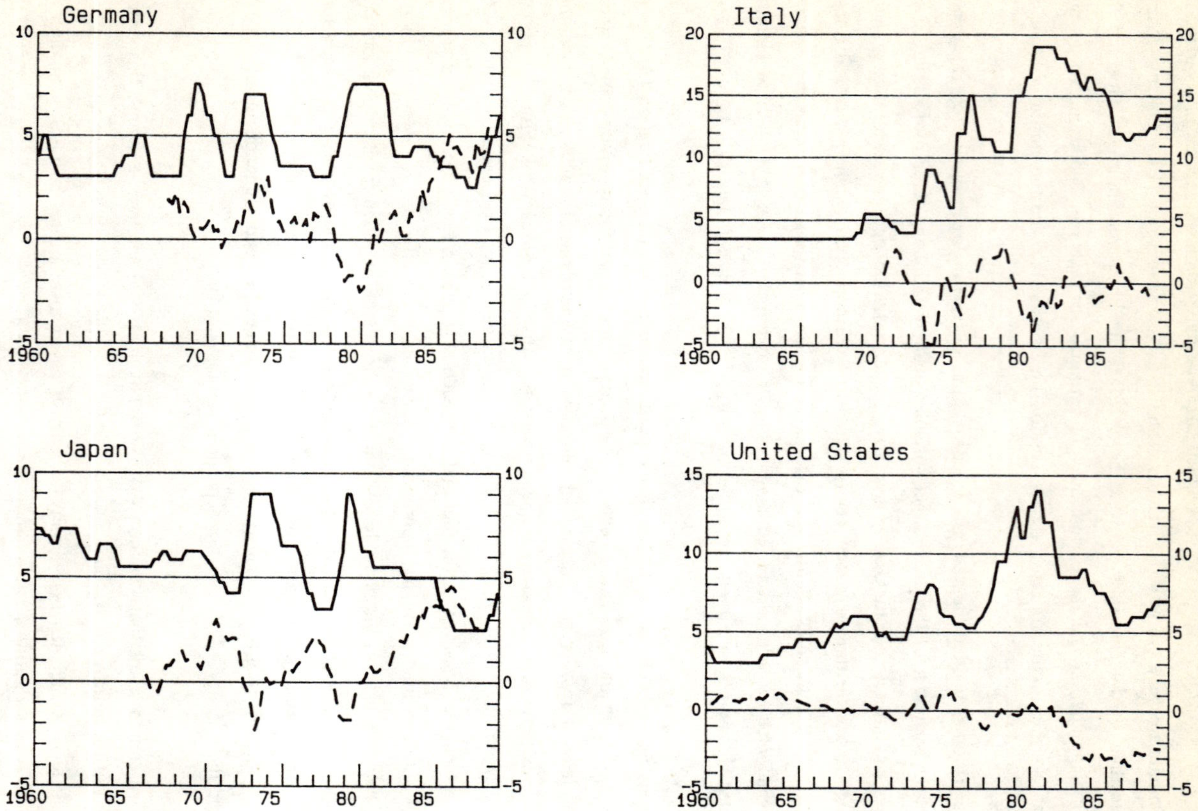

SP TU ANMA

The second issue has to do with the functional form of the reaction function (3). There is no particular reason — except simplicity — why the reaction function should be linear across the domain of various target variables. The monetary authority may not treat the deviations of actual values of the target variables from their desired levels in a symmetrical way. In particular, there may be asymmetricity so that while domestic ownership of foreign assets is regarded as "acceptable", foreign ownership of domestic assets is not regarded so. Under these circumstances the monetary authority may react differently depending on whether the current account is in deficit or in surplus and on whether the deficit is huge or not. And in principle, analogous behaviour may hold in the case of other target variables as well. Postulating this sort of asymmetric loss function also means that exogenous uncertainty about future development of the economy should affect the policy instrument. In what follows, no attempt has been made to control for this. (For implications of asymmetric loss functions, see Waud (1970) and Hosomatsu (1980).)

One way to account for the potential asymmetricities mentioned above is to use the so-called threshold models. Applying the threshold specification means that the coefficients of the independent variables are allowed to vary depending on their level. A simple way to account for this kind of switching phenomenon in the context of the current account variable ca (only) is to fit the following type of nonlinear specification to the data:

$$\Delta r_t = b_0 + b_1 p_t + b_2 p_{t-1} + b_3 y_t + b_4 y_{t-1} + b_5^* ca_t^* + b_6^* ca_{t-1}^* + \upsilon_t \quad \text{if} \quad ca \leq ca' \tag{5i}$$

$$\Delta r_t = b_0 + b_1 p_t + b_2 p_{t-1} + b_3 y_t + b_4 y_{t-1} + b_5^{**} ca_t^{**} + b_6^{**} ca_{t-1}^{**} + \upsilon_t \quad \text{if} \quad ca \leq ca' \tag{5ii}$$

Thus there is supposed to be some threshold value ca' so that if ca $\leq$ ca', then ca = ca* and (5i) holds, while in the case of ca > ca = ca** and (5ii) holds. (Notice that the residual υ_t is here assumed to be homoskedastic over the regimes.) The optimal threshold value — i.e. the value which gives the smallest residual variance — is obtained by using a simple search procedure.

This kind of piecewise-linear threshold specification might also be justified in Bayesian terms as follows: Suppose that the policy maker is uncertain about the effects of policy instruments on targets and tries to approximate this uncertain relationship by using a linear model with uncertain, but normally distributed coefficients. To decide whether the linear model is an acceptable approximation, the policy maker uses the loss function — which captures his (or her) tolerance to differences between the true and linear model — and makes a decision so as to minimize the expected loss function. Under certain quite natural assumptions this leads to a piecewise-linear threshold rule, according to which the policy maker resorts to a different approximating model – connecting the policy and target variables – depending on the values of the target variables (for a description of this idea, see Tong (1983), pp. 66–70; see also Smith and Harrison and Zeeman (1981) for some other possibilities and further analyses).

Of course, it may well be that the reaction function is linear but that the coefficients are time-varying rather than constant (see Beck (1983) for this kind of alternative). Clearly, it is not easy to discriminate between this alternative and some nonlinear specifications (see Koskela and Viren (1991), which contains some comparative analyses with all these models).

II.2 OLS and Threshold Estimation Results

The OLS estimation results for the specification (4) for alternative dependent variables RS and RD are reported in Table 1. They suggest that the linear reaction function specification performs reasonably well. In most cases coefficients of the target variables are of expected sign, though not always very precisely estimated. Nevertheless, the estimation results do not prevent the interpretation according to which the monetary authorities in the respective countries react to output growth, inflation and current account deficits by raising the interest rate or by behaving so that interest rates rise (the current account effect is hardly surprising given Figure 1). This conforms with the results reported in e.g. Artis and Bayomi (1989).

Naturally, this is something one might expect. Notice also that the results for the short-term market rate and the discount rate differ only marginally. Although their variability is somewhat different in all countries included in the data sample the coefficient estimates are typically of the same sign and magnitude.[3]

But as we suggested earlier, the linear specification (3) may be inappropriate after more careful consideration. More specifically, we would like to know whether the coefficient estimates are stable over time, and in particular, whether there are signs of nonlinearities in the specification. The test statistics, which are reported in Table 1 and in Koskela and Virén (1990), give conflicting evidence on both issues. This verdict does not seem to depend on the choice of the dependent variable.

First, as far as the parameter stability is concerned, the CHOW test statistic suggests that the parameters are stable in terms of the the first floating exchange rate period. The only minor caveat concerns the United States discount rate equation.

Second, as for the nonlinearities, both the RESET and RB (Utts' Rainbow test) indicate the existence of significant nonlinearities. Moreover, the Plosser-Schwert-White differencing test and White's information matrix test statistics can also be interpreted as supporting the existence of nonlinearities.

In the light of this evidence on nonlinearities we decided to estimate the piecewise-linear threshold specification for the reaction function using the current account and the inflation rate alternatively as the threshold variable. The idea of a threshold is not intended to be a general remedy for instabilities and/or nonlinearities in the estimating specifications. One purpose of the threshold specification is to try – particularly in terms of the current account variable – to capture potential asymmetric reactions of the monetary authorities to current account deficits and surpluses. Not surprisingly, experiments did not indicate any meaningful threshold in terms of the inflation rate. With the exception of Italy, the

---

[3] As pointed out earlier, one may suspect that the reaction functions for individual countries are not independent. This suggests that the equations should at least be estimated in a system form. Unfortunately, the sample periods for the four countries are very much different so that we cannot really make a proper comparison of results. We did, however, carry out some experiments with the sample period 1973Q4-1988Q4. The corresponding results indicated that the system form does not outperform the unrelated regression model in the case of treasury bill rates (the likelihood ratio test statistics for the diagonal covariance matrix did not exceed the standard significance levels) while in the case of discount rates the outcome was less clear (thus the test statistics failed to exceed the 5 per cent level when the equations contained a constant term and when this term was dropped the test statistics just exeeded the 5 per cent level). Obviously, this does not constitute a proof for the hypothesis that the reaction functions are independent of each other. To model a case where policy reactions in different countries are genuinely interrelated is unfortunately beyond the scope of this paper.

TABLE 1. OLS Estimates of the Reaction Function (4)

	FRG	Italy	Japan	USA	FRG	Italy	Japan	USA
$\hat{b}_0$	.188	-.963	-.157	-.437	-.268	-.506	-.070	-.372
	(0.56)	(2.39)	(0.71)	(2.96)	(1.51)	(1.49)	(0.46)	(3.78)
$\hat{b}_1$	-.217	.447	.046	.413	.127	.327	-.002	.275
	(1.04)	(2.83)	(0.61)	(2.90)	(1.14)	(2.44)	(0.03)	(3.11)
$\hat{b}_2$	.054	-.176	.078	-.186	.041	-.188	.049	-.061
	(0.24)	(1.10)	(0.97)	(1.22)	(0.36)	(1.39)	(0.89)	(0.65)
$\hat{b}_3$	.050	.081	-.011	.269	.060	.078	.030	.167
	(0.72)	(1.45)	(0.20)	(5.37)	(1.64)	(1.66)	(0.81)	(5.39)
$\hat{b}_4$	.217	.119	.099	-.028	.158	.131	.039	.008
	(3.32)	(2.30)	(1.87)	(0.60)	(4.53)	(3.01)	(1.08)	(0.28)
$\hat{b}_5$	-.048	.212	-.509	.313	-.014	-.178	-.321	.363
	(0.29)	(1.18)	(2.72)	(1.23)	(0.16)	(1.17)	(2.51)	(2.31)
$\hat{b}_6$	.094	-.442	.404	-.292	-.002	.061	.232	-.337
	(0.53)	(2.41)	(2.23)	(1.15)	(0.02)	(0.39)	(1.87)	(2.14)
R2	.184	.317	.276	.303	.286	.315	.231	.339
SEE	1.053	1.277	.766	.800	.561	1.082	.523	.496
DW	1.380	1.888	1.391	2.006	1.574	2.511	1.471	2.076
RESET	.791	.931	.921	.080	.663	.976	.959	.717
RB	.982	.059	1.000	1.000	.940	.402	1.000	1.000
DIF	.987	.402	.997	.997	.653	.962	.998	.999
IMT	.867	.907	.989	1.000	.908	.880	.991	.999
CHOW	.587	.159	.133	.898	.928	.008	.124	.981
Dep.var.	RS	RS	RS	RS	RD	RD	RD	RD
First obs.	68Q3	71Q3	67Q2	60Q3	68Q3	71Q3	67Q2	60Q3
Last obs.	89Q1	88Q4	89Q1	89Q2	89Q1	88Q4	89Q1	89Q2

Numbers in parentheses are t-statistics. RESET is a test for correctness of the functional form, RB is Utt's rainbow test, DIF is the Plosser-Schwert-White differencing test, IMT is White's information matrix test, and CHOW is CHOW's stability test in terms of 1973Q3. The probability figures reported for RESET, RB, DIF, IMT and CHOW denote points of cumulative probability distribution. Hence, for instance, .950 is the threshold for significance at the level .05.

TABLE 2. Threshold Model Estimates of the Reaction Function

	FRG	Italy	Japan	USA	FRG	Italy	Japan	USA
$\hat{b}_0$	-.015	-.466	-.410	-.344	.500	-.589	.166	-.327
	(0.05)	(0.81)	(2.20)	(1.54)	(2.86)	(1.84)	(1.19)	(2.35)
$\hat{b}_1$	-.187	.600	-.033	.409	.165	.409	-.059	.281
	(0.98)	(2.46)	(0.51)	(2.92)	(1.64)	(3.13)	(1.25)	(3.23)
$\hat{b}_2$	.220	-.589	.050	-.206	.089	-.212	.042	-.075
	(1.08)	(2.56)	(0.73)	(1.39)	(0.84)	(1.67)	(0.85)	(0.81)
$\hat{b}_3$	.085	.145	.013	.255	.076	.062	.027	.158
	(1.34)	(1.80)	(0.29)	(5.17)	(2.28)	(1.51)	(0.27)	(5.13)
$\hat{b}_4$	.257	.256	.083	-.028	.174	.127	.033	.008
	(4.20)	(3.48)	(1.88)	(0.61)	(5.74)	(3.11)	(1.03)	(0.29)
$\hat{b}_5^*$	-.281	.422	-1.368	.670	-.403	-.328	-.976	.551
	(1.57)	(1.07)	(4.85)	(1.95)	(2.37)	(1.48)	(5.07)	(2.67)
$\hat{b}_5^{**}$	.169	-.682	-.255	-.091	.056	-.164	.011	.107
	(0.49)	(1.87)	(1.42)	(0.25)	(0.56)	(0.92)	(0.08)	(0.43)
$\hat{b}_6^*$	-.096	-.978	.316	-.630	.130	.383	.502	-.516
	(0.54)	(2.44)	(1.12)	(1.85)	(0.87)	(1.60)	(3.00)	(2.56)
$\hat{b}_6^{**}$	-.194	.667	.296	.009	.006	-.059	-.038	-.126
	(0.53)	(2.13)	(1.72)	(0.03)	(0.05)	(0.35)	(0.27)	(0.53)
R2	.270	.441	.482	.316	.436	.429	.423	.395
DW	1.39	2.45	0.73	2.00	1.63	1.48	0.69	1.11
100*ca'	2.90	-1.10	-.40	-.40	.80	-1.90	.00	-.20
F(ca')	7.62	9.10	19.76	4.01	9.84	6.09	13.11	4.93
	(.999)	(1.000)	(1.000)	(.979)	(1.000)	(.996)	(1.000)	(.991)
F(0)	6.95	4.08	18.26	3.39	8.87	4.00	13.11	4.75
	(.998)	(.978)	(1.000)	(.963)	(1.000)	(.977)	(1.000)	(.989)
nl:ca < ca':n	67:83	24:70	10:88	39:116	47:83	13:70	21:88	47:116
dep.var.	RS	RS	RS	RS	RD	RD	RD	RD

The numbers in parentheses are asymptotic t-ratios (notice that the distribution of these values is probably affected by the search procedure in terms of ca'). F denotes the F test statistic for the hypothesis that the parameter values for ca* and ca** as well as ca(-1)* and ca(-1)** are equal. F(0) is the same test statistic but now the threshold value ca' is set to 0. The values of cumulative PD are in parentheses.

sample split - which may be formed by minimizing the residual variance - allocated less than 10 % of the observations to the smaller sample.[4] It is at least equally reasonable to consider these observations as mere outliers rather than as realizations of different policy regimes.

Let us now turn to consider the threshold model estimation results with the current account as the threshold variable. The estimation results of the specification (5) with one threshold value for each country are reported in Table 2. The following features of the results merit attention. First, and perhaps most important, the existence of one threshold with respect to the current account variable is clearly confirmed, with the United States being a sort of marginal case. The F-statistics computed for the threshold model — the null hypothesis being the linear model — indicate that the hypothesis according to which the coefficient estimates of the current account variable are equal below and above the threshold can be rejected at the standard significance level. The power of these F-tests here is somewhat unclear, hence some caution is needed in interpreting the corresponding test results. Second, and related, the explanatory power of the reaction function is now in each case higher than for the linear reaction function (4). Moreover, the coefficient estimates are now considerably more precise. Notice that imprecise coefficient estimates were a problem in the OLS estimation results of (4). Finally, as far as the size of coefficient estimates are concerned, it is of interest to scrutinize the sums of the coefficients of the current account variables ca* and ca(-1)* (and ca** and ca(-1)**).

Clearly, these numbers make a lot of sense. As one would expect, the current account variables have a considerably greater effect on the dependent variable in the case of deficits than in the case of surpluses, the United States (and in the case of the discount rate, also Italy) being an exception to this general pattern. An obvious, though not a very satisfactory explanation, may lie in the fact that monetary policy in the United States has not paid very much attention to the current account development owing to the relative "closedness" of the economy compared with other countries of the data sample.

We also estimated for each country an extended threshold model with two thresholds and thus three regimes, where the treasury bill rate was used as the dependent variable. Mostly, the explanatory power of the equations became better. This was reflected in the fact that the F test statistics for the hypothesis that there are two thresholds instead of one turned out to be: 1.50 for Germany, 30.74 for Italy, 4.82 for Japan and 6.70 for the United States. Thus only the value for Germany fails to exceed

[4] The threshold estimations with inflation as the threshold variable gave the following sample split of observations, when the residual variance was minimized: Germany 8/83, Italy 24/70, Japan 9/88 and United States 3/116.

the standard levels of significance. A major problem with "two threshold-three regime" reaction functions seems to be that typically it is difficult to interpret them meaningfully. Only in the case of Italy is the "corridor" between the two thresholds located around the zero current account. In other cases the threshold just seemed to pick up positive and negative extreme — outlier — observations. This conclusion is supported by the parameter estimates; they did not follow any systematic pattern. Thus we do not report them (for various specifications of and tests for threshold models, see Tong (1983) and Luukkonen (1990)).

TABLE 3. Summary of Long-Run Effects of the Current Account on Interest Rates

	FRG	Italy	Japan	USA	FRG	Italy	Japan	USA
OLS	-.142	-.230	-.105	.021	-.016	-.117	-.089	.026
SUR	-.052	-.224	.032	-.008	-.072	-.114	-.112	-.008
Threshold	-.232	-.200	-.083	-.041	-.128	-.171	-.134	.003
dep.var.	RS	RS	RS	RS	RD	RD	RD	RD

OLS denotes OLS estimation (see Table 1 for details), SUR denotes SUR estimation results from the period 1973Q4-1988Q4 and Threshold denotes the results from the threshold specification (5) (see Table 2 for details). In the latter case, the coefficients for different regimes are weighted by the corresponding number of observations.

Overall, the results are encouraging. Both the OLS, SUR and threshold estimation results of the reaction function suggest that the current account deficit leads to tighter money, ceteris paribus, the United States being an exception (see Table 3 for a summary of the effects). The threshold estimation results show, however, that the reaction function is nonlinear in terms of the current account variable; monetary policy — proxied by the discount rate or by the treasury bill rate — reacts more strongly to deficits than to surpluses and the coefficients relating to the current account become more precise when this asymmetricity is allowed. We are tempted to interpret the findings as giving considerable support for the notion that — with the exception of the United States — the current account has been a significant target for monetary policy over the observation period. Since the major effect of monetary policy is probably on private sector saving and investment, rather than on government balance, these data do not provide support for the hypothesis of Summers (1988) that it is fiscal policy that has been used to target the current account.

Before we conclude it is perhaps worthwhile shortly discussing possible endogeneity and causality problems connected with our reaction function specification. As pointed out earlier, it is not easy to determine the importance of such things. The problem is particularly severe here because we use quarterly data. It is quite clear that quarterly data are not very suitable in capturing the policy reactions. Unfortunately, we had no real alternative.

We did, however, try to scrutinize the causality structure of the model by estimating a four-variable VAR model in terms of (r, p, y and ca). This exercise indicated that (Granger) causality runs from the current account to interest rates rather than vice versa although both effects turned out to be rather weak in this setting. On the other hand, when we also computed cross-correlations between interest rates and the current account the latter variable seemed typically to lag behind the interest rate(s). As far as other variables are considered, important linkages seemed to exist between inflation and interest rates. The corresponding causality test statistics suggested that in the case of the United Staes causality is two-way while with other sample countries causality seems to run form interest rates (especially discount rates) to inflation. All in all, the evidence does not allow us to discriminate between competing views of interest rate determination. But the important thing is that the evidence is not totally at variance with the reaction function interpretation of the data.

3 Summary and Conclusions

This paper has scrutinized the possibility that monetary policy reactions might explain the behaviour of (certain) interest rates in Germany, Italy, Japan and the United States. In particular, we focused on the possibility that policy reactions to target the current account might explain the observed high saving-investment correlations.

Empirical results support the idea that there is indeed some systematic policy reaction function in terms of interest rates in these countries. The results suggest that inflation, output growth and the current account deficit lead to higher interest rates. The results are strikingly similar in these countries. The only notable exception is the current account effect, which cannot be discerned in the case of the United States. In addition to this general result we have obtained some evidence of asymmetric (nonlinear) policy reactions. Thus, interest rates react more strongly to deficits than to surpluses. This, in turn, suggests that empirical policy reaction functions are more complicated than is customarily assumed in the literature. The generally rather poor results obtained with these functions may merely be due to misspecification of the functional form. All in all, we are tempted to interpret the findings as giving considerable support for the notion that the current account has been a significant target for monetary policy and they might explain the high saving-investment correlations even in the presence of international capital mobility.

References

Abrams, R.K., Froyen, R. and Waud, R.N. "The State of the Federal Budget and the State of the Economy", Economic Inquiry 21, 1983, 485—503.

Artis, M., Bayomi, T., "Saving, Investment, Financial Integration, and the Balance of Payments". IMF Working Paper, WP 89/102, 1989.

Beck, N. "Time-Varying Parameter Regression Models", American Journal of Political Science, 1983, 557—600.

Black, S.W., "The Use of Monetary Policy for Internal and External Balance in Ten Industrial Countries". In: Frenkel, J. (Ed.), Exchange Rates and International Macroeconomics, NBER, University Chicago Press, Chicago, 1983, pp. 189—225.

Dagenais, M.G., "Application of a Threshold Regression Model to Household Purchases of Automobiles", Review of Economics and Statistics 57, 1975, 275—285.

Dooley, M., Frenkel, J., Mathieson, D., "International Capital Mobility: What do Saving-Investment Correlations Tell Us?", IMF Staff Papers 34, 1988, 503—530.

Feldstein, M., Bacchetta, P., "National Saving and International Investment". NBER WP 3164, 1989.

Feldstein, M., Horioka, C., "Domestic Saving and International Capital Flows", Economic Journal 90, 1980, 129—151.

Gregory, R.N. and Raynauld, J. "An Econometric Model of Canadian Monetary Policy over the 1970s", Journal of Money Credit and Banking 17, 1985, 43—58.

Hosomatsu, Y., "Asymmetric Loss Function and Optimal Policy Under Uncertainty: A Simple Proof", Decision Sciences 11, 1980, 577—585.

Joyce, J.P., "On the Specification and Estimation of Macroeconomic Policy Functions", Quarterly Journal of Business and Economics 25, 1986, 16—37.

Koskela, E. and Viren, M. "Monetary Policy Reaction Functions and the Saving Investment Correlations: Some Cross-Country Evidence", Bank of Finland Discussion Paper 11/90, 1990.

Luukkonen, R., "On Linearity Testing and Model Estimation in Non-Linear Time Series Analysis". Finnish Statistical Society, Statistical Studies, 10, 1990, Helsinki.

Obstfeld, M., "Capital Mobility in the World Economy: Theory and Measurement", Carnegie-Rochester Conference on Public Policy 24, 1986, 55—103.

Seehan, R.G. "The Federal Reserve Reaction Function: Does Debt Growth Influence Monetary Policy?", Federal Reserve Bank of Saint Louis, Review 67, 1985, 24–33.

Smith, J.Q., Harrison, P.J., Zeeman, E.C., "The Analysis of Some Discontinuous Decision Processes", European Journal of Operations Research 7, 1981, 30–43.

Summers, L., "Tax Policy and International Competitiveness". In: J. Frenkel (Ed.) International Aspects of Fiscal Policies, Chicago University Press, Chicago, 1988.

Tong, H., "Threshold Models in Non-Linear Time Series Analysis". Springer-Verlag, Berlin, 1983.

Waud, R.N., "Asymmetric Policymaker Utility Functions and Optimal Policy Under Uncertainty", Econometrica 44, 1976, 53–66.

AN EXPLANATION FOR THE WEAK EVIDENCE IN SUPPORT OF THE SYSTEMATIC RISK-RETURN RELATIONSHIP

D. J. Bradfield
Department of Mathematical Statistics
University of Cape Town, Rondebosch, 7700

ABSTRACT

Tests of the Capital Asset Pricing Model (CAPM) have mainly been conducted using the Fama-MacBeth methodolgy. Published results of these tests have shown relatively little empirical support for the theory and have led to conclusions that the theory may be invalid. Using a simulation approach we show that the power of the Fama-MacBeth methodology is low unless the test period exceeds 30 years. This provides a potential explanation for the lack of significance found in tests over shorter intervals and for the inability of subperiod tests to confirm significance found in overall periods. Our results suggest that lack of statistical power may be a more valid conclusion than rejection of the CAPM.

I. INTRODUCTION

At the heart of most financial models in the field of Modern Portfolio Theory is the notion that investors can expect to be rewarded (over the longer term) for bearing systematic risk. This notion forms an integral part of much of modern finance. To date, however, the statistical evidence in support of this hypothesis has been surprisingly weak, prompting several researchers to doubt the existence of a systematic risk/return tradeoff.

Most of this statistical evidence stems from tests using the Fama and MacBeth (1973) methodology, or a variation thereof. To date no evidence has been forthcoming documenting the statisical power of the test. Thus conclusions that the theory is invalid may be premature. Alternatives to the Fama-MacBeth test such as the multivariate tests of Gibbons (1982), Shanken (1987) and Gibbons, Ross and Shanken (1989) have been proposed. However, the power of these tests has been studied (e.g. by MacKinlay (1987)) and found to be low. Consequently the Fama-MacBeth methodology remains widely used and hence is the focus of this paper.

In this paper we offer an explanation for the weak evidence in support of the systematic risk/return hypothesis by considering the power of the test of this hypothesis. A simulation approach is used to investigate the power of the traditional Fama and MacBeth (1973) test. We demonstrate that the power of the test is generally extremely low when typical 5-year test periods are used and show that the power of the test usually only increases above .75 when the test period is longer than 30 years. Our evidence suggests that authors who have rejected the CAPM on the basis of weak statistical evidence based on tests of less than 30 years' duration may well have done so prematurely and should rather have expressed reservations regarding the power of the test. Furthermore our results clearly indicate that the Fama-MacBeth test has very low power during times when the market premium is low. Consequently we argue that failure to reject the CAPM in tests over such periods should not be construed as evidence against the CAPM.

In the next section we review some of the existing statistical evidence of prior studies on the risk/return hypothesis. In Section 3 we describe the simulation methodology and in section 4 the results are presented and compared to the existing evidence test results. Finally some conclusions based on the power of the test are given.

2. REVIEW

Fama and MacBeth (1973) proposed the following empirical analog to their model which they refer to as a stochastic generalization of the CAPM:

$$R_{pt} = \gamma_{0t} + \gamma_{1t}\,\hat{\beta}_{p,t-1} + \gamma_{2t}\,\hat{\beta}^2_{p,t-1} + \hat{\gamma}_{3t}\,\bar{S}_{p,t-1}(\hat{e}_i) + \eta_{pt},$$

where,

R_{pt} is the return on portfolio p at time t;

$\hat{\beta}_{p,t-1}$ is the beta of portfolio p at time t-1;

$\hat{\beta}^2_{p,t-1}$ is included to test the linearity of the CAPM;

$\bar{S}_{p,t-1}$ is the average of the standard deviations of the OLS market model residuals for the securities in portfolio p at time t-1; and

η_{pt} is the disturbance term which is assumed to have zero mean and to be independent of all other variables.

Fama and MacBeth use the coefficients of the model to test three testable implications of the CAPM (i.e. conditions C1, C2 and C3 as stated in Fama and MacBeth (1973)). Researchers following Fama and Macbeth however have mainly been concerned with the condition C3 which specifies the risk/return tradeoff, namely:

(C3) In a market of risk-averse investors, higher risk should be associated with higher expected return,

$$\text{i.e., } E(\gamma_{1t}) = E(R_{mt}) - E(R_{0t}) > 0,$$

where $E(R_{0t})$ is the expected return on a minimum variance zero-beta portfolio at time t, and R_{mt} is the return on the market portfolio in time t.

Furthermore, the traditional Sharpe-Lintner model (as opposed to the Black (1972) model in C3) imposes another constraint, namely

$$E(\gamma_{0t}) = R_{ft},$$

which should hold in a market setting where unrestricted riskless borrowing and lending at a known rate R_{ft} is possible. It should be noted that if the above hypothesis does not hold, the Black (1972) model can be used and the least squares intercept, $\hat{\gamma}_{0t}$ can be interpreted as the return on a zero-ß portfolio during month t.

Fama and MacBeth use t-statistics for testing their hypotheses that the $E(\gamma_1) = 0$, and refer to Officer (1971) for suitable justification. These t-statistics are computed using:

$$t(\hat{\gamma}_1) = \frac{\hat{\gamma}_1}{s(\hat{\gamma}_1)/\sqrt{n}}$$

where n is the number of months in the test period, which is also the number of estimates of $\hat{\gamma}_{1t}$ used to compute $\hat{\gamma}_1$ and $s(\hat{\gamma}_1)$, and $s(\hat{\gamma}_1)$ is the estimated standard deviation of the $\hat{\gamma}_{1t}$.

Although Roll (1977) has several pertinent criticisms relating to the hypothesis of Fama and MacBeth, the majority of researchers continue to concentrate on testing condition C3. For this reason we concentrate on C3 in the ensuing discussion and simulation.

The multitude of studies using the Fama-MacBeth (1973) cross-sectional test methodology to test condition C3 have yielded mounting evidence suggesting that the empirical support for a positive relationship between systematic risk and return is surprisingly weak. The test statistics of some of the more notable studies focussing on conditon C3 have been summarized in table 1 below.

Table 1. "t-statistics" for the hypothesis $H_0 : E(\gamma_{1t}) = 0$

Authors	Test period	Test period length (years)	t - statistic
Fama & Macbeth(1973)	1935-1940	5	0.79
	1941-1945	5	2.55
	1946-1950	5	0.48
	1951-1955	5	0.53
	1956-1960	5	-1.37
	1961-1968	8	2.81
	1934-1945	12	1.92
	1946-1955	10	0.70
	1956-1968	13	1.73
	1935-1968	34	2.57
Levy(1978)	1948-1968	21	2.10
Blume(1980)	1937-1946	10	1.19
	1947-1956	10	0.20
	1967-1976	10	0.30
	1936-1976	41	1.54
Tinic & West(1984)	1935-1958	23	1.55
	1969-1982	13	1.43
	1935-1982	47	2.57
Lakonishok & Shapiro(1986)	1962-1981	20	0.91

With reference to the summarized results in table 1, it was Schwert (1983) who first pointed out that the t-statistic for testing condition C3 (i.e. whether the slope coefficient of the risk-return relation is significant) in the Fama and MacBeth study is 2.57 for the 1935-68 sample period, but is only 1.92, 0.70 and 1.73 for the 1934-45, 1946-55, and 1956-68 subperiods respectively. From table 1 it can be seen that Tinic and West (1984) for example document a t-statistic of only 1.33 over the 1969-82 period. Several of the other researchers also find surprisingly weak evidence in support of this hypothesis. For example, Levy (1978) documents a t-statistic of 2.10 over the 1948-68 period, and Blume (1980) documents a t-statistic of 1.54 over the 1936-76 period as well as insignificant t-statistics in all four of his subperiods under study. Finally, Lakonishok and Shapiro (1986) document a t-statistic of only 0.91 over the 1962-81 period.

While Fama and Macbeth (1973) were satisfied that their statistically weak results showed support for the risk/return relationship most other researchers were clearly concerned with the implications of their weak statistical evidence. Levy (1978) for example, argues that the existence of imperfect divisibility of stocks and transaction costs might negate the CAPM, but nevertheless concludes "the well-known systematic risk of the traditional CAPM, β_i, has little to do with equilibrium price determination". Tinic and West (1984) question the length of the testing period, concluding that their results might simply show that ex post data, even from a period approaching a half-century, is insufficient to detect an ex ante relationship.

Lakonishok and Shapiro (1986) also find insignificant test statistics but are encouraged by the fact that the coefficient on beta in their study has the predicted sign. However they conclude that "investors appear to have no assurance whatsoever that taking higher risks as traditionally measured, leads to higher returns, even over relatively long periods of time". More recently Carroll and Wei (1988) compare their results to those of Tinic and West (1984) and conclude that both studies add to the growing empirical evidence inconsistent with the implication of the traditional CAPM.

Surprisingly, few of the above-mentioned studies have directly examined the power of their tests. Some, for example Tinic and West (1984) and Lakonishok and Shapiro (1986), do imply that their results may be caused by low power or inappropriate selection of significance levels. But, nowhere do they explicitly examine the power of the Fama-MacBeth methodology. This is particularly disturbing since it is well known that the power of such t-tests increase with increasing n. The fact that in all the above-mentioned studies the statistical evidence in support of the hypothesis over the overall periods was stronger than over the subperiods, further suggests that the power of the test is an important consideration.

A possible reason for the lack of examination of the power in Fama and MacBeth type tests, is that the distribution of the test statistic under the alternative is not known, and consequently the "exact power" of the test cannot be easily determined. It is for this reason that the ensuing power study deals with power from an empirical viewpoint. More specifically, stock return data is simulated assuming normality, and violations of the null hypothesis are introduced into this series of simulated return data. The percentage of times the null hypothesis is rejected at a given level of significance is then referred to as the "empirical power" of the test. Using this approach, the power of the Fama-MacBeth methodology is investigated under various controlled shifts in the parameters that characterize the market setting.

3. SIMULATION METHODOLOGY

The ensuing power study was conducted using return data simulated for 100 securities using the CAPM, assuming normally distributed returns, and using parameters characteristic of the NYSE. Thus all tests are performed under conditions in which the CAPM is the true generating model. In addition, sensitivity tests were performed for several relevant parameters in order to compare the power of the test under different market conditions.

To compensate for an obvious "errors-in-variables" problem, Fama and MacBeth grouped stocks into portfolios. More specifically, they formed 20 portfolios on the basis of the ranked beta values of the individual stocks. To avoid the "regression tendency" in betas, that is, the tendency for high and low betas to revert to the mean over time, they recomputed the portfolio betas in a subsequent time period. Finally, a third nonoverlapping subperiod was utilized to obtain the monthly returns on the portfolios and to estimate the cross-sectional relationship between return and risk. The same procedure was followed using the simulated data and is in essence identical to the procedure described in Fama and MacBeth (1973, pp. 615-18) (A detailed summary of the simulation procedure is available from the authors on request).

The relevant parameters required as inputs for the generation of return data are superscripted by P (to denote parameter), and are listed below:

$\mu^P_{R_m - R_f}$: the mean monthly excess return on the market portfolio (i.e., the market premium);

$\sigma^P_{R_m - R_f}$: the standard deviation of monthly excess return on the market portfolio;

$\bar{\sigma}^P_e$: the average residual standard deviation in the market model regressions;

μ^P_{beta}: the mean of the beta values across all stocks, which is usually taken to be equal to unity; and

σ^P_{beta}: the standard deviation of the beta values across stocks.

Table 2 shows the input parameters used in this study to examine the power of the Fama-MacBeth test. In order to obtain parameters which typify the NYSE, the results from several studies conducted on the NYSE were scrutinized. The values documented in those studies that were felt to be consistent with reasonable expectations were selected. Thus, for the simulation, the input parameters $\sigma^P_{R_m - R_f}$ and $\bar{\sigma}^P_e$ were extracted from the Fama-MacBeth (1973) study ranging from 1935 to 1968. The value for mean excess market return in the Fama-MacBeth study was uncharacteristically high for the NYSE (15.6% p a). Consequently, $\mu^P_{R_m - R_f}$ was extracted from the MacKinlay (1987) study by averaging the excess market return over periods ranging from 1954 to 1983. This results in 0.77 percent per month, or 9.24 percent per annum.

Table 2. Parameters Used in the Simulation

$\mu^P_{R_m - R_f}$	$\sigma^P_{R_m - R_f}$	$\bar{\sigma}^P_e$	μ^P_{beta}	σ^P_{beta}
0.0077	0.0610	0.0740	1	0.4600

All parameters were estimated from monthly return data on the NYSE. The mean market premium ($\mu^P_{R_m} - R_f$) is the average from 1954 to 1983 in MacKinley (1987). The standard deviations on the market premium ($\sigma^P_{R_m} - R_f$) and the market model residuals ($\bar{\sigma}^P_e$) were obtained from Fama and MacBeth (1973) for the period 1935-1968. The cross-security standard deviation of beta (σ^P_{beta}) was chosen from Kim and Zumwalt (1979) for the 1962-1977 period. Finally, the mean of the cross-security betas (μ^P_{beta}) was set equal to one.

This figure is probably more characteristic of typical expectations on the NYSE and compares favorably with the excess market return of 8.8 percent per annum documented by Ibbotson and Sinquefield (1977) over the 1926-1977 period. The parameter σ^P_{beta} was extracted from Kim and Zumwalt (1979) where the variance of a sample of 322 NYSE security betas was computed over the 1962-1976 estimation period.

The parameters specified in Table 2 were used to examine the power of the Fama-MacBeth methodology. These results should provide a reasonable indication of the power of this methodology to detect significance of the CAPM on the NYSE. To enable comparisons on other exchanges or in different time periods, several sensitivity analyses are performed by allowing the parameters to change over fairly wide ranges. This provides some indication of the sensitivity of this methodology to parameter specification.

4. RESULTS

Traditionally the test is formulated as follows:

H_0: $E(\gamma_{1t}) = 0$

H_a: $E(\gamma_{1t}) > 0$

It should be noted that rejection rather than acceptance of the null hypothesis implies consistency with the CAPM.

The empirical power of the test is examined by increasing the value of the parameter $\mu^P_{R_m\text{-}R_f}$ upwards over a plausible range starting at zero and noting the number of times H_0 is rejected in the simulation. In all cases a significance level of 5% is used. The results of this analysis are shown in Table 3 for the typical NYSE parameters listed in table 2. The choice of the significance level of 5% is arbitrary and is unlikely to affect the major conclusions of this study. For more general procedures where the significance level is selected relative to power, see Arrow (1960). Burgstahler (1987) presents a discussion of the impact of the power/size relationship on posterior beliefs.

The expectation of γ_{1t} is the excess return on the market; consequently violations of the null hypothesis are introduced into the series of returns by introducing a non-zero $\mu^P_{R_m\text{-}R_f}$ value in the simulation. The results shown in Table 3 reveal that when the test period is of short duration (e.g., 5 or 10 years), the test has low power over the range of reasonable economic expectations for the NYSE as specified in Table 1. For example, using a 5-year

Table 3. Power of the test at the 5% level of significance under various market premium scenarios

Duration of test period	Market premium scenarios (% per month)						
	0.00	0.50	0.77[d]	1.00	1.30[e]	1.50	2.00
5 years	.05	.17	.27	.40	.51	.59	.79
10 years	.05	.19	.33	.49	.69	.79	.95
20 years	.06	.32	.55	.76	.94	.98	1.00
30 years	.05	.44	.73	.92	.98	1.00	1.00
50 years	.04	.59	.91	.98	1.00	1.00	1.00

[d]The actual average monthly excess return on the NYSE over the period 1954-1983, reported in MacKinlay (1987).

[e]The actual average monthly excess return documented by Fama and MacBeth (1973) over the period 1935-1968.

test period, the power of the test at the 5% significance level is only 0.27 and is only 0.33 if the test period is doubled to 10 years. Even over a test period of 20 years the power is only .55. For longer periods (i.e., 30 and 50 years) the power is much higher, confirming Tinic and West's (1984) suggestion that long periods may be necessary to accurately capture the relationship. These results are also consistent with the empirical evidence which typically finds significance over long periods but no significance in shorter subperiods (e.g., Fama and MacBeth).

Given that the simulated data is from a CAPM world, these results raise serious questions concerning the usefulness of this methodology for testing the CAPM over short periods. In simulated periods when the monthly excess market return was higher than 0.77 percent per month (approximately 9.2% per annum), significant power gains are evident. However, from Table 3 it can be seen that for an excess market return of as much as 1.5% per month (or about 18% per annum) the power at the 5% level for a 5-year test period, although significantly greater, is still only 0.59. Finally, the results illustrate that, as expected, the power of the test equals the significance level when the mean market premium is zero. This confirms that testing the CAPM during times of small or zero market premium is of little value.

Other parameters that are likely to influence the power of the test is the variability of the excess market returns, and possibly the average variability of the market model residuals. We present the results for various plausible shifts of these parameters in the appendix in tables A1 and A2 respectively. Table A1 in the appendix reveals that an increase in the variability of excess market returns, i.e. $\sigma^{P}_{R_m-R_f}$ is seen to be associated with a reduction in power. Table A2 in the appendix reveals that the power decreases as the average standard deviation of the market model residuals, $\bar{\sigma}^{P}_{e}$, increases. These results suggest that on smaller markets where traditionally the variance of market returns as well as the variance of market model residuals are traditionally higher, the power of the test is even lower than on the NYSE (assuming the market premium is of the same order as the NYSE). This insight suggests that it would be relatively more difficult to detect a risk/return relationship on smaller markets if it existed.

It is worth noting that in the overall test period of Fama and MacBeth (approximately 30 years), the average excess market return was 1.3% per month. The results in Table 3 suggest that the power of their test (at the 5% level) was therefore about 0.98. For the subperiods, given this level of excess return on the market, the power of the test would be approximately 0.69. Thus, even if the CAPM were valid, the weak results they find in the three subperiods are not inconsistent with this level of power. Based on our results we have subjectively estimated the power relevant for the data sets used by the other researchers listed in table 1 as well.

From table 4 it can be seen that Lakonishok and Shapiro (1986) by contrast, conducted their test over a twenty year period having an average excess return of 0.62% per month. The estimated power shown in Table 4 suggest that the power of their test (at the 5% level) may be of the order of 0.45. It is thus not altogether surprising that they failed to find evidence in support of the CAPM. Similar comments apply to the studies of Tinic and West (1984) and Blume (1980) and hence we argue that our results indicate that the lack of statistical power in previous tests is a more acceptable conclusion rather than the invalidity of the CAPM.

Table 4. Estimated power for prior studies.

Authors	Test period			t statistic	Estimate of Power
	Years	Annual Market premium	Length		
Fama & Macbeth(1973)	1935-1940	15.8%	5	0.79	.31
	1941-1945	32.6%	5	2.55	.84
	1946-1950	8.4%	5	0.48	.27
	1951-1955	16.3%	5	0.53	.52
	1956-1960	8.4%	5	-1.37	.21
	1961-1968	13.3%	8	2.81	.76
	1935-1945	23.4%	11	1.92	.74
	1946-1955	12.4%	10	0.70	.59
	1956-1968	11.4%	13	1.73	.69
	1935-1968	16.8%	34	2.57	.98
Levy(1978)	1948-1968	11.9%	21	2.10	.88
Blume(1980)	1937-1946	22.8%	10	1.19	.70
	1947-1956	12.3%	10	0.20	.56
	1967-1976	9.4%	10	0.30	.33
	1936-1976	14.0%	41	1.54	.80
Tinic & West(1984)	1935-1958	16.4%	23	1.55	.76
	1969-1982	9.6%	13	1.43	.48
	1935-1982	14.0%	47	2.57	.99
Lakonishok & Shapiro(1986)	1962-1981	7.4%	20	0.91	.45

In sum the results presented here indicate that the Fama and MacBeth methodology has relatively low power when the test period is of short duration. However, the power of this test is sensitive to both the overall return and the standard deviation of return on the market premium with the power increasing as the risk premium increases and as the standard deviation decreases. Additional tests show that the power decreases as the residual standard deviation increases.

It should be stressed that the simulations in this study assume parameter stability over time and normality of all relevant distributions. Recent evidence (e.g., French, Schwert and Stambaugh (1987)) has suggested that the market premium may vary over time. In addition, numerous studies (e.g., Fama (1965) and Affleck-Graves and McDonald (1989)) have suggested that both security return and market model residuals may be nonnormal. Consequently the power results presented in this paper probably represent a "best case" scenario for the Fama-MacBeth test when using stock market data.

5. CONCLUSIONS

The results presented in this paper clearly show that for periods of short duration, the power of the Fama-MacBeth test of the CAPM is low for securities typical of those traded on the NYSE. As this test has been widely used in the literature, we argue that prior studies indicating lack of support for the CAPM, especially in subperiods, should be interpreted with caution. In particular, we believe that the magnitude of the power in subperiod tests is typically so low that conclusions that the CAPM is invalid are unwarranted. Rather, prior studies should have indicated that the power of the test is so low that a conclusion on the validity of the CAPM is not possible.

While the power tests in this study focused on the NYSE, the simulation methodology presented in this paper can be easily adapted to examine any particular set of parameters relevant for other markets. Researchers using the Fama-MacBeth methodology should note that substantial gains in power are associated with either an increase in the test period duration, an increase in the average return on the market premium or a decrease in the variability of the market premium.

Finally, even though we have offered a plausable explanation for the weak evidence in support of the CAPM we cannot discount the fact that other pricing models may exist which are superior to the CAPM, for example the Arbitrage Pricing Model (of which the CAPM is a subset). However the absence of a systematic risk/return relationship in these models would place much of the basic intuition of investment in jeopardy - and this seems far too tragic to take seriously.

REFERENCES

Affleck-Graves, J. F. and McDonald, B. Sept. 1989. Nonnormalities and tests of asset pricing theories. Journal of Finance 44, 889-908.

Arrow, K. J. 1960. Decision Theory and the Choice of a Level of Significance for the T-test. In Contributions to Probability and Statistics (I. Olkin et al., eds.). Stanford: Stanford University Press.

Black, F. July 1972. Capital market equilibrium with restricted borrowing. Journal of Business 45, 444-454.

Blume, M. Nov. 1980. Stock returns and dividend yields: Some more evidence. Review of Economics and Statistics 62, 567-577.

Burgstahler, D. Jan. 1987. Inference from accounting research. Accounting Review 62, 203-214.

Carrol, C. and Wei, J. Oct. 1988. Risk, return and equilibrium: An extension. Journal of Business 61, 485-499.

Fama, E. F. Jan. 1965. The behavior of stock market prices. Journal of Business 38, 34-105.

Fama, E. F. and MacBeth, J. D. May/June 1973. Risk, return and equilibrium: Empirical tests. Journal of Political Economy 81, 607-636.

French, K. R., Schwert, G. W. and Stambaugh, R. Sept. 1987. Expected stock returns and volatility. Journal of Financial Economics 18, 3-30.

Gibbons, M. R. Mar. 1982. Multivariate tests of financial models: A new approach. Journal of Financial Economics 10, 3-27.

Gibbons, M. R., Ross, S. A. and Shanken, J. Sept. 1989. A test of efficiency of a given portfolio. Econometrica 57, 1059-1090.

Ibbotson, R. G. and Sinquefield, R. A. 1988. Stocks, Bonds, Bills, and Inflation: The Past and the Future. Charlottesville: The Finanical Analysts Research Foundation.

Kim, M. K. and Zumwalt, J. F. Dec. 1979. An analysis of risk in bull and bear markets. Journal of Financial and Quantitative Analysis 14, 1015-1025.

Lakonishok, J. and Shapiro, A. C. 1986. Systematic risk, total risk and size as determinants of stock market returns. Journal of Banking and Finance 10, 115-132.

Levy, H. Sept. 1978. Equilibrium in an imperfect market: A constraint on the number of securities in the portfolio. American Economic Review 68, 643-58.

MacKinlay, A. C. June 1987. On multivariate tests of the CAPM. Journal of Financial Economics 18, 341-371.

Officer, R. R. 1971. A time series examination of the market factor of the New York Stock Exchange. Ph.D. dissertation, University of Chicago.

Roll, R. Mar. 1977. A critique of the asset pricing theory's tests--Part 1: On past and potential testability of the theory. Journal of Financial Economics 4, 129-176.

Schwert, W. G. June 1983. Size and stock returns, and other empirical regularities. Journal of Financial Economics 12, 3-12.

Shanken, J. Dec. 1987. A Bayesian approach to testing portfolio efficiency. Journal of Financial Economics 19, 195-215.

Tinic, S. and West, R. Dec. 1984. Risk and return: January vs. the rest of the year. Journal of Financial Economics 13, 561-74.

PRESENT VALUE DECOMPOSITION OF FOREIGN CURRENCY ASSETS[1]

Mariacristina Uberti
Istituto di Matematica Finanziaria - Universita' di Torino
Via Assarotti, 3 - 10121 Torino (Italy)

Introduction

With the opening of international stock-markets, financial decision-makers have the opportunity to diversify the composition of their portfolio by assets in different foreign currencies. If on one hand this opening enlarges the possibility of both investment and financing, on the other financial tools are needed to subdue, to limit or to exclude the exchange risk. In particular it may be useful to analyse how contingent variations of exchange rates can influence a portfolio evaluation in a multiperiod context.

Among several approaches used for the portfolio evaluation, it is well known the Net Present Value (NPV) method. Recently, on the basis of such a method, Peccati [1989] has proposed a new general methodology effective in a multiperiod environment. In fact, such a metodology involves a inter/infra-period NPV decomposition which allows a careful financial analysis of portfolio. We refer to Peccati [1990] for both the explanation of the new methodology and its interesting applications.

In this paper, an extension and an application of the new general Peccati's method are developed. In particular deterministic and stochastic models are studied for the decomposition of the NPV of financial assets in foreign currencies within a multiperiod framework. In such a context it is also showed the existence of the International Fisher Effect for both

[1] Research financed by the "Ministero dell'Universita' e della Ricerca Scientifica e Tecnologica".

investment and financing in an exchange environment.

This paper is organized as follows. In section 1 the basic Peccati's method is outlined. The deterministic version of our model is supplied in sections 2 and 3 while the stochastic one is in sections 4 and 5. In both formulations a foreign currency investment is entirely financed by own capital (sections 2, 2.1 for a zero-coupon bond, and 4) or by debt capital in another foreign currency (sections 3.1 and 5.1). Finally in sections 3.2 and 5.2 some leverage policies involving debt capital in a foreign currency are analysed. Summary and extensions follow in section 6.

1. The basic model

In this section the general structure of Peccati's method is outlined and some notations are given too. Constantly we refer to them for the successive extensions.

In a n-period framework, with the not restrictive assumption of period with equal lenght, both investment and financing are considered.

Let $\{f_s\}$ be the cash-flows of an investment at the corresponding times $s=0,\ldots,n$ and discount coefficient be $\varphi(t,\tau) = \Pi_{\tau+1}^{t}(1+x_s)^{-1}$, $t\geq\tau$, $\varphi(0,0)=1$. We say that a function φ is an Internal Financial Law (IFL) for the investment if the NPV

$$G[\varphi] = \Sigma_0^n f_s\varphi(s,0) = 0$$

where the "internal" period rates

$$x_s = \frac{\varphi(s-1,0) - \varphi(s,0)}{\varphi(s,0)} \tag{1}$$

characterize φ. By x_s it is possible to calculate the outstanding capitals

$$w_s = w_{s-1}(1 + x_s) - f_s; \quad s=1,..,n-1; \; w_0=-f_0, \; w_n=0 \tag{2}$$

that are crucial for the time decomposition of NPV.

As regards the loan, let $\{r_s\}$ be the corresponding period instalments and $\{\delta_s\}$ be the period costs of debt capital such that the following evolution of sinking fund is described by:

$$d_s = d_{s-1}(1 + \delta_s) - r_s; \qquad s=1,\ldots,n; \; d_0=-r_0$$

If investment is partially funded with debt capital, we assume that for the s-th period leverage ratio be $\vartheta_s=d_{s-1}/w_{s-1}$.

Moreover the model includes "external" cash-flows $\{\Xi_s\}$ which a financial project can involve such as, for example, tax payments and transaction costs.

Finally, if ρ_s are the opportunity costs between the times s-1 and s, $1 \le s \le n$, and $\Phi(s,0)=\Pi_1^s (1+\rho_t)^{-1}$, the NPV decomposition

$$G[\Phi] = \Sigma_0^n (f_s - r_s + \xi_s)\ \Phi(s,0)$$

turns out to be

$$G[\Phi] = \Sigma_1^n g_s$$

with period components

$$g_s = w_{s-1}\ [(1-\vartheta_s)(x_s-\rho_s) + \vartheta_s(x_s-\delta_s) + \xi_s]\Phi(s,0) \tag{3}$$

and $\xi_s = \Xi_{s-1}/w_{s-1}$, $1 \le s \le n$.

Here we do not dwell upon comments on the general Peccati's method and its applications even if of fundamental importance to appreciate its uselfuness as a new financial tool, but it is possible to refer to Peccati [1989, 1990] for a more complete analysis and references quoted therein. Nevertheless, as far as the aim of this paper it is important to stress that every period component g_s of the NPV consists of three distinct parts: the first one is linked to investment, the second one is connected to the loan and the last one concerns external cash-flows.

2. Investment in a foreign currency

In this section the case of an investment in a foreign currency[(2)] (f.c., in the following) is analysed in absence of debt capital. Therefore, let $\{F_s\}$ be the cash-flows of such an investment and Φ be a IFL with associated period rates X_s such that $G[\Phi]= \Sigma_0^n F_s\Phi(s,0)=0$. The outstanding capitals in f.c. turn out to be

$$W_s = W_{s-1}\ (1 + X_s) - F_s \tag{4}$$

that are similar to (2).

If at each date s=0,..,n the exchange rates - between f.c. and domestic currency (d.c., from now on) - are E_s and their relative variations during the periods are e_s, s = 1,...n, such that

$$E_s = E_{s-1}\ (1 + e_s),$$

(2) From now on, we use capital letters for the parameters which refer to foreign currency assets, while the small ones for the corresponding domestic currency values.

the following results:

$$E_s = E_0 \Pi_1^s (1+e_i)$$

where E_s is simply expressed in terms of initial value E_0 and period variations e_s of the exchange rates of previous periods.

On the other hand, for the corresponding investment in d.c. it follows that the cash-flows $\{f_s\}$, where $f_s = F_s \cdot E_s$, satisfy the relations[(3)] already mentioned in section 1 with $\vartheta_s = \xi_s = 0$.

At this point it is interesting to analyse for each period, how f.c. interest rate X_s and variations e_s affect the interest rate x_s of the equivalent investment in d.c. and how this dependence touches the NPV decomposition.

First of all, dividing (2) by E_s and comparing it with (4) we get that

$$x_s = X_s + e_s + X_s \cdot e_s. \qquad (5)$$

This last relation points out that the International Fisher Effect (IFE) holds for equity returns within each period, under the assumptions of movements in exchange rates perfectly anticipated and no inflation in domestic and foreign economy[(4)].

Finally, as regards the period component of the NPV in d.c., it results

$$g_s = w_{s-1} (X_s + e_s + X_s \cdot e_s - \rho_s)\Phi(s,0). \qquad (6)$$

From the last expression it follows that for each period, besides the f.c. interest rate X_s and the variation e_s of exchange rate, also product $X_s \cdot e_s$ interfere in g_s. And this last product is necessary because $w_{s-1} \cdot X_s \cdot e_s$ represents the distorsion that, at time s, d.c. interests $w_{s-1} \cdot X_s$ undergo because of e_s.

Before going on the explanation of models with liabilities in f.c., the following section hints a special application which is also interesting from a practical point of view.

2.1 Zero-coupon bonds in f.c.

---

(3) In this version of the paper the proofs are omitted. For proofs and further comments see Uberti [1990].

(4) See Hodder & Senbet [1990] for an uniperiodal analysis of IFE for interest rates in an inflationary and taxation environment. See also Jaffe & Madelker [1976] for an empirical study on the interaction between inflation and the return to risky assets.

Let us consider a zero-coupon bond investment with f.c. cash-flows $F_0=-A$, $F_s=0$, $s=1.....n-1$ and $F_n=R$. The corresponding d.c. cash-flows are: $f_0=a=A\cdot E_0$, $f_s=0$, $s=1,...,n-1$ and $f_n=r=R\cdot E_n$.

As far as the evaluation of the period return of bond and, hence, the NPV decomposition we note that a d.c. decision maker can have two different points of view:

(a) to consider the zero-coupon bond in f.c. to which constant period rates $X_s=X^*$ correspond;

(b) to think of the investment in d.c. as if it were a zero-coupon bond in d.c. with costant period rates $x_s=x^*$.

The two approaches are both interesting. In fact in the case (a) it can be useful to think of the zero-coupon bond in f.c. with constant period rates X^* so that the rates x_s absorb possible variations of exchange rates. On the contrary, with the approach (b), the investment in d.c. has constant period rates x^* "as if" such asset were a zero-coupon bond in d.c., while X_s is variable.

The possibility to apply the model in both cases, emphasize again the flexibility of Peccati's method as an actual evaluation tool for a financial decision maker.

Therefore let us consider the case (a). It is easy to show that the internal period rates of return in d.c. can be decomposed as:

$$x_s = y + e_s + y\cdot e_s \tag{7}$$

where

$$y = \left(\frac{r}{a\cdot \Pi_1^n \, (1+e_s)} \right)^{1/n} -1.$$

Again the IFE holds for bond returns. In fact, value y can be interpreted as the real rate of return of a "zero-coupon bond" in d.c. of emission price a $(=A\cdot E_0)$ and price at maturity $r/[\Pi_1^n(1+e_s)]$ $(=R\cdot E_0)$. Namely, the nominal period rate x_s is the "correction" of real rate y by variation e_s during the s-th period.

From (7) it is easy to calculate g_s by substituting (7) into (3).

As far as the second point of view, the internal rate of d.c. investment is

$$x^* = [\Pi_1^n(1 + e_s)]^{1/n} \, (R/A)^{1/n} -1$$

In this case it is interesting to notice that the presence of the period variations e_s of exchange rates is synthetized by the geometric mean of exchange rates all over periods.

By rate x^* it is possible to evaluate the f.c. corresponding period rates

$$X_s = \frac{x^* - e_s}{1 + e_s}$$

that, once more, emphasize the existence of IFE between domestic and foreignreturns in a multiperiod framework. Moreover

$$g_s = a\ (r/a\ )^{(s-1)/n} \cdot (X_s + e_s + X_s \cdot e_s - \rho_s)\Phi(s,0).$$

As announced, this last two expressions show (a) how it is possible to go back again to a "fictitious" zero-coupon bond in d.c. with nominal rate of return x^*, so that the variations e_s of exchange rates can be absorbed from the real period rates X_s of a corresponding f.c. bond and (b) how such dependences interfere in each period component g_s of NPV.

3. Debts in a foreign currency

3.1 Whole funding with debt capital

Let us assume that $\{R_s\}$ are the sequence of instalments in f.c. and that $\{\Delta_s\}$ are the one of cost rates corresponding to the loan in f.c.. Between sinking funds the following recursive relation turns out

$$D_s = D_{s-1}\ (1 + \Delta_s) - R_s\ .$$

On the other hand, if the sequence of instalments in d.c. are $\{r_s\}$ we get $r_s = R_s \cdot T_s$, where the exchange rates T_s of the f.c. refer to loan; and if the period variations of exchange rates are $\{\tau_s\}$, then $T_s = T_{s-1}(1+\tau_s)$.

Let δ_s be the cost rates of debt capital in d.c. so that $d_s = d_{s-1}(1+\delta_s) - r_s$ are the sinking fund in d.c.. As in section 2, it is easy to show that IFE holds for the cost rates within each period

$$\delta_s = \Delta_s + \tau_s + \Delta_s \cdot \tau_s \qquad (8)$$

so that the cost rates in d.c. can be evaluated by the cost rate in f.c. and the variations of exchange rate.

In the absence of constraints on borrowing/lending behaviour on international financial markets so that both investment and financing are in (possibly different) foreign currencies, then g_s can be split up as follows:

$$g_s = w_{s-1}[\underbrace{(X_s - \Delta_s)}_{(a)} + \underbrace{(e_s - \tau_s)}_{(b)} + \underbrace{X_s e_s - \Delta_s \tau_s}_{(c)}]\Phi(s,0) \qquad (9)$$

Also for representation (9), a consideration holds like that of investment case. In fact, by comparing the parameters associated to investment and financing, the components of g_s well show the spreads between : (a) assets and liabilities rates referred to the two foreign currencies, (b) the variations of exchange rates, (c) the influence of the last ones on assets and liabilities rates.

Finally, we notice that if (9) is compared with the period NPV components (3) of the basic model (with $\vartheta_s=0$) the last three addenda of (9) can be considered as the "external cash-flows" which correct the spread between rates X_s and Δ_s.

3.2 Leverage

As in section 1, let $\vartheta_s=d_{s-1}/w_{s-1}$ be the leverage ratio referred in d.c., for the sake of simplicity.

In this case, by relations (5) and (8) it is easy to obtain the following NPV decomposition

$$g_s = w_{s-1}[(1-\vartheta_s)(X_s-\rho_s)+\vartheta_s(X_s-\Delta_s)+\xi_s]\Phi(s,0),$$

which involves the parameters of loan in f.c. as well as the changes of exchange rates and where the "external cash-flows" $\xi_s=(1+X_s)e_s-\vartheta_s(1+\Delta_s)\tau_s$, multiplied by w_{s-1}, gather the components g_s that are tightly connected to the shifts e_s and τ_s of the two exchange rates.

4. Non-random investment in random f.c.

In this section and in the following ones, the investment in f.c. is assumed non-random, that is: cash-flows $\{F_s\}$, internal rates X_s and outstanding capitals W_s are non-random. We also assume that opportunity costs ρ_s be non-random.

In the more realistic stochastic case that we consider in the following, randomness is introduced by random rates $\tilde{e}_s$ which have given expected value $\bar{e}_s=E(\tilde{e}_s)$ and variance $\sigma^2(\tilde{e}_s)$. From this follows that, given E_0, exchange rates

$\tilde{E}_s$ are random, $1 \le s \le n$, with

$$\bar{E}_s = E_0 \cdot E[\Pi_1^s (1+\tilde{e}_i)] \qquad \text{and} \qquad \sigma^2(\tilde{E}_s) = E_0^2 \cdot \sigma^2[\Pi_1^s (1+\tilde{e}_i)].$$

As a consequence, investment in d.c. turns out to be random: cash-flows $\tilde{f}_s = F_s \cdot \tilde{E}_s$ are random with

$$\bar{f}_s = E(\tilde{f}_s) = F_s \cdot \bar{E}_s \qquad \text{and} \qquad \sigma^2(\tilde{f}_s) = F_s^2\, \sigma^2(\tilde{E}_s)$$

and internal rates of return $\tilde{x}_s$ are random as well as the corresponding IFL $\tilde{\varphi}$, such that $G[\tilde{\varphi}] = 0$.

First of all, as in deterministic case, the IFE exists even for random returns. In fact, comparing the parameters of non-random investment in f.c. with the ones of the equivalent random investment in d.c., we obtain that random interest period rates can be split as follows

$$\tilde{x}_s = X_s + \tilde{e}_s + X_s \cdot \tilde{e}_s$$

with moments:

$$\bar{x}_s = E\,(\tilde{x}_s) = X_s + \bar{e}_s + X_s \cdot \bar{e}_s$$

$$\sigma^2(\tilde{x}_s) = (1+X_s)^2\, \sigma^2(\tilde{e}_s).$$

The last expression shows that the rate risk $\sigma^2(\tilde{x}_s)$ increases not only with the exchange risk $\sigma^2(\tilde{e}_s)$ but also with period rate X_s in f.c..

As far as the decomposition of random NPV, an IFL can be chosen in a standard way as suggested in Luciano and Peccati [1990], according to wide spread and traditional financial evaluation methods. In our case, a standard IFL $\bar{\varphi}$ can be obtained by using the expected value $\bar{f}_s$ of cash-flows in d.c. and the associated interest rates x_s such that $G[\bar{\varphi}]=0$. It follows that the outstanding capitals w_s and x_s are non-random.

As regards the random d.c. investment it is possible to gather the randomness on rate $\tilde{x}_s$. In fact $\tilde{x}_s$ depends on $\tilde{f}_s$ by

$$\tilde{x}_s = \frac{w_s - w_{s-1} + \tilde{f}_s}{w_{s-1}}$$

Moreover, the expected value of $\tilde{x}_s$ is

$$\bar{x}_s = E(\tilde{x}_s) = \frac{w_s - w_{s-1} + \bar{f}_s}{w_{s-1}} = x_s$$

that is equal to period rate x_s corresponding to the d.c. investment with expected cash-flows; and variance

$$\sigma^2(\tilde{x}_s) = \frac{1}{w_{s-1}^2}\, \sigma^2(\tilde{f}_s) \qquad s = 1, \ldots, n$$

whose dependence on $\sigma^2(\tilde{f}_s)$ is weighed by outstanding w_{s-1} at the beginning of period.

From the last two expressions of the variance of $\tilde{x}_s$ it is easy to obtain $\sigma^2(\tilde{f}_s)$ depending on $\sigma^2(\tilde{e}_s)$ and the internal rate of investment in f.c.:

$$\sigma^2(\tilde{f}_s) = w^2_{s-1} (1+X_s)^2 \sigma^2(\tilde{e}_s).$$

Therefore it is possible to conclude that given $\bar{e}_s$ and $\sigma^2(\tilde{e}_s)$, at each period the expected value and the variance of random interest rate $\tilde{x}_s$ as well as the ones of the random cash-flow $\tilde{f}_s$ of investment in d.c. depend on the interest rate X_s of f.c. investment.

Finally, the s-th random component of the NPV decomposition is

$$\tilde{g}_s = w_{s-1}(X_s + \tilde{e}_s + X_s\tilde{e}_s - \rho_s)\Phi(s,0)$$

with expected value

$$\bar{g}_s = E(\tilde{f}_s) = w_{s-1}(X_s+ \bar{e}_s+X_s\bar{e}_s-\rho_s)\Phi(s,0)$$

and variance

$$\sigma^2(\tilde{g}_s) = [w_{s-1}(1+X_s)]^2 \sigma^2(\tilde{e}_s)\Phi^2(s,0) = \sigma^s(\tilde{f}_s)\Phi^2(s,0).$$

which stress, once again, the period quote dependence on X_s, $\bar{e}_s$ and $\sigma^2(\tilde{e}_s)$.

5. Non-random funding in random f.c.

In the following both whole and partial funding are considered. The results obtained in the first case are used to analyse the more realistic - and complicate - one of leverage involving randomness of f.c..

5.1 Whole funding

Referring to section 3.1 for the notations connected to fund with debt capital in a f.c. and arguing about randomness as in section 4, it follows that once more the IFE holds for costs rates

$$\tilde{\delta}_s = \Delta_s + \tilde{\tau}_s + \Delta_s \tilde{\tau}_s.$$

The expected value

$$\bar{\delta}_s = E(\tilde{\delta}_s) = \Delta_s + \bar{\tau}_s + \Delta_s \cdot \bar{\tau}_s$$

and variance

$$\sigma^2(\tilde{\delta}_s) = (1+\Delta_s)^2 \sigma^2(\tilde{\tau}_s)$$

depend on the cost rate Δ_s of debt capital in f.c. and the random variation $\tilde{\tau}_s$

of exchange rate.

Moreover random instalments $\tilde{r}_s$ have expected values $\bar{r}_s=E(\tilde{r}_s)$ and variances $\sigma^2(\tilde{r}_s) = d^2_{s-1}(1+\Delta_s)^2\ \sigma^2(\tilde{\tau}_s)$. In this case sinking fund dynamics $d_s=d_{s-1}(1+\delta_{s-1})-\bar{r}_s$ will be stated by the non-random d.c. loan to which expected instalments $\bar{r}_s$ corresponds.

As regards the NPV decomposition, the s-th random component $\tilde{g}_s$ is

$$\tilde{g}_s = w_{s-1}[(X_s-\Delta_s) + (\tilde{e}_s-\tilde{\tau}_s) + X_s\cdot\tilde{e}_s - \Delta_s\tilde{\tau}_s]\Phi(s,0)$$

with moments

$$\bar{g}_s = E(\tilde{g}_s) = w_{s-1}[(X_s-\Delta_s) + (\bar{e}_s-\bar{\tau}_s) + X_s\bar{e}_s - \Delta_s\bar{\tau}_s]\Phi(s,0)$$

$$\sigma^2(\tilde{g}_s) = w^2_{s-1}[(1+X_s)^2\ \sigma^2(\tilde{e}_s) + (1+\Delta_s)^2\ \sigma^2(\tilde{\tau}_s)+$$

$$- 2(1+X_s)(1+\Delta_s)\cdot\rho(\tilde{e}_s,\tilde{\tau}_s)\cdot\sigma(\tilde{e}_s)\cdot\sigma(\tilde{\tau}_s)]\Phi^2(s,0)$$

where ρ is the correlation coefficient and σ represents the standard deviation.

Arguing as in Luciano & Peccati [1990], in our case we can conclude that the randomness of $\tilde{g}_s$ comes down if $\tilde{e}_s$ and $\tilde{\tau}_s$ are positively correlated. Moreover, for given X_s and Δ_s, $\sigma^2(\tilde{g}_s)$ reduces as the correlation between $\tilde{e}_s$ and $\tilde{\tau}_s$ increases.

In the special case of perfect positive correlation, $\rho(\tilde{e}_s,\tilde{\tau}_s)=1$, i.e. $\tilde{\tau}_s=\alpha_s\tilde{e}_s+\beta_s$, then variance $\sigma^2(\tilde{g}_s)$ is null iff in addition holds:

$$\alpha_s = \frac{1 + X_s}{1 + \Delta_s}\ .$$

Moreover, if $\rho(\tilde{e}_s,\tilde{\tau}_s)=1$ and the expected values of the period variations of the exchange rates are equal (i.e. $\bar{\tau}_s=\bar{e}_s$) then the variance $\sigma^2(\tilde{g}_s)$ vanishes if and only if $\Delta_s = X_s$. Obviously, in this last case also $\bar{g}_s=0$.

5.2 Leverage

Let $\vartheta_s= d_{s-1}/w_{s-1}$ be the non-random ratio of debt capital referred to d.c..

By the results in sections 4 and 5.1, it is easy to obtain a decomposition of random NPV with random investment and random financing in f.c. but evaluated in d.c.. In fact, we get

$$\tilde{g}_s=w_{s-1}\{(1-\vartheta_s)(X_s+\tilde{e}_s+X_s\tilde{e}_s-\rho_s)+\vartheta_s[X_s+\tilde{e}_s+X_s\tilde{e}_s-(\Delta_s+\tilde{\tau}_s+\Delta_s\tilde{\tau}_s)]\}\Phi(s,0)$$

and expected value and variance turn out to be, respectively:

$$\bar{g}_s=w_{s-1}\{(1-\vartheta_s)(X_s+\bar{e}_s+X_s\bar{e}_s-\rho_s)+\vartheta_s[X_s+\bar{e}_s+X_s\bar{e}_s-(\Delta_s+\bar{\tau}_s+\Delta_s\bar{\tau}_s)]\}\Phi(s,0)$$

$$\sigma^2(\tilde{g}_s) = w^2_{s-1}[(1+X_s)^2\ \sigma^2(\tilde{e}_s)+\vartheta^2_s(1+\Delta_s)^2\ \sigma^2(\tilde{\tau}_s)]+$$

$$-2(1+X_s)(1+\Delta)\vartheta_s\cdot\rho(\tilde{e}_s,\tilde{\tau}_s)\cdot\sigma(\tilde{e}_s)\cdot\sigma(\tilde{\tau}_s)]\Phi(s,0).$$

As in the previous section a positive correlation between $\tilde{e}_s$ and $\tilde{\tau}_s$ reduces $\sigma^2(\tilde{g}_s)$. Furthermore if $\rho(\tilde{e}_s,\tilde{\tau}_s)$ is equal to 1 and

$$0 < \alpha_s < \frac{1+X_s}{1+\Delta_s}$$

then the risk associated to $\tilde{g}_s$ is null iff the leverage policy

$$\vartheta_s = \alpha_s\ \frac{1+X_s}{1+\Delta_s}$$

is chosen.

This leverage policy is interesting because it involves the non-random interest rates of assets and liabilities in f.c. as well as the correlation coefficient between the two corresponding exchange rates.

6. Summary and extensions

In this paper we propose deterministic and stochastic models to decompose the NPV of foreign currency assets in a multiperiod framework. Such a decomposition turns out to be very significant because, within each period, (i) the IFE holds for both equity returns and interest rates referred to assets in domestic and foreign currencies, and (ii) each component of NPV is split up in addenda which involve separately the parameters of investment, financing and exchanges. Therefore at each period it is possible to separate the effects of the shifts of the exchange rates of currencies from the spreads among interest rates, the cost of debt capital and the opportunity cost.

Moreover, it is worth noticing that stochastic models work with no one assumptions of independence on random variables among periods. Nevertheless, if inside to a period the assumption of perfect positive correlation between variations of exchange rates of currencies is made, a leverage policy exists in order that the risk of corresponding period NPV component is null.

Further research should focus on the NPV decomposition under different (i) assumptions on the stochastic processes which govern the variation rates of exchange rates in foreign currencies and the relations among several studied variables (interest rates, debt capital and opportunity cost) as well as (ii) leverage policies. Moreover the scheme could be enriched with the inclusion of an inflationary and taxation environment (for example see Hodder & Senbet [1990], Levi [1977], Howard & Johnson [1982]).

References

J. E. HODDER, L. W. SENBET [1990] "International capital structure equilibrium", *The Journal of Finance,* XLV, no. 5, pp. 1495-1516.

D. H. HOWARD, K. H. JOHNSON [1982] "Interest rates, inflation, and taxes. The Foreign Connection", *Economic Letters*, 9, pp. 181-184.

J. F. JAFFE, G. MANDELKER [1976] "The 'Fisher Effect' for risky assets: an empirical investigation", *Journal of Finance*, 31, no. 2, pp. 447-58.

M. D. LEVI [1977] "Taxation and 'abnormal' international capital flows", *Journal of Political Economy*, 85, no. 3, pp. 635-646.

E. LUCIANO, L. PECCATI (1990) *The decomposition of random discounted cash flows*, Seventh Meeting of the EURO working Group on Financial Modelling, Sirmione (I), April 5-7.

L. PECCATI (1989) *Multiperiod analysis of a levered portfolio*, Proceedings of the Fifth Meeting of the Euro Working Group on Financial Modelling, Catania (I), April 20-21, Special Issue of *Rivista di matematica per le scienze economiche e sociali,* 12, pp. 157-166.

L. PECCATI (1990) "Valutazione analitica e sintetica di attivita' finanziarie", *Quaderni della Rivista Milanese di Economia*, to appear.

M. UBERTI (1990) "Present value decomposition of foreign currency assets", *Quaderno n.59, Serie III, dell'Istituto di Matematica Finanziaria di Torino*, Torino.

INSTITUTIONALLY HETEROGENEOUS AGENTS IN AN IMITATIVE STOCK-MARKET

L. Ferrari - E. Luciano - L. Peccati
Ist. di Mat. Fin. – Fac. di Ec. e Comm. – Università
Piazza Arbarello, 8 – 10122 Torino – Italia

1 Introduction

The host of anomalies and the bulk of difficulties in explaining the stock-market (S.M.) behaviour, according to standard criteria only, are well-known. As a counterpart, the explicit use of agents' heterogeneity and "imitation" supplies a more realistic grasp of some relevant market features, although in highly simplified and theoretical models. In this framework the aim of this paper is to stress two points, by using a single-stock model where only market orders are allowed[1].

The first point is agents' heterogeneity arising from the fact that they enter the market at different times. With this aim, we distinguish between two classes of agents :

(i) professional traders, who make their investment choices throughout the t.d., in accordance with the current price.

(ii) non-professional investors, who buy or sell at the beginning of the t.d., on the basis of the information about the previous closing price.

The second point, which follows also from agents' heterogeneity as described by the first point, is the distinction between two different equilibrium prices:

(i) the short-run equilibrium price, which can be thought of as the listed price for a single trading day (t.d.);

(ii) the long-run price, which in turn is the equilibrium value of the short-run prices.

Both of these points justify the presence of imitation in the stock market.

The paper is structured as follows. In section #2 we analyze a first model of interaction among agents of heterogeneous types, without considering imitation. In section #3 we study a special case of imitation between agents, while in section #4 we consider a general model.

[1]For the distinction between *market* and *limit* orders see for instance PAGANO-ROELL (1990a). The former are placed with a dealer or a specialist, the latter with brokers or a specialist. As a consequence, the distinction between market and limit orders enlarges to that between markets with dealers or a specialist acting as a dealer, and markets with brokers or a specialist acting as a broker. The rôle of dealers has been analysed for instance by GARMAN (1976), STOLL (1978), HO-STOLL (1980), CONROY-WINKLER (1986) and PAGANO-ROELL (1990b). The rôle of the specialist acting both as a dealer and as a broker is studied for instance in USHC (1972). See also the review article CHEN-MAIER-SCHWARTZ-WHITCOMB (1979). Important contributions through simulation methods come also from LOISTL-LANDES (1989) and from the more recent LOISTL-LANDES (1990).

2 Heterogeneous agents, with speculative attitudes only

2.1 The constant parameter case

It is evidently impossible to analyze a S.M., without making precise assumptions on its organization. heterogeneous organizations and rules of negotiation bring about heterogeneous problems, quotations and paths to the equilibrium price. As for this paper, we consider a single-equity economy with market orders only.

We have only three types of agents[2]:

(i) **The Specialist** (S.), who is obliged to make a price on the stock. His aim is to clear the market, not to make a profit. This is because, in order to prevent unbounded monopoly profits, we assume he has no stock. He maintains the position he desires through a sequel of transactions in the unique stock of this market.

(ii) **Professional traders** (P.T.) – The agents who continuously negotiate with the specialist[3]. They are assumed to act as speculators and to have a representative agent.

(iii) **Non-professional traders** (N.P.T.) – Speculators, who decide to buy or to sell, before the beginning of the t.d., placing irrevocable orders . The N.P.T., aware of their weak position in the market, can decide, also, to imitate professional investors decisions. The models we propose from sec. # 3 onwards do incorporate this hypothesis.

The general set-up of the model can be suitably presented with reference to the taxonomy we have recalled.

A premise about time must be made. A first clock counts the t.d.'s through the index $T = 1, 2, 3, \ldots$, and we need values for the state variables at $T = 0$.

Another clock counts the order placements during each t.d.. Let S be the common duration of each t.d.. For each of them we introduce a "local" time variable with origin at its beginning and unity fixed so that the terminal epoch of the t.d. is S. For the T-th t.d. we then have a monotonically increasing sequence of order placement epochs $t_n(T)$ converging to S. In symbols:

$$t_n(T) < t_{n+1}(T) \ \forall n = 0, 1, 2, \ldots \ \text{ and } \ n \to +\infty \Rightarrow t_n(T) \to S$$

It is reasonable to assume that the initial (final) epochs of consecutive t.d. are equidistant, while the sequences of order placement epochs cannot share this property[4].

In this framework, at each epoch of the sequence $\{T\}$ the S. formulates a price. At this price both the P.T. and N.P.T. place an order, which is executed at the S. price. If during this first trade supply and demand do not clear, the S. revises his price. Since he has no stock in fact, he aims at clearing the market during each t.d.. He acts knowing that his counterpart is formed by speculators. When the S. fixes a new price, N.P.T. do not react – they wait until the next t.d. in order to place an eventual new order – while the P.T. places new ordes. These orders, which are carried out at the price fixed by the S., are again based on speculative criteria. After the first instant, within a t.d., the market is then characterized by the interaction of the P.T. and the S. only.

[2]The following definitions are partially connected with the ones proposed in FLAVELL (1989).

[3]They could do this via intermediaries (brokers). The rôle of brokers however will be studied at a later stage of this research.

[4]A complement to this paper (available on requesT) shows how a sequence $\{t_n(T)\}$ can be endogenously generated, based on the price history.

Behaviour equations for the N.P.T.

Let $m = 1, 2, \dots M$ be the index counting the agents of this type. For the m-th N.P.T. in the T-th t.d. we assume the following behaviour equation:

$$q_m(T) = -\alpha_m[P(T-1) - r] \tag{1}$$

where $q_m(T)$ is the value of the market order for the T-th t.d., $P(T-1)$ is the specialist price, at which the N.P.T.'s orders are carried out; r_m is the fundamental value (F.V.) of the stock, which is common belief to N.P.T.. Finally, α_m is a positive reaction parameter[5], so that negative values of $q_m(T)$ represent sale orders, and positive values buy ones.

Define $Q(T)$ as the sum of the $q_m(T)$. Adding up the equations for the $q_m(T)$'s, in this simple model one gets:

$$Q(T) = -a[P(T-1) - r] \tag{2}$$

where α is the sum of the α_m. This relation substitutes (1) in this section.

Behaviour equations for P.T.

We model the behaviour of the (representative) P.T. within any t.d. substantially in the same way as for N.P.T., *i.e.*, as a speculative one. However, the P.T. continuously revises his position in accordance with the current specialist price.

Reminding that $n = 0, 1, 2, \dots$ is the index counting the order placement epochs $t_n(T)$, and letting $B_n(T)$ be the total amount of orders placed by the P.T. till to the n-th epoch (included), so that $B_0(T) = 0$, the transactions carried out at $t_n(T)$ are then:

$$B_n(T) - B_{n-1}(T) = -\beta[p_{n-1}(T) - h] \tag{3}$$

where $p_{n-1}(T)$ is the S. price, at which these orders will be carried out[6], β is the P.T. (positive) reaction parameter and h is the P.T.'s F.V..

The total amount of transactions by the P.T. in the T-th t.d. is $B^*(T) \stackrel{d}{=} \lim_{n\to+\infty} B_n(T)$, provided that the latter limit exists.

Behaviour equation for the specialist

As a consequence of the general framework explained above, the S. fixes an initial price and then formulates a sequence of prices according to the following rule: he increases (decreases) the price with respect to the fundamental value as long as there is total net demand (supply).

Let us denote with $p_0(T)$ the initial price for the T-th t.d.. We assume that the S. sets its value[7] equal to the closing price of the last t.d.:

$$p_0(T) = P(T-1) \tag{4}$$

As concerns the ensuing prices of the T-th t.d., $p_n(T)$ for $n \geq 1$, the S. behaviour can be formalized with the following equation:

$$p_n(T) = k + \eta[Q(T) + B_n(T)] \tag{5}$$

where η is a positive parameter and k is the F.V. he attributes to the stock.

---

[5]This equation is substantially the same used in FERRARI-PECCATI (1991) to describe the agents' behaviour in the non-imitation case.

[6]It is possible to take into acount in equation (3) the bid-ask spread by adding to the price at the $n-1$-th call an expression like the following: $\epsilon(B_n - B_{n-1}) \cdot | B_n - B_{n-1} |$, where ϵ is proportional to the signum function. This destroys the linearity of the model, but it is easy to check that it doesn't affect its equilibrium.

[7]Which - as we demonstrate - will not affect the ultimate output of the trading process.

Short-run and long-run equilibria

To get a complete system we need to formalize the connection between the time paths of prices $\{p_n(T)\}$ at which the orders of the P.T. have been carried out during the T-th t.d. and the corresponding closing price. We assume that the closing price $P^*(T)$ is the short-run stable equilibrium point, if it exists:

$$P^*(T) \stackrel{d}{=} \lim_{n \to +\infty} p_n(T) \tag{6}$$

$P(0)$ is assumed to be given.

Our model is then represented by the system (1)—(4).

Within this model we analyze both a short-run equilibrium, which concerns a single t.d., and a long-run one, *i.e.*, an inter-day one. The former is determined by the behaviour of equations (3) and (5), the latter by equation (2).

As concerns the short-run equilibrium, note that an equilibrium point $[p^*(T), B^*(T)]$ must satisfy:

$$p^*(T) = k + \eta[B^*(T) + Q(T)]$$

$$B^*(T) = B^*(T) - \beta(p^*(T) - h)$$

or:

$$p^*(T) = h$$

$$B^*(T) = (h - k)/\eta - Q(T)$$

The coefficient matrix of the system (3) and (5), has eigenvalues 0 and $1 - \eta\beta$. Then the equilibrium is stable iff $\mid 1 - \eta\beta \mid < 1$ or $0 < \eta\beta < 2$. The economic meaning of this condition is quite evident. It requires that the "global" reaction intensity of the agents represented by the product $\eta\beta$ is not too high. Within the t.d. the N.P.T. are neutral, from the point of view of the stability, and the equilibrium can be reached iff the product of the reaction parameters of the P.T. and the S. is under two. In other words, an equilibrium can be reached also in the presence of – say – an overreactive S. if the P.T. react mildly enough.

The closing prices $P(T)$ are equal to the F.V., as viewed by the P.T.. This implies that a long-run price is reached at $T = 1$.

2.2 The variable parameter case

Assume now that the F.V. estimate of the P.T. and of N.P.T. is no longer constant, but evolve according to the signals coming from the market.

In the former model the trade $[B(T) + Q(T)]$ is proportional to the discrepancy between h and k. We assume that the P.T. adjusts his F.V. $h = h(T)$, through a relation of the type:

$$h(T+1) = h(T) - \Omega[B(T) + Q(T)]$$

where Ω is a positive adjustment speed. This equation can be justified by assuming that he believes that the estimate of the F.V. by the S., k, is more accurate than his own. Since the traded amount is proportional to the difference between h and k $(B + Q = (h - k)/\eta)$, from the sign of $B(T) + Q(T)$ he infers the sign of the difference $h - k$.

As concerns the N.P.T., assume that he adjusts his opinion about the F.V. of the stock by observing its closing price each t.d.:

$$r(T) = (1 - \omega)r(T-1) + \omega P(T-1)$$

where $\omega \in (0,1)$ is an adjustment speed parameter. As it is well known in Insurance Theory, such an equation can be interpreted in terms of Credibility Theory as result of a Bayesian information updating process.

With these new hypotheses, the short-run equilibria, if they exist, are characterized by $p^*(T) = h(T)$ and $B^*(T) = (h(T) - k)/\eta - Q(T)$, while the dynamical system describing the evolution from t.d. to t.d. – and eventually the long-run equilibrium – is the following:

$$\begin{cases} Q(T) = -\alpha[P(T-1) - r(T)] \\ P(T) = h(T) \\ h(T) = h(T-1) - \Omega[B(T-1) + Q(T-1)] \\ B(T) = [h(T) - k]/\eta - Q(T) \\ r(T) = (1-\omega)r(T-1) + \omega P(T-1) \end{cases} \tag{7}$$

It substitutes eq. (2) in the original formulation, and its equilibria – provided that they are stable – may be understood as the long-run equilibria of our market.

The equilibria for the system above are characterized by:

$$P^* = h^* = r^* = k \;;\; B^* = 0 \;;\; Q^* = 0 \tag{8}$$

The stability properties of this equilibrium, since h and P have the same value for $T \geq 1$, can be studied through the system with state variables $[Q(T) \;\; P(T) \;\; B(T) \;\; r(T)]^T$ (where ^{T} denotes transposition). In turn its asymptotic behaviour depends on whether the eigenvalues of its coefficients matrix fall in the unit circle of the complex plane or not.

These eigenvalues are: 0 (double), $1-\omega$, $1-\Omega/\eta$.

It is then clear that the condition under which the equilibrium is approached is $\Omega < 2\eta$. By recalling the meaning of the two parameters Ω and η it is possible to provide an economic interpretation for this condition. Precisely, Ω is the price adjustment parameter of the P.T., while η is the S. reaction parameter. Our condition requires that this reaction parameter must be sufficiently high with respect to the adjustement parameter of the P.T.: $\eta > \frac{1}{2}\Omega$. When this condition is violated an eigenvalue of the coefficient matrices is < -1. This fact entails an explosive and oscillating component in the time path of the system. This unstabilizing element disappears when the price choices of the S. are sufficiently strong to succeed in containing the reactions by the P.T..

If the mentioned condition is fulfilled the equilibrium is stable and the long-run evolution of the market is decribed by (8).

3 Different agents and imitation w. r. t. the P.T. The variable parameter case

From a more realistic point of view, it can be assumed that, in a market with different possibilities of anticipating the movements of the market, different economic power positions and beliefs, the imitative behaviour among agents is widespread. In a very simple and idealized S.M., like the one introduced in section 1, there may be a very large number of possible imitative networks at work. Two of them seem to us particularly relevant:

1. homogeneous imitation of N.P.T. with respect to the P.T. and
2. imitation of the N.P.T. among each other and heterogeneous imitation with respect to the P.T..

They are analysed respectively in this and in the following section.

When the N.P.T. takes his investment decisions in part comparing the current price and the F.V., in part imitating the behaviour of the P.T., in the system (7) only the first equation must be modified:

$$Q(T) = -\alpha[P(T-1) - r(T)] + \gamma B(T-1) \tag{9}$$

where γ is a positive parameter which increases demand or decreases supply whenever in the last t.d. the P.T. bought the stock, and vice-versa when he sold it.

In the present case, the trading process between S. and P.T., and then the short-run equilibrium, are not touched by imitation. The closing price of the T-th t.d. and the quantities traded by P.T. remain unchanged.

The long-run equilibrium values too are not affected by imitation. However, as concerns stability, the dynamics of the system (7) with (9) instead of its first equation is decided by the following eigenvalues: 0, $1-\omega$, $-g$,$1-\Omega/h$. A further condition to be fulfilled to get for stability is then $|\gamma|< 1$. This further constraint deserves some comment. Large values of γ (precisely: $\gamma > 1$) introduce in the solution of the system an explosive-oscillatory component which prevents stability. In other words: there is no problem for the market stability if the N.P.T. mildly imitates the P.T.. If this imitative behaviour induces transactions globally larger than the imitated one, instability is assured. It's worthwhile to remark that in presence of *many N.P.T.'s* imitating the same P.T. this could happen. Recent anti-imitation measures studied for introduction into the London Stock-Exchange can find a simple justification even in our over-simplified world.

4 Different agents and generalized imitation by N.P.T. The variable parameter case

Let us assume now that N.P.T. not only imitate the P.T. in a manner possibly different from agent to agent, but also that they try to learn from each other. As in the previous section, the short-run equilibrium is unaltered.

As for the long-run one, in the presence of imitation among the M N.P.T. and possibly unequal imitative behaviour with respect to each other it is impossible to replace this class of agents with a representative agent. Equation (2), in fact, becomes now:

$$q_m(T) = -\alpha_m[P(T-1) - r(T)] + \gamma_m B(T-1) + \sum_{s=1}^{M} e_{m,s)q_m(T-1)} \tag{10}$$

where γ_m is the m-th investor imitation parameter with respect to the P.T. orders at $T-1$, $e_{m,s}$ is the m-th agent imitation coefficient with respect to th s-th N.P.T. orders at $T-1$. Define the transactions vector $\mathbf{q}(T) \in \mathbf{R}^M$:

$$\mathbf{q}(T) \stackrel{d}{=} \begin{bmatrix} q_1(T) \\ q_2(T) \\ \vdots \\ q_M(T) \end{bmatrix}$$

Define also the square matrix $\mathbf{E}$ of order M, collecting the imitation coefficients among N.P.T., $\mathbf{E} \stackrel{d}{=} [e_{m,s}]$, the vector $\mathbf{g} \in \mathbf{R}^M$ collecting the imitation coefficients of N.P.T. towards the P.T. and $\mathbf{a}^*$, the M-th order diagonal matrix having on its principal diagonal the α_m. Finally, let us denote with $\mathbf{1}$ the M-vector with unitary components and let $\mathbf{r}(T)$ be the M-vector collecting the opinions of N.P.T. about the F.V.. The last equation becomes:

$$\mathbf{q}(T) = -\mathbf{a}^*[P(T-1)\mathbf{1} - \mathbf{r}(T)] + \mathbf{g}B(T-1) + \mathbf{E}\mathbf{q}(T-1) \tag{11}$$

which substitutes (9).

As concerns the short-run equilibrium, we still have $p^*(T) = h(T)$, while the equation defining the closing price becomes:

$$B(T) = [h(T) - k]/\eta - \mathbf{1}^T\mathbf{q}(T) \tag{12}$$

As concerns the long-run equation, and then the system (7), the closing price is still given by:

$$P(T) = h(T) \tag{13}$$

The opinion evolution equations become:

$$lh(T) = h(T-1) - W[B(T-1) + 1q(T-1)] \tag{14}$$

$$\mathbf{r}(T) = (\mathbf{I} - \mathbf{w}^*)\mathbf{r}(T-1) + \mathbf{w}^*\mathbf{1}^T P(T-1) \tag{15}$$

where $\mathbf{I}$ is an $M \times M$ identity matrix and $\mathbf{w}^*$ is the $M \times M$ diagonal matrix of N.P.T. adjustment speeds with respect to the F.V..

Any equilibrium point of the system must satisfy the following system of linear equations in the $2M+3$ unknowns $\mathbf{q}^*, P^*, B^*, h^*, \mathbf{r}^*$:

$$\begin{aligned}
&\mathbf{q}^* = \mathbf{a}^*(\mathbf{1}P^* - \mathbf{r}^*) + \mathbf{g}^*B^* + \mathbf{E}\mathbf{q}^* \\
&B^* = [h^* - k]/\eta - \mathbf{1}^T\mathbf{q}^* \\
&P^* = h^* \\
&h^* = h^* - \Omega(B^* + \mathbf{1}^T\mathbf{q}^*) \\
&\mathbf{r}^* = (\mathbf{I} - \mathbf{w}^*)\mathbf{r}^* + \mathbf{w}^*\mathbf{1}P^*
\end{aligned}$$

The fourth equation provides $B^* + \mathbf{1}^T\mathbf{q}^* = 0$. The second one, remembering the fourth, gives $h^* = k$. Hence $P^* = k$ too. Under the hypothesis of nonsingularity for $(\mathbf{I} - \mathbf{E})$ we get from the first equation: $\mathbf{q}^* = (\mathbf{I} - \mathbf{E})\mathbf{g}B^*$, since from the last equation we have $\mathbf{r}^* = \mathbf{1}P^*$. By substituting in the fourth equation we get:

$$B^*[1 + \mathbf{1}^T(\mathbf{I} - \mathbf{E})\mathbf{g}] = 0$$

where the expression in square brackets may be zero for special matrices $\mathbf{E}$. If we assume that the imitation among N.P.T. is sufficiently small, then $\mathbf{I} - \mathbf{E}$ is nonnegatively invertible, the expression in square brackets is positive and we must have $B^* = 0$. This entails $\mathbf{q}^* = \mathbf{0}$.

To sum up we have a long-run equilibrium characterized by:

1. same opinions of all the agents about the F.V.,

2. price equal to the F.V.,

3. trade vanishing in the long-run.

These characteristics of the long-run equilibrium may disappear in the presence of more realistic random or nonlinear relations between the variables. On these points see respectively LUCIANO (1992), who studies the effect of random disturbances in a world with symmetric information, and CORNAGLIA (1992), who introduces nonlinearities in our model.

AKNOWLEDGEMENTS

We thank for some interesting remarks about a previous version of this paper M. Cenci, A. Cerquetti, R. Flavell, L. Ghezzi and O. Loistl.

REFERENCES

K.J. COHEN, S.F. MAIER, R.A. SCHWARTZ, D.K. WHITCOMB (1979): 'Market Makers and the Market Spread: a Review of Recent Literature', *Journal of Financial and Quantitative Analysis*, **14**, pp. 813-835.

R.M. CONROY, R.L. WINKLER (1986): 'Market Structure: The Specialist as Dealer and Broker', *Journal of Banking and Finance*, **10**, pp. 21-36.

A. CORNAGLIA (1992): 'A Nonlinear Model of Stock-Market Behaviour with Imitation', in this volume.

L. FERRARI , L. PECCATI (1991): 'Stock-Market Behaviour and Imitation: a Simple Model', in A. CORNAGLIA - L. FERRARI - E. LUCIANO - L. PECCATI (1991): *Some Models of imperfect financial Markets*, Quaderni dell'Istituto di Matematica Finanziaria dell'Università di Torino, serie III, n. 62.

R. FLAVELL (1989): 'A Model of a Trader", *6th Meeting of the EURO Working Group on Financial Modelling*, Liège.

M.B. GARMAN (1976): 'Market Microstructure'. *Journal of Financial Economics*, **3**, pp. 33-53.

T. HO, H.R. STOLL (1980): 'On Dealer Markets under Competition'. *Journal of Finance*, **35**, pp. 259-267.

O. LOISTL , T. LANDES (1989): *The Dynamic Pricing of Financial Assets*, McGraw-Hill, Hamburg.

O. LOISTL , T. LANDES (1990): 'Complexity Models in Financial Markets - The Interdependencies of non-observable value estimates and observable price quotations'. Unpublished Manuscript.

E. LUCIANO (1992): 'Market making with noise: the case of a financial market with heterogeneous traders', in this volume.

M. PAGANO, A. ROELL (1990a): 'Shifting Gears: An Economic Evaluation of the Reform of the Paris Bourse', Unpublished Manuscript.

M. PAGANO, A. ROELL (1990b): 'Mercati d'asta, Mercati di dealers e rischio di esecuzione', Unpublished Manuscript.

H.R. STOLL (1978): 'The supply of Dealer Services in Securities Markets', *Journal of Finance*, 33, pp. 1133-1151.

UNITED STATES HOUSE COMMITTEE ON INTERSTATE AND FOREIGN COMMERCE AND FINANCE (USHC) (1972): 'Securities Industry study: Report and hearings', *U.S., 92nd Congress*, 1st and 2nd t.d.s.

PRICING CONTINGENT CLAIMS: FIRST- AND SECOND-ORDER EFFECTS FROM STOCHASTIC INTEREST RATE DEVELOPMENT

Bjarne Astrup Jensen, Institute of Finance, Copenhagen Business School, Rosenørns Alle 31,3., DK-1970 Frb. C.

Jørgen Aase Nielsen, Dept. of Operations Research, Institute of Mathematics, B 530, Aarhus University, Ny Munkegade, DK-8000 Aarhus C.

Acknowledgements

Part of this research was supported by the Danish Social Science Research Council. We appreciate comments on an earlier version of this paper from participants at the European Finance Association's 17th Annual Meeting in Athens, August 1990. In particular we would like to thank Peter Carr and Jin-Chuan Duan.

Abstract

Applying an intertemporal and arbitrage-free binomial lattice model for the development of the term structure of interest rates, we derive the equations that determine prices of interest rate contingent claims.
The theoretically correct, arbitrage-free premiums for call options on bonds are compared with the "pseudo premiums" obtained by adopting the common practice of treating the short term rate of interest as a constant. This practice has been justified by referring to an assumed second-order effect on option premiums.
We find that the deviations between the arbitrage-free premiums and the "pseudo premiums" cannot be discarded as second-order effects. For a certain range of the exercise price the deviations constitute an essential first-order effect.

1. Introduction

In recent years it has been recognised that converting standard models for pricing contingent claims from a scenario of interest rate **certainty** to a scenario of interest rate **uncertainty** is far from being an easy step.
In the pricing models of the Black-Scholes type, the binomial type etc. it is often either assumed that the short term rate of interest is developing in a deterministic manner; or, in case a stochastic development is allowed for, the short term rate of interest is brought to disappear from the scene by substituting the instantaneously maturing bond in the duplicating portfolio with a zero-coupon bond maturing at the expiration date for the option.
The latter approach to contingent claims pricing under interest rate uncertainty was first developed in Merton(1973). It relies on an assumed homogeneity of the pricing function, which requires that the type of stochastic process for the dynamic development of the zero-coupon bond price must be chosen accordingly.[1]
Neither of these modeling strategies are theoretically valid for the pricing of contingent claims written on bonds. However, taking account of interest rate uncertainty in a strictly adequate manner will add considerable complications to the standard models for pricing contingent claims and deprive them of most of their unquestionable elegance. To overcome some of these complications, various authors have

---

1) The approach mentioned is incompatible with the fundamental requirements for the stochastic processes for bond prices. The restrictions on these processes are analysed in detail in Jensen&Nielsen(1988).

suggested a short cut, when the underlying bonds are "longer term" bonds and the time until expiration on derivatives is "short". It is conjectured that the inaccuracies induced by assuming stochastically varying "long rates" and constant "short rates" are second-order effects in the sense that the prices of derivatives are relatively insensitive to the modeling of short rates compared to the modeling of long rates. E.g., in their continuous-time, duration based model, Schaefer&Schwartz(1987) deliberately assumed the instantaneous riskless rate of return to be a constant. They did so with the following remarks (ibid., p. 1120-21):

> "In theory, it would be easy to include a stochastic short rate of interest in our model, but doing this would involve considerable complication in its practical application.... .
> Given the empirical evidence on the performance of the Black-Scholes model, it appears that the influence of random variation in the short-term rate on option prices is a second-order effect."

Similar arguments can be found in Buser, Hendershott&Sanders(1990), who compared bond prices as well as prices of derivatives for some continuous-time models. They found that the deviations in bond prices, calculated according to different models, were typically first-order effects, whereas the deviations in the prices of derivatives were typically second-order effects.

Whether the assumed deterministic short term rate of interest causes first- or second-order effects on the prices of contingent claims written on bonds can only be assessed by applying an intertemporal and arbitrage-free model, allowing the short term rate of interest to develop stochastically. Such models have been developed by a number of researchers in recent years, e.g. Ho&Lee(1986) and Pedersen, Shiu& Thorlacius(1989)[2] in discrete time[3] and by Heath, Jarrow&Morton(1989) in continuous time.

The paper is organised as follows.

In section 2 we state a concentrated version of the PST-model together with the necessary formulas and theorems to be applied later in the paper. In section 3 we calculate forward- and futures-prices on zero coupon bonds in order to examine the difference between these two prices under interest rate uncertainty. We conclude that, within the PST-model, these prices are indistinguishable for any practical purpose. This is in accordance with the vast majority of the empirical findings reported in the literature.

In section 4 we calculate the theoretically correct prices for european call-options on zero-coupon bonds. Furthermore, we calculate some "pseudo option prices" based on the (erroneous) assumption that the successive one-period interest rates during the lifetime of the option are constant and equal to the initial yield to maturity on the zero-coupon bond maturing at the expiration date of the option. These pseudo prices are then compared to the theoretically correct prices. We take the difference between these prices as a measure of the effect of stochastic short term rates of interest.

In section 5 we summarise the paper.

---

2) Henceforward termed the PST-model.

3) For an exhaustive characterisation of the entire class of binomial lattice models we refer to Jensen&Nielsen(1991).

2. The PST-model

In a widely cited article, Ho&Lee(1986) described a binomial lattice model for the development of the entire term structure of interest rates. However, it has been recognised that their model, although arbitrage-free, normally allows for negative interest rates.

The model we consider is the binomial lattice model developed in Pedersen, Thorlacius and Shiu (1989) along the same lines as the Ho&Lee model, but modified in a way that eliminates the occurence of negative interest rates.

The variable t, $t=0,1,2,\ldots$, denotes time, and $t=0$ is our starting point ("now"). The variable s is a counting variable keeping track of the number of "up movements" recorded since time 0. During each period, s either remains unchanged or increases by 1. States are assumed to be fully described by the coordinates (t,s), $0 \leq s \leq t$, and from any given (t,s) we may move to either (t+1,s+1) or (t+1,s) according to whether an "up movement" has occurred or not.

In order that asset prices can be represented as functions of t and s it is necessary that the prices are path-independent. Only the time t and the number of "up movements" recorded since time 0 are relevant, whereas the timing of the occurences of "up movements" is irrelevant.

Bonds are assumed to be such assets, whose prices are functions of t and s. The price at date-event (t,s) of a unit discount bond maturing at time T is denoted by D(T;t,s).

It is well known that an arbitrage-free bond market in the binomial lattice model is equivalent to the following property:

(P1) At each node (t,s) there exists a number $\theta(t,s)\epsilon(0,1)$, which solves all the equations in (2.1) simultaneously:

$$D(T;t,s) = D(t+1;t,s) \cdot [\theta(t,s) \cdot D(T;t+1,s+1) + (1-\theta(t,s)) \cdot D(T;t+1,s)] \tag{2.1}$$

for $T=t+1$, $t+2$, ... and so forth up to the longest maturity of any bond in the market.

Equations (2.1) will determine $\theta(t,s)$ uniquely, provided $T>t+1$.

To derive a tractable model, a parameterisation must be imposed on θ and/or bond prices in order to limit the degrees of freedom.

Following Pedersen, Thorlacius and Shiu(1989) we first assume that $\theta(t,s)$ is state independent, but possibly time varying. Secondly, we assume that $D(t+1;t,s+1)=c(t) \cdot D(t+1;t,s)$ for a state independent, but possibly time varying, function $c(t)>0$. The latter parameterisation implies that

$$D(t+1;t,s+j) = [c(t)]^j \cdot D(t+1;t,s) \qquad \text{for } 0 \leq j \leq t-s. \tag{2.2}$$

Inserting (2.2) into (2.1) and chaining these one-period relations sequentially, a multi-period bond pricing model is derived, where bond prices can be expressed in closed form. Without proof we state the result as theorem 1.[4)]

---

4) For an exact derivation we refer to the original article by Pedersen, Shiu&Thorlacius(1989) or to Jensen&Nielsen(1991).

Theorem 1.

Let the function g(k,j), $0 \leq k \leq j$, be defined as:

$$g(k,j) = 1-h(k)+h(k)\cdot\left[\prod_{v=k+1}^{j} c(v)\right], \quad g(k,k) \equiv 1 \tag{2.3}$$

Then D(T;t,s) can be expressed in terms of the initial forward rate discount function $\frac{D(T;0,0)}{D(t;0,0)}$ as shown in (2.4):

$$D(T;t,s) = \left[\prod_{k=0}^{t-1} \frac{g(k,t-1)}{g(k,T-1)}\right] \cdot \left[\prod_{v=t}^{T-1} c(v)\right]^{s} \cdot \frac{D(T;0,0)}{D(t;0,0)} \tag{2.4}$$

While property (P1) is equivalent to the "no arbitrage" condition in the bond market, it is a desirable property - maybe even a "must" - that interest rates generated within the model remain positive. I.e.

$$0 < D(T;t,s) < 1 \tag{2.5}$$

Requiring interest rates to be positive is equivalent to require that all forward rates within the model are positive. The following inequalities are shown by PST to give a sufficient condition on the function c(t) in order to ensure the absence of non-positive forward rates:

$$\frac{D(t+1;0,0)}{D(t;0,0)} < c(t)^{t} < \frac{D(t;0,0)}{D(t+1;0,0)} \tag{2.6}$$

These inequalities show a way to construct the c(t)-function from a given initial term structure of interest rates. For any $\Delta \epsilon (0,1)$, the function

$$c(t) = \Delta\cdot\left[\frac{D(t+1;0,0)}{D(t;0,0)}\right]^{(1/t)} + (1-\Delta)\cdot\left[\frac{D(t;0,0)}{D(t+1;0,0)}\right]^{(1/t)} \tag{2.7}$$

will satisfy the requirements in (2.6). We will use this method of generating c(t) in the rest of the paper.

3. Forward and futures prices

Let T_U be the maturity date of the zero-coupon bond underlying forward as well as futures contracts. The maturity date of these contracts will be denoted by T_f for forward contracts and T_F for futures contracts.

The **forward price** and the **futures price** at date-event (t,s) are denoted by $f(T_f,T_U;t,s)$ and $F(T_F,T_U;t,s)$, respectively.

The **forward price** is the solution to equation (3.1):

$$0 = D(T_U;t,s) - f(T_f,T_U;t,s)\cdot D(T_f;t,s) \Leftrightarrow f(T_f,T_U;t,s) = \frac{D(T_U;t,s)}{D(T_f;t,s)} \tag{3.1}$$

In order to find the **futures price** $F(T_F,T_U;t,s)$ one observes that a futures contract maturing at T_F is equivalent to **a sequence of one period contracts**. Entering a futures contract at date-event (t,s) gives rise to the following payments at time t+1:

$F(T_F,T_U;t+1,s+1) - F(T_F,T_U;t,s)$ in case s increases by 1

$F(T_F,T_U;t+1,s) - F(T_F,T_U;t,s)$ in case s remains unchanged

The **futures price** $F(T_F,T_U;t,s)$ is determined so that the contract has value 0 at date-event (t,s). The **futures price** at time t+1 - $F(T_F,T_U;t+1,\cdot)$ - is determined such that the **remainder** of the contract, **after** the payment of $F(T_F,T_U;t+1,\cdot) - F(T_F,T_U;t,s)$, has value 0 at date-event $(t+1,\cdot)$. Hence, these futures prices are the solution to the following backwards difference equation:

$$0 = \theta(t,s)\cdot[F(T_F,T_U;t+1,s+1)-F(T_F,T_U;t,s)] + (1-\theta(t,s))\cdot[F(T_F,T_U;t+1,s)-F(T_F,TU;t,s)] \Leftrightarrow$$

$$F(T_F,T_U;t,s) = [1-\theta(t)]\cdot F(T_F,T_U;t+1,s) + \theta(t)\cdot F(T_F,T_U;t+1,s+1) \tag{3.2}$$

At maturity, $F(T_F,T_U;T_F,s) \equiv D(T_U;T_F,s)$.

It is well known, cf. e.g. Cox, Ingersoll & Ross(1981), that the **forward price** and the **futures price** are identical under interest rate certainty. This will only be so under interest rate uncertainty by pure coincidence.

In this section we examine the difference between the **forward price** and the **futures price** within the PST-model. Although the results reported here are merely en example, they appear to be representative for numerous other examples investigated.

The initial term structure used in this and the following section is given by the discount function

$$D(t;0,0) = 1 - 0.000011\cdot(\frac{t}{52})^3 + 0.00205\cdot(\frac{t}{52})^2 - 0.0792\cdot(\frac{t}{52}) \tag{3.3}$$

where t denotes time measured in weeks, corresponding to one period in the PST-model. In figure 1 the term structure is calculated according to (3.3) as

$$r(t)\cdot 100 = -\frac{1}{t}\cdot 52\cdot 100\cdot \ln(D(t;0,0)) \tag{3.4}$$

It is shown graphically for $t \leq 520$ (=10 years).

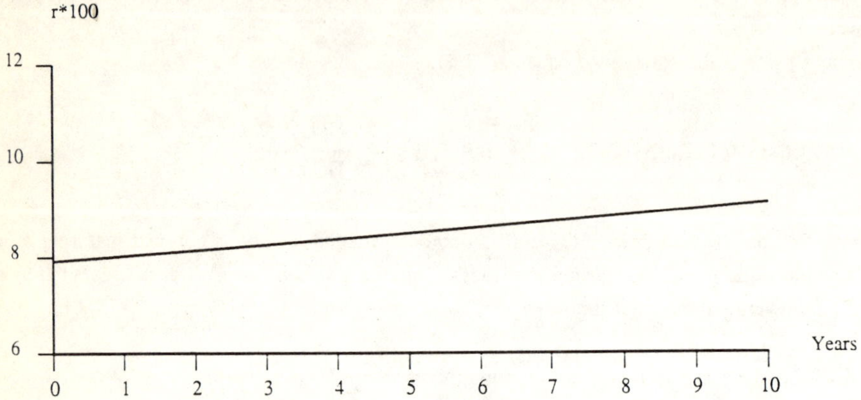

Figure 1. The initial term structure.

The function $\theta(t)$ is chosen in all our calculations as the constant $\theta=0.4$. The parameter Δ determining the c-function, cf. (2.7), has been chosen to be 0.01.

The 40 term structures after 39 weeks, i.e. after the elapse of 3 quarters of a year, are shown graphically in figure 2.

Looking at forward- and futures contracts expiring after 39 weeks and written on zero-coupon bonds maturing at T_U, we found that the differences between forward and futures prices were generally very small and not suitable for graphical illustration. In table 1 we give some representative figures for $T_F=T_f=0.75$.

T_U	$f(0.75,T_U;0,0)$	$F(0.75,T_U;0,0)$
1	97.992	97.991
2	90.227	90.225
5	69.432	69.429
10	42.687	42.684

Table 1.

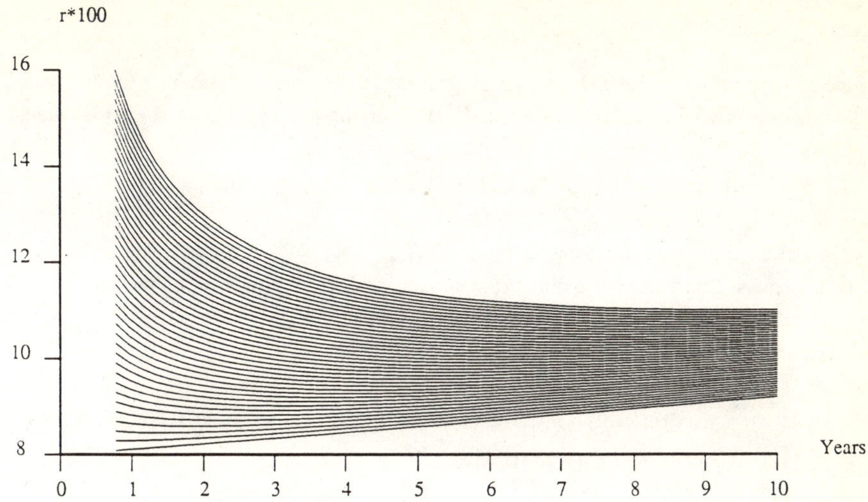

Figure 2. The 40 possible term structures after 39 weeks.

We performed a number of different calculations. E.g., with 10 year contracts written on a 20 year zero-coupon bond, and with the time period in the PST-model equal to 1 year, we found - by varying the values of Δ and θ - the maximal deviation between forward- and futures prices to be 1.3 %.
We conclude from all of the cases examined that the differences between forward- and futures prices for zero-coupon bonds are negligible.

4. European call option premiums

The premium on a european call-option at date-event (t,s) will be denoted by $C(T_C,T_U,X;t,s)$, where

T_C = expiration date of the option
T_U = expiration date of the underlying zero coupon bond
X = exercise price on the european call-option

It is calculated in accordance with the pricing formula (2.1). The only difference between the zero coupon bonds in (2.1) and the options is the boundary condition:

$$C(T_C,T_U,X;T_C,s) = \max\{0,D(T_U;T_C,s)-X\} \tag{4.1}$$

We next calculate a "pseudo option premium" based on the (erroneous) assumption that the short term rate of interest is a constant. This constant is denoted by R and chosen at time 0 as the yield to maturity on a zero coupon bond maturing at date T_C. I.e.

$$R = (D(T_C;0,0))^{-(1/T_C)} - 1 \tag{4.2}$$

The pseudo option premium is found by a stepwise, backward dynamic programming procedure. At each date-event (t,s) we solve for the "pseudo $\theta(t,s)$'s". Denoting these as $\phi(t,s)$, we solve the equations

$$D(T_U;t,s) = (1\text{-}R)^{-1}\cdot\{\phi(t,s)\cdot D(T_U;t+1,s+1) + (1\text{-}\phi(t,s))\cdot D(T_U;t+1,s)\} \tag{4.3}$$

The pseudo option premiums are denoted by $C^*(T_C,T_U,X;t,s)$. They are calculated in an analogous manner by a stepwise, backwards dynamic programming procedure. However, as the solutions to (4.3) are not guaranteed to be positive, we might eventually have a negative pseudo premium. In such a situation we force the pseudo premium to zero:

$$C^*(T_C,T_U,X;t,s) = \max[0,(1+R)^{-1}\cdot\phi(t,s)\cdot C^*(T_C,T_U,X;t+1,s+1)+(1\text{-}\phi(t,s))\cdot C^*(T_C,T_U,X;t+1,s)\}] \tag{4.4}$$

We apply the same discount function, (3.3), as in section 3 and the same parameter values as those underlying table 1.

In figure 3 we show the typical pattern of C and C^* as functions of X, with T_C=0.75 year and T_U=2 years. The deviation between C and C^* is largest for exercise prices close to the forward price of the underlying bond. And the C values are found to be below the values of C^* for all X.

A strong indication for $C^*\text{-}C \geq 0$ can be given theoretically. In an analogous setting we show in Jensen& Nielsen(1991) that

$$\begin{aligned} C(T_C,T_U,X;t,s) = {} & E[D(t+1;t,s)\cdot D(t+2;t+1)\cdot \ldots \cdot D(T_C;T_C\text{-}1)]\cdot E[C(T_C,T_U,X;T_C)] + \\ & \text{cov}[D(t+1;t,s)\cdot D(t+2;t+1)\cdot \ldots \cdot D(T_C;T_C\text{-}1),C(T_C,T_U,X;T_C)] \end{aligned} \tag{4.5}$$

where E denotes the expectation with respect to the probability measure induced by the θ's applied in this paper. When the underlying asset is a bond, we expect the covariance term to be negative. Assuming (erroneously) that the short term rate of interest is developing deterministically, this covariance term disappears giving a bias in the direction found in this paper.[5]

In order to visualise the difference depicted in figure 3 more clearly we show in figure 4 the ratio C/C^* together with the results for three other zero coupon bonds with varying maturity dates serving as underlying assets.

The abscissa value for the thin vertical lines drawn are the respective forward prices for the underlying bonds. It is apparent from figure 4 that the differences between C and C^* are located narrowly around the forward prices. However, within these neighborhoods the deviations turn out to be of quite dramatic proportions.

---

5) The approach in this paper is not exactly portrayed in (4.5). However, the bias has an entirely analogous form, although the θ's here may eventually be outside (0,1). The difference can be traced back to the exact interpretation of "assuming the short term rate of interest to develop in a deterministic manner."

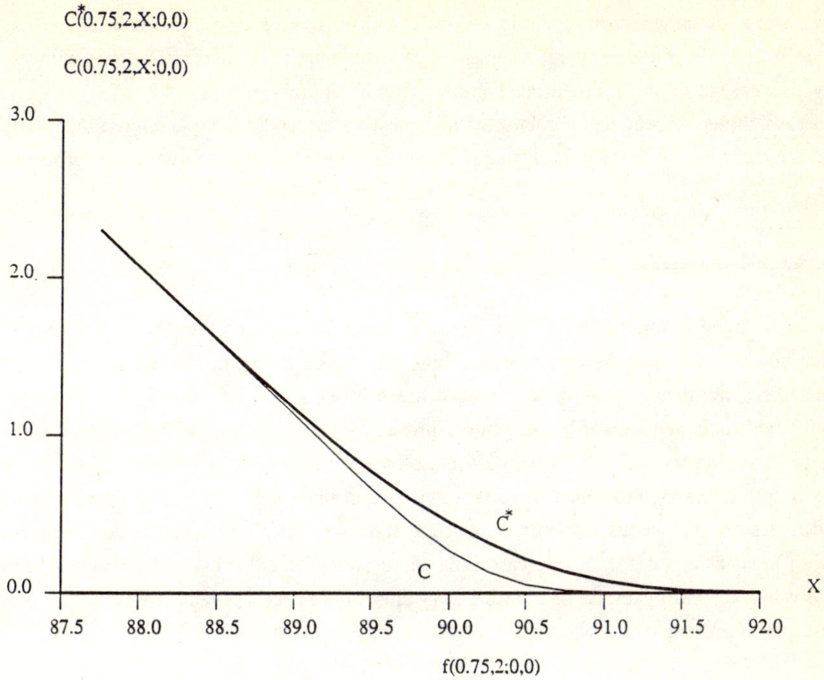

Figure 3. Arbitrage-free call option premiums (C) versus pseudo option premiums (C^*) as functions of X. T_C = 0.75 years. T_U = 2 years.

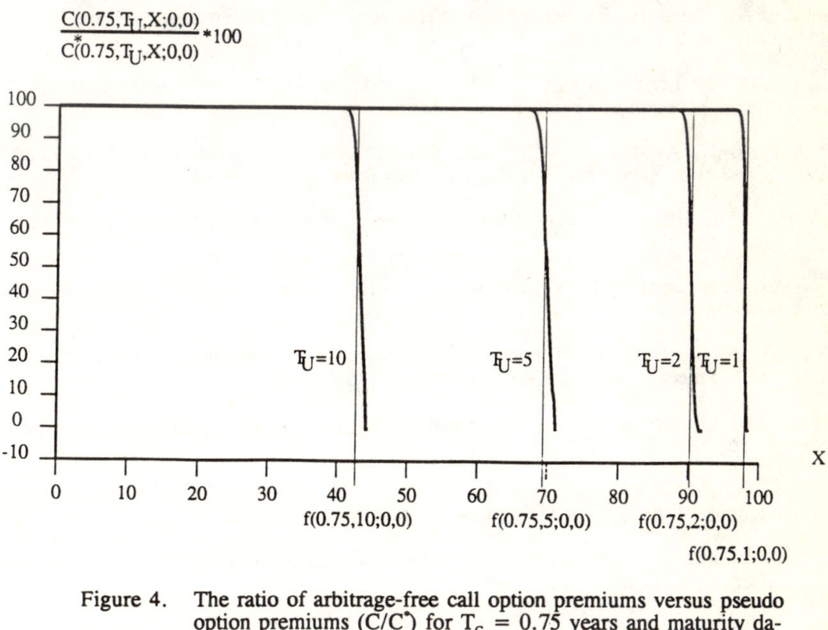

Figure 4. The ratio of arbitrage-free call option premiums versus pseudo option premiums (C/C^*) for T_C = 0.75 years and maturity dates T_U = 1 year, 2 years, 5 years and 10 years, respectively.

The curves will eventually return to the level 100% with increasing exercise prices. However, as the absolute level of both prices converge rapidly to zero we might encounter problems with numerical instability. Hence, we have discarded these minor parts of figure 4.
The properties shown appear to be robust with respect to the choice of parameters and initial term structure. We calculated a number of different examples showing the same qualitative properties.

5. Summary and conclusion

In this paper we have examined the effect of interest rate uncertainty on the prices of derivatives. The vehicle for this analysis was the arbitrage-free binomial lattice model developed in Pedersen, Shiu& Thorlacius(1989), the main results of which were stated in section 2.
In section 3 we calculated forward- and futures prices. We also gave some representative numerical examples to show that the differences between these two prices are negligible.
In section 4 we compared theoretically correct call option premiums with some "pseudo premiums" calculated under the (erroneous) assumption that the short term rate of interest is constant. We found that these differences could not in any reasonable sense be discarded of as second-order effects. Although the values for most exercise prices were very close, the effect was remarkably large over a range of exercise prices around the forward price of the underlying bond.

References

Buser, Stephen A., Patric H. Hendershott&A.B. Sanders(1990): "Determinants of the value of call options on default-free bonds." Journal of Business, vol. 63, pp. 33-50.

Cox, J.C., J.E. Ingersoll & S.A. Ross(1981): "The relation between forward prices and futures prices." Journal of Financial Economics, vol. 9, pp. 321-346.

Heath, D, R. Jarrow & A. Morton(1989): "Bond pricing and the term structure of interest rates: A new methodology." Technical Report no. 900, Cornell University.

Ho, T.S.Y. & S. Lee(1986): "Term structure movements and pricing interest rate contingent claims." Journal of Finance, vol. 41, pp. 1011-1029.

Jensen, B.A.&J.Aa.Nielsen(1988): "Options on bonds - II". Working Paper 88-2, Institute of Finance, Copenhagen Business School.

Jensen, B.A.&J.Aa.Nielsen(1991): "The structure of binomial lattice models for bonds". Working Paper 91-1, Institute of Finance, Copenhagen Business School. (Submitted).

Merton, R.(1973): "Theory of rational option pricing." Bell Journal of Economics and Management Science, vol. 4, pp. 141-183.

Pedersen, H.W., E.S. Shiu & A.E. Thorlacius(1989): "Arbitrage-free pricing of interest-rate contingent claims." Transactions of the Society of Actuaries, vol. XLI, pp. 231-279.

Schaefer, S.M. & E.S. Schwartz(1987): "Time-dependent variance and the pricing of bond options." Journal of Finance, vol. 42, no. 5, pp. 1113-1128.

MARKET MAKING WITH NOISE: THE CASE OF A SPECIALIST FINANCIAL MARKET WITH HETEROGENEOUS TRADERS

Elisa Luciano

Istituto di Matematica Finanziaria, Università di Torino,

Via Assarotti 3, 10121 Torino

Several efforts have been recently devoted to the study of the microstructure of financial markets in the presence of a specialist, mostly as a short-cut for approaching the complex issue of dealers'pricing.[1)]

As it is well-known, the interaction between the public - the traders - and the specialist depends crucially on

i) the nature of the orders placed with the former;

ii) the state of information, the decision rules and the objectives of both.

As concerns the first question, the standard distinction between market and limit orders applies. Most papers focus on traders' market orders, i.e. orders for a prespecified quantity, at a price imposed by the specialist[2)]. At this price he acts as a single dealer, i.e., he guarantees immediate clearing.

As regards the second one, the theoretical contributions on market making with a specialist can be divided into two strands: the first analyses the optimal behavior of the specialist only, the second of both counterparts[3)].

In both cases the representative agent hypothesis is used for traders. Furthermore, standard rational behavior is assumed respectively for the specialist or for both him and the traders.

As for this paper, we intend to concentrate on market orders, taking into consideration both the fact that not all traders are alike - in particular, they do not enter the market with the same frequency - and the fact that they may have different decision criteria.

---

1) See for instance Conroy and Winkler (1986), and the references therein. The comparison between specialist and dealers holds when market orders only are allowed (see below in the text).

2) They also disregard limit orders, i.e. orders entailing a reservation price, which usually are not immediately executed, and may be not executed at all. The point behind the choice of market orders is that a dealer or a specialist quoting a price is like an investor deciding a reservation price.

3) The seminal paper of the first strand is Garman (1976). See for instance Amihud and Mendelson (1979), Ho and Stoll (1981), Mildenstein and Schleef (1983). In the second strand see for instance Gould and Verrecchia (1985) or Glosten and Milgrom (1985).

In order to reach the first goal, we distinguish between two classes of agents: non-professional and professional traders. As for decision criteria, the first class may exhibit an imitative behavior - with respect to professional traders - in addition to a speculative behavior. The imitative behavior is due to the awareness of the greater professional traders' familiarity with the market, i.e. of their superior information. The second class, professional traders, presents a speculative demand too. It can deviate from it by a zero-mean random component of demand, which is meant to include constraints and adjustment lags as well as hedging and imitative effects[4]. The zero-mean assumption however implies that these effects are not as strong as among non-professional traders. A zero-mean deviation from the main objective may characterize the specialist too[5].

The paper is structured as follows: in section 1 we outline the basic model, with non-professional traders acting as speculators. In section 2 we define the concept of equilibrium of our model. In section 3 we study both the solutions and the equilibria of the basic model. In section 4 we extend the basic model to the case of non-professional traders with imitative and speculative decision criteria. Section 5 suggests further extensions.

1. The basic model

1.1. TRADERS AND TIME

As mentioned above, we have two classes of traders, each represented by a single agent: professional (Pts) and non-professional ones (Npts) (ass. 1), who trade in a single stock (ass.2).

Npts enter market orders only at discrete times, while Pts act continuously, as a consequence of their profession and of their lower costs of information[6].

---

[4] See footnote 7.

[5] The paper differs from Ferrari, Luciano and Peccati (1990), in the following sense: in the latter we focused on the role of Npts. Here we are interested in studying in greater detail the relationship between Pts and the S. As a consequence, we enrich the description of their behavior, by explicitly introducing uncertainty. At the same time, we disregard some learning effects and the fact that the fundamental value may vary across investors and over time. We adopt continuous time. In the complete version of this paper - which can be obtained from the author - the deterministic model in continuous time is studied too.

[6] Our distinction between Npts and Pts can be understood in two ways, depending on the market the reader intends to focus on. Here we refer to the first interpretation. The second is explained in the complete version of this paper (see above).

1.2. GENERAL SET UP

At each epoch of a sequence denoted with the parameter T - say T-1 - the specialist (S) fixes a price and both Npts and Pts submit orders which are carried out at the stated price. After this initial action, Npts do not enter the market up to the next (discrete) epoch, while Pts and the S act in the continuum as follows. The S reformulates his price at each point in time, in order to clear total buy and sell orders received from the last clearing date on (in our example from an instant before T-1). He must clear these tenders because, in order to prevent infinite monopoly profits, we assume that he has no stock (ass. 3). He attains his goal by increasing (decreasing) price with respect to the fundamental value as long as there is total net demand (supply). In fact, he knows that a price higher (lower) than the fundamental value decreases (increases) demand. Pts' behavior after the first instant in fact consists for sure in decreasing (increasing) their buy tenders for the period from T-1 to T whenever the current S price is above (below) the fundamental value. Each addition to the initial order is carried out at the price updated by the specialist. A new price is revealed to Npts, as soon as there is no more sure quantity adjustment by Pts. The corresponding price in fact is considered as the new S price (ass. 4).

1.3. UNCERTAINTY AND EXPECTATIONS

Uncertainty enters the model in two ways.

The first source of uncertainty is due to the nature of market orders: the S fixes a price without knowing the reaction (demand) of traders.

Secondly, uncertainty enters into the model because both Pts and the S change their initial demand and price partly according to a standard speculative objective (to be specified below), partly to collateral goals, constraints and adjustment lags, imitation on the part of Pt included. We describe the latter bulk of criteria as a random component of demand[7]. The exact functional form of this component is specified below.

Expectations connected to the first source of uncertainty are fully rational, in the sense that the expected quantity is the true one (ass. 5).

---

[7] For a similar approach see Pagano and Roell (1990a, p.29).

1.4. TRADERS' DEMANDS

Up to section 4 we assume that **Npts** are speculators: at time T, they place an order Q(T) which is a buy order if the current price is below the fundamental value, an ask order if the opposite inequality holds between price and fundamentals. We take a linear specification of their demand function (ass. 6):

$$Q(T) = - \alpha[P(T-1) - k],$$

where k is the fundamental value of the traded asset, α is a positive parameter, P(T-1) is the current price. P(0) is assumed to be a known constant.

As for **Pts**, at time T they act exactly like Npts: they place an order $b_0(T)$ based on P(T-1). Formally, we translate this hypothesis into the following linear demand (ass. 7):

$$b_0(T) = - \beta[P(T-1) - k],$$

where β is a positive parameter, so that a buy (sale) order is placed - $b_0 >(<) 0$ - whenever the price is below (above) the fundamental value.

As a consequence, orders from Npts and initial orders from Pts are either both sale or buy. As we see in a moment, the initial S price in the two cases is on average below and above the fundamental value respectively. This means that there is a disequilibrium due to the impossibility for the S to carry out the orders received (see ass. 3).

Professional traders' behavior after the first instant consists for sure in decreasing (increasing) their buy tenders whenever the current S price is above (below) the fundamental value. In addition, they show the random component of demand discussed above.

Taking for these components a linear specification too, for $t \geq 0$ we have (ass. 8):

$$db_t(T) = -\tau(p_t(T)-k) + \Sigma^1{}_n \, (C_i b_t(T) + c_i)dw^i{}_t,$$

where τ is a positive parameter, $p_t(T)$ is the price quoted by the S at time t, C_i and c_i are constants, $dw^i{}_t$ are independent white noises.

1.5. THE SPECIALIST PRICE

The S reformulates his price at each point in time - with the purpose of clearing total buy and sell received from the last clearing date on - as explained above, in 1.2.

However, adjustment and information lags as well as external constraints may cause the actual price to deviate from the clearing one. Formalizing the effect of lags and constraints as a random component of price quoting, and maintaining linearity, we have (ass. 9):

$$p_0(T) = k + \delta[Q(T) + b_0(T)],$$

$$dp_t(T) = \delta db_t(T) + \Sigma^1{}_n\ (D_i p_t(T) + d_i)dw^i{}_t,$$

with δ a positive constant, D_i and d_i constants.

2. Definition of solutions and equilibria

The basic model outlined above is described by the system

$$Q(T) = -\ \alpha[P(T-1) - k], \qquad (1)$$

$$b_0(T) = -\ \beta[P(T-1) - k], \qquad (2)$$

$$db_t(T) = -\tau(p_t(T)-k)dt + \Sigma^1{}_n\ (C_i b_t(T) + c_i)dw^i{}_t, \qquad (3)$$

$$p_0(T) = k + \delta[Q(T) + b_0(T)], \qquad (4)$$

$$dp_t(T) = \delta db_t(T) + \Sigma^1{}_n\ (D_i p_t(T) + d_i)dw^i{}_t. \qquad (5)$$

First of all, for each sequence of interactions between Pts and the S we want to know the behavior of b_t, the total Pts demand or supply, and p_t, the corresponding price. This study is accomplished by considering the system of equations (3) and (5) with boundary conditions (2) and (4) respectively.

We are particularly interested in the asymptotic properties of the solutions of this system, since, under a condition to be specified below,

$$\lim_{t\to+\infty} b_t(T) \quad \text{w.p.1}$$

represents B(T), the overall traded assets by Pts between two successive Npts' interventions (in T-1 and T). At the same time

$$\lim_{t\to+\infty} p_t(T) \quad \text{w.p.1}$$

represents the corresponding S price, P(T).

The condition under which these limits make sense is that they both correspond to the points of equilibrium $b^*(T)$ and $p^*(T)$ of the differential equations for $b_t(T)$ and $p_t(T)$ implied by our system:

$$\lim_{t\to+\infty} b_t(T) = b^*(T), \quad \lim_{t\to+\infty} p_t(T) = p^*(T), \quad \text{w.p.1.}$$

In fact, in this case only the price revealed to Npts (P(T)) and the total quantity traded (Q(T)) are an equilibrium - in the economic sense[8] - for the S and for Pts respectively. This is the short-run equilibrium of our model.

At a later stage we determine the value and we study the asymptotic behavior of Q(T) and P(T), since these represent the long-run market equilibrium. This analysis is accomplished by using relation (1).

In what follows we distiguish between the following subcases of the model:

i) random changes in Pts demands only;

ii) random changes in prices and Pts demands,

analysing first their short, then their long-run behavior.

3. Solutions and equilibria in the basic model

3.1. RANDOM CHANGES IN PT DEMANDS ONLY.

Suppose that uncertainty impinges on Pts only, so that in the system above $D_i = d_i = 0$ for all i, and

$$p_t(T) = k + \delta[Q(T) + b_t(T)]. \qquad (6)$$

In order to analyze the **short-run** behavior of the model we need to substitute (6) into (3) and to solve the so-obtained stochastic differential equation:

$$db_t(T) = -\tau\delta(Q(T) + b_t(T))dt + \Sigma^1{}_n\,(C_i b_t(T) + c_i)dw^i{}_t, \qquad (3')$$

with initial condition (2).

By standard methods[9] we get the unique solution:

$$b_t(T) =$$

$$\Phi_t(b_0 - (\tau\delta Q(T) + \Sigma^1{}_n C_i c_i)\int_0^t \Phi_s{}^{-1} ds + \Sigma^1{}_n \int_0^t \Phi_s{}^{-1} c_i\ dw^i{}_s), \qquad (7)$$

where

$$\Phi_t = \exp\{-(\tau\delta + \Sigma^1{}_n C_i{}^2/2)t + \Sigma^1{}_n \int_0^t C_i\ dw^i{}_s\},$$

which reduces to:

[8] The difference between a point of equilibrium in the economic and mathematical sense mentioned here is the classical one: see for instance Hahn (1982).

[9] See for instance Arnold (1974) for this results and the following standard ones.

$b_t(T)$ =

$$Q(T)[\exp(-\tau\delta t)-1] + \exp(-\tau\delta t)[b_0 + \Sigma^1{}_n \int_0^t \exp(-\tau\delta s)c_i dw^i{}_s], \quad (8)$$

when uncertainty does not depend on the current level of demand, i.e. when the equation is linear in the narrow sense (LNS): $C_i = 0$ for all i.

In both cases the expected value of b_t, Eb_t, is the solution of the corresponding model without uncertainty:

$$Eb_t(T) = -(\alpha+\beta)[P(T-1)-k]\exp(-\tau\delta t) + \alpha[P(T-1)-k], \quad (9)$$

with

$$\lim_{t\to+\infty} Eb_t(T) = -Q(T).$$

In the second LNS case (equation 8) the variance of b_t, v_t, is $v_t = [1 - \exp(-2\tau\delta t)](\Sigma^1{}_n c_i{}^2)/2\tau\delta$. Its asymptotic value is evidently finite and equal to $\Sigma^1{}_n c_i{}^2/2\delta\tau$.

The main difference between the models (7) and (8) however is the fact that in the former case the first two moments are unable to characterize the overall distribution of b_t; in the latter case instead we know that b_t is normally distributed, non-stationary but with independent increments, so that Pts demand is completely characterized by the moments $Eb_t(T)$ and v_t.

The same applies to the price p_t, which is given by (6), and in both cases admits as expected value

$Ep_t(T) = = k - \delta(\alpha+\beta)(P(T-1)-k)\exp(-\tau\delta t)$.

In the LNS case this price is normally distributed (instant by instant and asymptotically) with variance $\delta^2 v_t$. It maintains also the properties of non-stationarity and independent increments of b_t. In the other case instead the price is not fully characterized by its first two moments.

There is also an important distinction between the general and the LNS model, from the point of view of the meaning of equilibrium. As mentioned in the previous section in fact in order to study the **long-run** behavior of our financial market we are interested in those short-run solutions which converge with probability one to an equilibrium point of the differential equation for $b_t(T)$ and $p_t(T)$. In our model in fact an equilibrium point for b_t implies also dp_t = 0 (both for the random and the non-random components), since p_t is given by (6).

However, an equilibrium position for b_t in the general case (equation 7) does not exist, unless $c_i = Q(T)C_i$ for all i.

In the LNS too there does not exist an equilibrium position properly defined: however, since the variance of b_t exponentially reaches its equilibrium position, the solutions (8) globally converge with probability 1 to the equilibrium position for their deterministic part[10]:

$$\text{Prob}\ (\lim_{t\to+\infty} b_t(T) = -Q(T)) = 1.$$

The definition of p_t (6) implies also that prices are globally asymptotically stable:

$$\text{Prob}\ (\lim_{t\to+\infty} p_t(T) = k) = 1.$$

As a consequence, in the LNS case we have: $B(T) = -Q(T)$ and $P(T) = k$ with probability one, as we would have without uncertainty. There is no net demand (supply) and the quoted price equals the fundamental value.

The distinction between the general and the LNS equilibrium applies also to the long-run equilibrium of the model.

In the general case the existence of the long run is questionable, due to the absence of a short-run standard equilibrium.

In the LNS case on the contrary from relation (1) we get:

$$\text{Prob}\ (Q(T) = 0\ ) = 1.$$

which holds for $T > 1$ and means that the market immediately reaches an equilibrium where no more transactions are needed.

3.2. RANDOM CHANGES IN PRICES AND PT DEMANDS

When uncertainty impinges not only on demand formation, but also on the price response of the S, we need to study the whole system (2)-(5) in order to characterize the **short-run** equilibrium of the model. Using (1), the system itself can be rewritten as

$$\begin{matrix} db_t(T) \\ dp_t(T) \end{matrix} = \left\{ -\tau \begin{bmatrix} 0 & 1 \\ 0 & \delta \end{bmatrix} \begin{bmatrix} b_t(T) \\ p_t(T) \end{bmatrix} + \tau k \begin{bmatrix} 1 \\ \delta \end{bmatrix} \right\} dt$$
$$+ \Sigma^1{}_n \left\{ \begin{bmatrix} C_i & 0 \\ \delta C_i & D_i \end{bmatrix} \begin{bmatrix} b_t(T) \\ p_t(T) \end{bmatrix} + \begin{bmatrix} c_i \\ \delta c_i + d_i \end{bmatrix} \right\} dw^i{}_t, \qquad (10)$$

with

---

[10] The result mentioned here - a variance exponentially approaching its equilibrium position implies stochastic stability - is for instance in Gihman and Skorohod (1972, p. 331).

$p_0(T) = k - \delta(\alpha+\beta)[P(T-1) - k],$

$b_0(T) = - \beta[P(T-1)-k].$

As in the previous section, the system above behaves quite differently in the general and the LNS case, i.e. in case respectively of dependence and independence of the stochastic components on the current level of p_t and b_t.

In the general case the system (10) does not admit a closed-form solution, but we know that:

$$Eb_t(T) = b_0(T)\exp(-\tau\delta t) - Q(T)(1-\exp(-\tau\delta t)),$$
$$Ep_t(T) = p_0(T)\exp(-\tau\delta t) + k(1-\exp(-\tau\delta t)).$$

In the LNS case on the contrary it can be demonstrated that total demand or supply from Pts is normal with the same mean than in the general case and variance

$$\Sigma^1{}_n \; d_i{}^2\delta^{-2}t + 2 \;\; d_i\delta^{-2} \;\; (\exp(-\tau\delta t)-1)(\delta\tau)^{-1} \;\; +$$
$$- \; (\delta c_i+d_i)\delta^{-2}(\exp(-2\tau\delta t)-1)(2\tau\delta)^{-1}.$$

The corresponding price is normal too, with the same mean than in the general case and variance

$$(1-\exp(-2\delta\tau))(2\delta\tau)^{-1}\Sigma^1{}_n(\delta c_i + d_i)^2.$$

As concerns the **long-run** analysis, a reasoning analogous to that used in section 3.1. applies.

In the general case there is no room for an equilibrium position, unless there exists a constant solution b such that $C_i b = -c_i$, for all i, and in addition $kD_i = d_i$ for all i.

In the LNS case there is not an equilibrium point stable with probability one both for the stochastic and the non-stochastic components of the motion of b_t and p_t. However, if $d_i = 0$ for all i, the solutions converge with probability one to the (globally asymptotically stable) equilibrium position for the non-random part, $b_t(T) = -Q(T)$, $p_t(T) = k$:

$$\text{Prob}\,(\lim_{t\to+\infty} p_t(T) = k) = 1,$$

$$\text{Prob}\,(\lim_{t\to+\infty} b_t(T) = - Q(T)) = 1.$$

As a consequence, also for this LNS specification the S price is the fundamental value and total transactions are null with probability one: $P(T) = k$, $B(T) = -Q(T)$ with probability one.

4. Solutions and equilibria with imitation on the part of Npts

The model described above may be enriched with the introduction of imitative behavior on the part of Npts. It is conceivable in fact that naïve agents on the financial market, such as our Npts, be affected by the decisions of better informed agents, such as Pts.

This affects the long-run equilibrium only, and can be formalized by substituting (1) above with the following:

$$Q(T) = -\alpha[P(T-1) - k] + \epsilon B(T-1), \qquad (1')$$

where ϵ is a positive parameter, which makes Npts' demand at T depend on Pts' one at T-1.

In the case of section 3.1. above - i.e. when uncertainty impinges on quantities only - if in addition uncertainty does not depend on the current level of demand (LNS case) - we know that

$$\text{Prob}\,(\lim_{t\to+\infty} b_t(T-1) = -Q(T-1)) = 1,$$

$$\text{Prob}\,(\lim_{t\to+\infty} p_t(T-1) = k) = 1,$$

and consequently $B(T-1) = -Q(T-1)$, $P(T-1) = k$ with probability one.

This implies that with probability one $Q(T) = -\epsilon\, Q(T-1)$, and total demand from Npts exhibits an oscillatory behavior, damped if $0 < \epsilon < 1$, explosive if $\epsilon > 1$.

In the general case of uncertainty on Pts' demand, depending also on the current level of the latter, nothing can be said, since - for the reasons explained in section 3 above - B(T-1) is not properly defined.

As concerns the model with uncertainty on both prices and demand, in the LNS case the same results of the previous LNS case hold, provided that $d_i = 0$ for all i.

5. Further extensions

For the sake of simplicity we have studied a model in which each class of agents is homogeneous: a straightforward extension of our work - in the spirit of the previous joint paper Ferrari, Luciano, Peccati (1990) - is to an economy without a representative agent for each class. The interest of this extension is mainly connected to the possibility of better understanding the imitative behavior.

A further extension of the present work is to a market with random demand components for Npts too. We expect that the long run equilibria depend on these components and on the stochastic dependence of Npts and Pts' demands.

Finally, we would be interested in the effects of heterogeneous believes about the fundamental value, which have proved to be noteworthy in the discrete-time case under certainty (Ferrari, Luciano and Peccati (1990)).

References

Amihud, Y., Mendelson, H., Dealership Market: Market-Making with Inventory, Journal of Financial Economics, 8 (1979), pp. 31-53.

Arnold, L., Stochastic Differential Equations: Theory and Applications, J. Wiley, New York, 1974.

Conroy, R.M., Winkler, R.L., Market Structure: the Specialist as Dealer and Broker, Journal of Banking and Finance, 10 (1986), pp. 21-36.

Ferrari, L., Luciano, E., Peccati, L., Institutionally heterogeneous agents in an imitative stock market, in this volume.

Garman, M. B., Market Microstructure, Journal of Financial Economics, 3 (1976), pp. 33-53.

Gihman, I.I., Skorohod, A.V., Stochastic Differential Equations, Springer Verlag, Berlin, 1972.

Glosten, L., Milgrom, P., Bid, Ask and Transaction Prices in a Specialist Market with Heterogeneously Informed Traders, Journal of Financial Economics, 14 (1985), pp. 71-100.

Gould, J., Verrecchia, R., The Information Content of Specialist Pricing, Journal of Political Economy, 93 (1985), pp.66-83.

Hahn, F., Stability, in Arrow, J.K., Intriligator, M.D. (eds), Handbook of Mathematical Economics, vol. II, North Holland, Amsterdam, 1982.

Ho, T., Stoll, H.R., On Dealer Markets under Competition, Journalof Finance, 35 (1980), pp. 259-267.

-------------------, Optimal Dealer Pricing under Transactions and Return Uncertainty, Journal of Financial Economics, 9 (1981), pp.47-73.

Mildenstein, E., Schleef,H., The Optimal Pricing Policy of Monopolistic Marketmakers in the Equity Market, Journal of Finance, 38 (1983), pp.218-231.

Pagano, M., Roell, A., Shifting Gears: an Economic Evaluation of the Reform of the Paris Bourse, Preliminary Working Paper, Banca Commerciale Italiana, 1990a.

----------------------, Mercati d'asta, mercati di dealer e rischio di esecuzione, ibidem, 1990b.

CAN SUBJECTIVE EXCHANGE RATE FORECASTS BE IMPROVED?

Mary E. Wilkie and Andrew C. Pollock

Department of Mathematics, Glasgow Polytechnic,
Cowcaddens Road, Glasgow, G4 0BA.

1 Introduction.

In the volatile and rapidly changing financial environment, human judgement is essential to currency forecasting. Recent events like German reunification, Yugoslavian upheaval, Iraq's invasion of Kuwait and the breakup of the USSR are a striking reminder that quantitative models alone cannot predict the future. Reliable currency forecasting requires subjective input, using the expertise of the person or persons making the forecast. Ignoring this knowledge can be a serious handicap: exchange rate movements are often influenced by unique events that can often be broadly foreseen, but cannot easily be incorporated into conventional models. People have many advantages over quantitative models, especially flexibility and their ability to take the unexpected into account.

The importance of judgemental input is recognised in many practical forecasting situations. Procedures tend to incorporate the use of quantitative models to provide initial estimates, which are subsequently updated by the views of a currency analyst or group of analysts. The final prediction, then, is a mixture of both quantitative and subjective analyses. But even though this composite framework is extensively used in practice, there has been surprisingly little academic research directed towards judgemental accuracy. Extensive research has focused on time series, econometric and technical analysis techniques. But the major aspect of real world currency forecasting has been virtually neglected: human judgement.

In view of this neglect, the present article concerns judgemental currency forecasting, its possible limitations and how it might be improved. In relation to this, three important issues are outlined and discussed below.

The first issue concerns the influence of cognitive biases on the currency forecaster's predictions. In recent decades, judgmental psychologists have identified a wide range of biases and limitations which seriously affect the quality of human decision making. Through skilful experimental studies some very important and, indeed, fascinating findings have emerged concerning the nature of human thought processes. This work illustrates that limitations in the human ability to process information lead people to adopt mental strategies or heuristics, which are subject to bias but simplify the task of judgement and choice. The psychological study of judgmental error and the processes of decision uncertainty can certainly be applied to exchange rate forecasting.

The second issue concerns the need for a probabilistic approach (which requires a prediction together with a probability associated with it) to currency forecasting. Such an approach not only allows identification of the effects of bias on the ability of the forecaster to make predictions, but provides invaluable feedback that is likely to substantially improve judgement.

The final issue concerns the effect of the forecaster's expertise on bias. That is, whether cognitive biases are related to the forecaster's ability to analyse information and make probabilistic predictions.

In currency forecasting situations, it is important to realise that all three issues are interrelated. Hence, they should be examined within an integrated framework.

2 What are Heuristics and Biases?

Subjective forecasting decisions, like many other decisions, tend to be based on beliefs concerning the likelihood of uncertain events, such as the future value of the yen/pound exchange rate. From the psychological literature we know that individuals tend to rely on a limited number of heuristic principles to simplify the complex tasks of assessing probabilities and predicting values - currency analysts are unlikely to be an exception to this. Such strategies may have served us well in the past, optimizing a trade off between the need for an accurate response and the psychological demands of processing information. And, indeed, they may still be effective in many decision making situations. It can be argued, however, that human conceptual skills may not be adequate in many decision making situations in which accuracy is essential.

The five biases addressed below, we feel, are particularly relevant to exchange rate forecasting situations. (For a collection of the most important work in this area, see Kahneman, Slovic and Tversky, 1982). Forecasters should be aware that in making subjective exchange rate forecasts, they often take mental short cuts. They should all be aware of their limitations. The highlighting of these biases and an understanding of their psychological causes, will, in the opinion of the authors, result in improved forecasts, even in forecasters who have high relative efficiency.

(i) The 'availability' bias (Tversky and Kahneman, 1973) refers to the tendency to judge the probability of an event by the ease with which it is retrieved from memory. Thus, readily available information tends to be judged as more important or more frequent than less easily accessed information. Weaknesses in the ability of a forecaster to imagine sources of uncertainty are associated with this bias. It relates to the ease by which a person can construct relevant hypothetical situations that play an important role in the evaluation of probabilities.

(ii) The 'Illusory correlation', as described by Chapman and Chapman (1969), refers to the tendency to see correlations or associations in data which are not statistically present, but which are expected to take place on the basis of prior beliefs.

(iii) The 'representativeness' bias (Kahneman and Tversky, 1972) refers to the tendency that individuals have of judging the probability of a event by how frequent it is in a class of such events. It arises where perceived similarity takes dominance over prior probabilities. 'Illusion of validity' is associated with this bias and relates to the tendency of setting an outcome that is most representative of a set of inputs, even where the inputs are are highly correlated. Individuals subject to this bias neglect colinearity between inputs.

(iv) The 'anchoring' bias (Slovic and Lichtenstein, 1971) relates to the tendency to make insufficient adjustments to an initial forecast value. In forecasting situations, experts often make predictions by starting at an initial value which is then adjusted as the assessment process proceeds. However, the adjustments made are usually inadequate. That is, varying the initial value results in differing predictions, which are biased towards the initial values.

(v) Hindsight bias, as described by Fischhoff and Beyth (1975), refers to the fact that individuals are rarely surprised by events that have happened even though the they may have found predicating these events extremely difficult. Although information from the past may be useful, in hindsight people often exaggerate what would have been anticipated with foresight. People can explain quite easily why an outcome was predictable- 'they knew it all along'. This self-flattery is not conscious, however. Rather, it is based on internalised beliefs which are genuine. Finding out that an event has occurred appears to restructure memory. People do not remember the uncertainties of the past: due to the strong, human motivation to understand and control the environment, past events are restructured in a way which makes coherent sense to the individual. The trouble with hindsight bias is that people do not learn from their mistakes.

3 How Relevant are Heuristics and Biases to Judgemental Currency Forecasting?

Psychological literature has illustrated that cognitive heuristics and biases play a key role whenever judgement is used. They cannot be overlooked when judgemental inputs (which are always necessary) are made in an exchange rate forecasting procedure. Judgement if not used directly in the procedure will certainly be used indirectly. Judgement is needed whenever decisions are made as regards the choice of model, the choice of analytical techniques and in the interpretation of the output. Even those who believe in the Efficient Market Hypothesis (MEH) are making a judgement!

The MEH, nevertheless, provides the most compelling reason for not examining human judgement in currency forecasting. The foreign exchange market is viewed as efficient if exchange rates adjust quickly to information. The strong form of EMH, as it implies that market participants cannot systematically beat the market, questions the use of forecasting models based on econometric, time series, technical analysis or, in fact, judgemental methods. If the market is efficient, however, there is no need to undertake currency forecasting; and no need to examine cognitive biases. As a wide range of commercial forecasting agencies exist, are we to believe that they are wasting their time and their clients wasting their money? There does appear some scope, at least, for examining judgement: unless we all believe in the EMH.

Given that judgement has a key role in any currency forecasting procedure, it is important to examine if there exists evidence of cognitive errors in the behaviour of foreign exchange market participants.

Direct evidence from the foreign exchange market is very limited. Nevertheless, the authors feel that this is not be a reason for ignoring the issue: in fact, it is a good reason for its study. There exists indirect evidence in the market that cognitive errors do exist. Frankel and Froot (1987,1990) and Ito (1990) using survey data, have illustrated that foreign exchange market participants are heterogeneous in the way they form their expectations about currency movements. They show expectations are not 'rational' and that the basis on which forecasters make expectations in the short term (which tend to be of the bandwagon type) is different from long term (which tend to be regressive). Heterogeneous expectations are, also, consistent with the behaviour of financial organisations which often use a wide range of commercially available forecasting information in their decision making procedures. Further, commercial forecasting agencies and publications (for example, *The Currency Forecasters' Digest*) use composite forecasts in their currency predictions. The cognitive biases of market participants are clearly a factor that could explain these variations between exchange rate expectations.

There also exists evidence from markets closely related to the foreign exchange market (particularly the stock market) that these biases exist. The work of De Bondt and Thaler (1985,1987,1990) has illustrated that overreaction is a feature of predictions by stock market professionals. Andreassen's (1990) study suggests that this type of overreaction is, to a large extent, caused by 'news' events increasing the salience of any trend present. In addition, Steal von Holstein (1972) and Yates, McDaniel and Brown (1991) suggest that professionals may tend to be overconfident in their probabilistic predictions.

4 Why is Probabilistic Forecasting Important in Examining Bias?

The efficient use of human judgement in currency forecasting and the identification of the effects of cognitive biases requires not only a prediction (directional or value) but a probability estimate (probability or confidence interval) associated with the prediction. A probabilistic framework is essential in detecting the presence of biases. For example, biases that cause overconfidence and overreaction cannot adequately be examined if there exists no information on the forecaster's assessment of the uncertainty that surrounds his/her predictions. The problem, at present, is that available currency forecasts tend to be only directional or point estimate predictions. It is, therefore, not surprising that the examination of cognitive biases in currency forecasting is in its infancy.

Once forecasts have been made in a probabilistic framework measures of overall probability judgement accuracy can be obtained. Further, overall accuracy can be broadly decomposed into two components; calibration and resolution.

Calibration or reliability refers to the ability an individual has in expressing accurately the probability or confidence bands for his/her predictions. This is particularly important for a corporate treasurer who has exposure in a particular currency and wishes to know the likelihood of a fall in the value of that currency. His/her actions may be different if the assigned probability is 0.51 compared with 0.99. It is very important that the assessment of probability is reliable.

Resolution or discrimination reflects a different kind of judgemental insight to calibration. Resolution reflects the ability to assign higher probabilities or shorter confidence bands in situations when the predicted event occurs from when it does not. Resolution is more important than calibration to currency traders who are required to discriminate between currencies or periods when the currency is likely to move in a particular direction from when it is not.

Relatively easy to compute measures of overall probability judgemental accuracy and its components have been developed. A fairly simple explanation of these is contained in Yates (1990). These techniques can easily be applied to directional forecasting. Furthermore, if assumptions are made concerning the distribution of forecast errors and forecasters specify parameters, probability judgement accuracy techniques can be applied to value forecasts. The present authors (Pollock and Wilkie, 1991) have outlined a methodology to examine calibration in this situation. The application of statistical techniques that can be used to assess calibration in forecasting situations are also discussed in Lichtenstein, Fischhoff and Phillips (in Kahneman, Slovic and Tversky, 1982) and Kling and Blesser (1989).

The most documented cause of poor calibration in psychological literature is overconfidence. In various studies people have been shown to be far more confident about their beliefs than they should be. It appears that additional information significantly increases confidence, but this increase in confidence is rarely justified by a corresponding increase in accuracy of conclusions. (Kahneman, Slovic and Tversky (1982) have reviewed much of the work on this area).

All of the biases discussed above can result in overconfidence. The 'availability' heuristic can lead to overconfidence when important information is not taken into account. 'Representativeness', when satisfied, can make people more confident about their beliefs than they should be. Beliefs about associations, derived from the the 'illusory correlation', can certainly contribute to overconfidence. Finally, 'hindsight' and 'anchoring' also lead to overconfidence.

O'Connor and Lawrence (1989) list a number of conclusions that have emerged from empirical studies. These are: (i) People are generally overconfident in predictions, (ii) Familiarity with the topic reduces overconfidence, (iii) Familiarity with probabilistic forecasting reduces overconfidence, (iv) Overconfidence is more likely to occur in difficult tasks, (v) Training does not necessarily overcome the problem of overconfidence. However, when forecasters are asked to state the reasons for their assessments the problem is reduced.

The overconfidence problem may be serious in subjective exchange rate forecasting because of the criteria on which forecasts are judged (point forecast errors and profitability). Further, forecasters operating in a highly competitive, stressful, financial environment, where large losses and gains can be made in the short and immediate term and where exchange rates are subject to continued movement, will often ignore some elements of uncertainty.

Poor calibration in value currency predictions can occur where a tendency exists to persistently overestimate or underestimate a currency value. The 'representativeness' heuristic might come into play where analysts persistently overestimate an upward movement in a 'strong' currency or downward movement in a 'weak' currency.

Poor calibration may also arise due to inconsistent probability estimates from the forecaster. Yates (1990) refers to this as 'scatter'. 'Scatter' reflects variation in assessed probabilities that is not related to variations in the outcome; unexplained variation. In currency forecasting this might arise when the forecaster applies different decisions to essentially similar situations or looks for patterns (such as cycles in the data) that may not be relevant. A particularly important heuristic in this context is the 'illusory correlation' which can cause chartists to see things that are not there: they go for a random walk.

Poor resolution, like poor calibration, can result from a wide range of cognitive biases. Individuals with good resolution have the ability to identify information that is relevant. The 'availability' heuristic is particularly a barrier to good resolution as it encourages the forecaster to be influenced by more salient information and to discount fundamental information. 'Anchoring' can also be an important barrier to good resolution. A forecaster may use the current exchange rate as the initial input and make insufficient adjustment in the subsequent judgemental updates. The random walk forecaster, of course, has no resolution.

It should also be pointed out that aggregating individual probability forecasts need not necessarily reduce the influence of biases in currency forecasting: it may make them worse!

While the aggregating of individuals' probabilistic currency forecasts may improve calibration (particularly when overconfidence is the problem and the individuals make different directional predictions), it can seriously deteriorate resolution. Data from composite forecasts (as used by Frankel and Froot, 1987,1990 and Ito, 1990) may not be appropriate in examining the biases of currency forecasters.

5 What Effect does Expertise have on Forecasting Bias?

Currency analysts are, of course, experts. It is, therefore, important to examine the effect of their expertise on and judgemental accuracy. In this connection, it is important to appreciate that there are a two forms of ability needed for accurate probabilistic forecasting: 'substantive' and 'normative'. 'Substantive goodness' reflects the forecaster's knowledge and understanding of the currency market while 'normative goodness' reflects his/her ability to apply probabilistic techniques. Generally, it is much easier to correct for biases that cause weaknesses in the 'normative' sense (which tend to influence calibration) than to correct for biases that cause weaknesses in the 'substantive' sense (which tend influence resolution).

The authors' current research, examined the judgemental accuracy of professional currency forecasters on a time series extrapolative task. It was found that these experts exhibited inferior judgemental accuracy to a simple AR(1) model. In addition, the currency professionals performance was compared to that of mathematicians (who had virtually no understanding of the currency markets). The result of this comparison was striking: currency professionals were no better than the mathematicians.

A very likely cause of this is a lack of 'normative goodness': currency professionals are not usually required to assign probabilities to their forecasts. People often have difficulty in eliciting probabilistic forecasts that are consistent (different probability assessment routes give similar probabilities for the same event) and coherent (probability laws are obeyed). (This is examined in Ayton and Wright, and Phillips; both in Wright and Ayton, 1987). All the currency professionals, of course, had a high degree of 'substantive goodness'; they all had a good knowledge of the currency market. Assigning appropriate probabilities is a skill that requires practice and patience, but the valuable feedback that it provides is likely to improve performance substantially. O'Connor's (1989) review points out that this was the case with weather forecasters in the U.S. who are now extremely reliable (Murphy and Winkler, 1977), but incidentally, did not perform particularly well until probabilistic forecasting became a requirement of the job. Why should the same not apply to currency forecasting?

Another cause may be from what is termed 'the curse of knowledge' which implies that experts may not ignore irrelevant information. Camerer, Loewenstein and Weber (1989) illustrate in an experiment using company earnings data that this effect can be important.

There are other studies which suggest that bias may still be present despite professional expertise. Stael von Holstein (1972), for instance, found in stock market forecasting, professionals were subject to substantial overconfidence. This, at least in part, was attributed to task difficulty. Yates, McDaniel and Brown (1991) found similar results in a replication study, with financial undergraduates significantly outperforming graduates.

6 How Can the Biases Be Reduced?

A number of suggestions which, the authors feel will reduce the impact of bias in currency forecasting are outlined below.

(i) Forecasts should be made in a probabilistic framework. It is impossible to examine, for example, biases that cause overconfidence if its presence cannot be detected. If overconfidence can be identified then particular biases that cause it may also be recognised.

(ii) Forecasters should be provided with adequate feedback on the past accuracy of the probabilistic assessments. It has been illustrated by O'Connor (1989) and Sharp, Cutler and Penrod (1988) that feedback can improve calibration and resolution.

(iii) The information contained in feedback should be thoroughly analysed. At the onset of a forecasting session some key issues should be examined. It is important that forecasters examine the mistakes made on previous forecasts and consider them critically so that they can be avoided in the future. Taking account of the 'hindsight' bias is, of course, very relevant in this situation especially since feedback based on unaided observation alone is unlikely to reduce this bias. Camerer, Loewenstein and Weber (1989) show, in relation to company earnings data, that the 'hindsight' bias may still be strong, even with high monetary incentives.

(iv) Currency forecasters should not only examine carefully all the available information, but should take special care not to overweight the impact of salient events. In other words, they should take notice of the 'availability' bias. Forecaster's should take care not to overreact to changes in market conditions. Froot and Frankel (1989) illustrate this in their examination of 'excessive speculation' using survey currency data. To examine the extent of overreaction, it is necessary to use a probabilistic framework. Overreaction to dramatic news events tends to be underestimated when it is measured only by the forecast error. This measurement fails to take into account that such events are likely to increase uncertainty such that the confidence bands surrounding the forecast are widened. Probabilistic forecast measures take this into account.

(v) Subjective currency forecasting in practical situations often relies heavily on the use of mental simulations to construct scenarios that examine possible future economic, political and market dominated events. The 'availability' heuristic can be very important in this situation. The quest for causal links in the construction of scenarios results in bias whereby dramatic events (such as the Iraqi invasion of Kuwait) have a relatively greater impact than slow but more fundamental changes. In addition, there may exist bias towards events where a single plausible scenario can be found and against events that may be produced in a variety of unlikely ways. In currency forecasting the authors feel that alternative scenarios need to be examined such that the overall effect (in a probability framework) can be built up. Forecasters need a clear understanding of uncertainty and probability in building up scenarios.

(viii) The use of quantitative models as an input in a subjective forecasting procedure requires special care. In this situation the 'anchoring' bias can be particularly a problem. It is important for forecasters to realise that, although models can improve accuracy, unjustifiable reliance should not be put on a model's predictions at the expense of judgemental factors. It is important that forecasters understand the strengths and weaknesses of the models they use and the importance of their own judgement.

7 Conclusion.

Human judgement has an essential role to play in currency forecasting but it is not without limitations. A number of psychological biases that are, arguably, pertinent have been examined. These biases can be broadly classified under the headings; 'availability', 'illusory correlation', 'representativeness', 'anchoring' and 'hindsight'. Identification of psychological biases in subjective exchange rate forecasting is an essential requirement in obtaining predictions that are accurate and reliable. The authors point out that to examine the impact of these cognitive biases on accuracy, it is necessary to use a probabilistic approach. This approach broadly divides accuracy into calibration and resolution. Furthermore, it is pointed out that expertise may not necessarily reduce these biases and can even make them worse. Above all the authors' views are that cognitive biases need to be analysed in an integrated framework that uses probabilistic forecasting approaches with experts in currency forecasting situations. At present, probabilistic currency forecasts are not usually made and this causes a serious impediment to the examination of the impact of these biases. The examination of currency experts' cognitive biases in a probabilistic framework appears to be an obvious direction for future research. The authors believe that the development of this area and its practical application will substantially improve the quality of judgemental currency forecasts.

References.

Andreassen P.B. (1990),
Judgement, Extrapolation and Market Overreaction: On the Use and Disuse of News.
Journal of Behavioral Decision Making, **3**:153-174.

Camerer C., Loewenstein G. and Weber M. (1989),
The Curse of Knowledge in Economic Settings: An Experimental Analysis.
Journal of Political Economy, **97**:1232-1255.

Chapman L.J. and Chapman J.P. (1969),
Illusory Correlation as an Obstacle to the Use of Valid Psychodiagnostic Signs.
Journal of Abnormal Psychology, **74**:271-280.

The Currency Forecasters' Digest.
(monthly periodical)
Tech A (publisher), White Plains, New York.

De Bondt W.F.M. and Thaler R.H. (1985),
Does the Stock Market Overreact.
Journal of Finance, **15**:793-808.

De Bondt W.F.M. and Thaler R.H. (1987),
Further Evidence on Investor Overreaction and Stock Market Seasonality.
Journal of Finance, **17**:557-581.

De Bondt W.F.M. and Thaler R.H. (1990),
Do Security Analysts Overreact?
American Economic Review, **80**:52-57.

Fischhoff B. and Beyth R. (1975),
'I Knew It Would Happen' - Remembered Probabilities of Once - Future Things.
Organisational Behavior and Human Performance, **13**: 1-16.

Frankel J.A. and Froot K.A. (1987),
Using Survey Data to Test Standard Propositions Regarding Exchange Rate Expectations.
American Economic Review, **77**:133-153.

Frankel J.A. and Froot K.A. (1990),
Chartists, Fundamentalists, and Trading in the Foreign Exchange Market.
American Economic Review, 80:181-185.

Froot K.A. and Frankel J.A. (1989),
Forward Discount Bias: Is it an Exchange Risk Premium?
Quarterly Journal Of Economics, **104**:139-161.

Ito T. (1990),
Foreign Exchange Rate Expectations: Micro Survey Data.
American Economic Review, **80**:434-449.

Kahneman D. and Tversky A. (1972),
Subjective Probability: A Judgment of Representativeness.
Cognitive Psychology, **3**:430-454.

Kahneman D., Slovic P. and Tversky A. (ed), (1982),
Judgment under Uncertainty; Heuristics and Biases.
Cambridge University, London.

Kling J.L. and Blesser D.A. (1989),
Calibration-Based Predictive Distributions: An Application of Prequential Analysis to Interest, Money, Prices and Output.
Journal of Business, **62**:477-499.

Murphy A.H. and Winkler R.L. (1977),
Reliability of Subjective Probability Forecasts of Precipitation and Temperature.
Journal of the Royal Statistical Society, Series C, **26**:41-47.

O'Connor M. (1989),
Models of Behaviour and Confidence in Judgement: A Review.
International Journal of Forecasting, **5**:159-169.

O'Connor M. and Lawrence M. (1989),
An Examination of the Accuracy of Judgmental Confidence Intervals in Time Series Forecasting.
Journal of Forecasting, **8**:141-155.

Pollock A.C. and Wilkie M.E (1991),
Briefing - Forex Forecasting.
Euromoney, June, 123-124.

Stael von Holstein C.A.S. (1972),
Probabilistic Forecasting: An Experiment Related to the Stock Market.
Organisational Behavior and Human Performance, **8**:139-158.

Sharp G.L., Cutler B.L. and Penrod S.D. (1988),
Performance Feedback Improves the Resolution of Confidence Judgments.
Organisational Behavior and Human Decision Processes, **42**:271-283.

Slovic P. and Lichtenstein S. (1971),
Comparison of Bayesian and Regression Approaches to the Study of Information Processing In Judgment.
Organisational Behavior and Human Performance, **6**:649-744.

Tversky A. and Kahneman D. (1973),
Availability: A Heuristic for Judging Frequency and Probability.
Cognitive Psychology, **5**:207-232.

Wright G. and Ayton P. (1987),
Judgemental Forecasting.
Wiley, London.

Yates J.F. (1990),
Judgment and Decision Making.
Prentice Hall, New Jersey.

Yates J.F., McDaniel L.S. and Brown E.S. (1991),
Probabilistic Forecasts of Stock Prices and Earnings: The Hazards of Nascent Expertise.
Organisational Behavior and Human Decision Processes, **49**:60-79.

A NONLINEAR MODEL OF STOCK MARKET WITH INSTITUTIONALLY DIFFERENT AGENTS AND IMITATION

Anna Cornaglia
Ist. Mat. Fin. – Fac. di Ec. e Comm. – Università
Piazza Arbarello, 8 – 10122 Torino – Italia

1 Introduction

The present paper represents only one step of a research on the behaviour of a stock market which is not necessarily characterized by the usual hypothesis of rational agents and perfect information.

The model being used here, to the purpose of studying the possibility to reach an equilibrium on the stock market, is the one proposed by FERRARI – LUCIANO – PECCATI (1992), except for the distinguishing feature that non-linearity is allowed in some relations.

There are fundamentally two hypotheses underlying the model: a distinction among different kinds of agents in the stock market, and a distinction between two different time periods leading on to some notion of equilibrium.

This model is far more subtle than the original one, that didn't take into consideration the two distinctions above described, which originated the works by FERRARI – PECCATI (1991), LUCIANO (1991), CORNAGLIA (1991).

The research model is anyway far from being definitive: ideas about how to improve it, so that it can better represent the real behaviour of small and imperfect stock markets, like some European ones, are already on discussion.

The present paper is structured as follows: hypotheses and conclusions of the model with no "irrational" behaviour are presented in section 2; section 3 takes into consideration the possibility of a particular kind of irrationality, namely an imitation effect among the agents; section 4 is a conclusive note, where also some possible improvements and variations of the model are underlined.

All the results about the conditions granting that an equilibrium is reached at the end are obtained under very general hypothesis on the behavioural equations. Namely, the linearity assumption of FERRARI – LUCIANO – PECCATI's (1992) model is substituted qualitative properties of the relations involved.

2 The model without imitation

2.1 Hypothesis of the model

While a detailed discussion of the hypothesis of the model can be found in FERRARI – LUCIANO – PECCATI (1992), we give here only a brief summary, in order to explain the symbols used. Two different time periods are taken into consideration: the sequence of the stock market sessions ($T = 1, 2, \ldots$) and, inside each one of these sessions, the the sequence of call epochs $t_n(T)$ ($n = 0, 1, 2, \ldots$). The distance between two subsequent calls is not established, while the duration of each session is invariably S. So $t_n(T) \to S^-$ when $n \to \infty$. We do not investigate here the mechanism that generates the $t_n(T)$ sequence, and we treat it as exogenous.

Three kinds of agents enter the stock market: first of all there are non-professional traders (NPT), that give irrevocable orders to banks before the beginning of each session: these orders will be executed at the fixing price, unknown by the investors, who base their requests on the latest session price.

The offered transaction by agent m ($m = 1, 2, \ldots, M$) is in fact a function (a_m) of the difference between the latest session price ($P(T-1)$) and the fundamental value of the stock r_m, as believed by the agent himself at time T.

$$q_m(T) = -a_m[P(T-1) - r_m(T)]$$

The value of $a_m(.)$ has the meaning of a proposed purchase if it is positive, of a proposed sale if it is negative. The function a_m can be assumed monotonically increasing with graph through the origin. The M relations can be added up to obtain a a new relation

$$Q(T) = -a[P(T-1) - r(T)] \tag{1}$$

where $Q(T) = \sum_m q_m(T)$, a is the sum of all the a_m functions, and will obviously be monotonic too. Moreover, if the a_m are continuous functions, there will be an $r \in [r_{min}, r_{max}]$ such that $P - r = 0$ implies $Q = 0$. a will then have graph passing through the origin too.

The second class of agents is formed by a single professional trader (PT), that can also be considered as a representative agent substituting without any loss of generality a set of several professional traders. The total amount of orders placed by the PT till the n-th call is B_n, so that the transactions which are carried out at $t_n(T)$ on the basis of the spread between the preceeding call price ($p_{n-1}(T)$) and the fundamental value h, as seen by the PT at time T, are given by:

$$B_n(T) - B_{n-1}(T) = -\beta[p_{n-1}(T) - h(T)] \tag{2}$$

β is again an increasing function with graph through the origin.

The total amount of transactions by the PT in the T-th session is:

$$B(T) = \lim_{n \to +\infty} B_n(T) \tag{3}$$

The third category of agents is represented by a specialist (SP), that is a market maker who makes teh price valuing the irrevocable orders by the non-professional traders and the offered transactions by the professional trader

$$p_n(T) = k + \phi[Q(T) + B_n(T)] \tag{4}$$

Again, ϕ is an increasing function with graph through the origin and k is the specialist opinion about the fundamental value of the stock. The specialist will increase (decrease) the price with respect to the fundamental value as long as there is total net demand (supply). The initial price will obviously be:

$$p_0(T) = k + \phi[Q(T)] \tag{5}$$

Leaving aside how the opinions of the specialist evolve over time (we can for instance suppose that he won't change his mind), the following relations for the time evolution of the opinions of professional and non-professional traders seem quite reasonable:

$$h(T) = h(T-1) - \mu[B(T-1) + Q(T-1)] \tag{6}$$

(with the usual hypothesis that $\mu(.)$ is monotonically increasing with graph through the origin) and

$$r(T) = (1-w)r(T-1) + wP(T-1) \tag{7}$$

($0 \leq w \leq 1$, then $r(T)$ represents a mean value of $r(T-1)$ and $P(T-1)$).

For the model to be complete, we need one more relation, that formalizes the connection between the time path of prices $p_n(T)$ during a session and the clearing price $P(T)$.

$$\lim_{n\to\infty} p_n(T) = P(T) \tag{8}$$

The model results from the equations from (1) to (8); it does not need to be solved, or analyzed, simultaneously, as we can study the equilibrium inside a single session, and then use the results of such an analysis for studying the long period equilibrium.

2.2 The equilibrium inside the negotiation

The system of equations describing the trading process during a session is given by (2) and (4):

$$B_n(T) = B_{n-1}(T) - \beta[p_{n-1}(T) - h(T)]$$

$$p_n(T) = k + \phi[Q(T) + B_n(T)]$$

Equilibrium values for the price and the total amount of transactions by the PT must satisfy the following system:

$$\begin{aligned} B^* &= B^* - \beta(p^* - h) \\ p^* &= k + \phi(Q + B^*) \end{aligned}$$

It's easily verified that:

$$\begin{aligned} B^* &= \psi(h-k) - Q \\ p^* &= h \end{aligned}$$

where $\psi(.) \stackrel{d}{=} \phi^{-1}$.

It's now worth spending some words about stability. A sufficient condition for the equilibrium to be globally asymptotically stable is the fact that:

$$\left|1 - \beta'\left[k + \phi(Q+B_n) - h\right]\phi'(Q+B_n)\right| \leq j \quad (j<1)$$

To prove this assertion it is sufficient to substitute (4) into (2). We obtain:

$$B_n = B_{n-1} - \beta\left[k + \phi(Q+B_n) - h\right] = f(B_{n-1})$$

Thanks to Banach's fixed point theorem (see for instance STOKEY-LUCAS (1989)), if $f(.)$ is a contraction, every sequence satisfying $B_n = f(B_{n-1})$ converges to the same equilibrium point (unique) and globally stable.

The function $f(.)$ is a contraction if

$$\frac{|f(B+h) - f(B)|}{|h|} \leq j$$

with $j < 1$, for all $B \in \mathbf{R}$ (as f is defined on the whole real set).

With a passage to limit, if ϕ and β are differentiable on $\mathbf{R}$, the condition becomes: $|f'(B)| \leq j < 1$, or:

$$\left|1 - \beta'\left[k + \phi(Q+B_n) - h\right]\phi'(Q+B_n)\right| \leq j \quad (j<1)$$

As ϕ and β are increasing, so that their first derivatives are positive, an equivalent condition is:

$$\beta'\left[k+\phi(Q+B_n)-h\right]\phi'(Q+B_n)\leq J<2$$

We can introduce a natural qualitative hypothesis about further properties of ϕ and β. We assume now that these functions are convex for negative values of their argument, concave for positive ones. That implies that $\sup\beta'[k+\phi(Q+B_n)-h]\phi'(Q+B_n)=\beta'(0)\phi'(0)$. A sufficient condition for the equilibrium to be stable is then $\beta'(0)\phi'(0)<2$.

Its economic meaning is that the equilibrium can be reached if near it the reaction parameters of both the professional trader and the specialist are jointly sufficiently small.

2.3 The long period equilibrium

Thanks to equations (3) and (8), we can consider the equilibrium values B^* and p^*, reached at the end of session T, as the clearing price and the total amount of transactions by the professional trader for the T-th session.

The dynamical system describing the evolution from session to session results by combining equations (1)-(6)-(7)-(9)-(10) and turns down to be the following

$$\begin{cases} Q(T)=-a[P(T-1)-r(T)] \\ h(T)=h(T-1)-\mu[B(T-1)+Q(T-1)] \\ r(T)=(1-w)r(T-1)+wP(T-1) \\ P(T)=h(T) \\ B(T)=\psi[h(T)-k]-Q(T) \end{cases}$$

It can be easily seen that the equilibrium values for the long run system are the following:

$$P^*=r^*=h^*=k;\quad Q^*=B^*=0$$

The proof is immediate. The equilibrium values must satisfy:

$$\begin{cases} Q^*=-a(P^*-r^*) \\ h^*=h^*-\mu(B^*+Q^*) \\ r^*=(1-w)r^*+wP^* \\ P^*=h^* \\ B^*=\psi(h^*-k)-Q^* \end{cases}$$

The equality $\mu(B^*+Q^*)=0$ implies $B^*=Q^*$. So $\psi(h^*-k)=0$, that implies $h^*=k$. The last relation gives $r^*=P^*=k$. So $Q^*=0$ and $B^*=0$ too.

The long run equilibrium is then characterized by fixing prices converging to the fundamental value, as seen by the specialist, and limit zero position of alla agents.

As we can see, conclusions do not change with respect to the linear case if we allow for non-linearity.

Moreover, if $\mu'(0)<1$ and $a'(0)(1-w)<1$, that is if the reaction parameter of the NPT and the adjustment speed of the PT's opinions are sufficiently small, the equilibrium is locally asymptotically stable.

The proof stems from trivial manipulations of the long run dynamical system, which becomes

$$\begin{cases} Q(T)= & -a\{(1-w)[P(T-1)-r(T-1)]\} \\ P(T)= & P(T-1)-\mu[B(T-1)+Q(T-1)] \\ B(T)= & \psi\{P(T-1)-\mu[B(T-1)+Q(T-1)]-k\}+ \\ & +a\{(1-w)[P(T-1)-r(T-1)] \\ r(T)= & (1-w)r(T-1)+wP(T-1) \end{cases}$$

that can be written as

$$\mathbf{Y}(T) = \mathbf{G}[\mathbf{Y}(T-1)]$$

where:

$$\mathbf{Y}(T) = \begin{bmatrix} Q(T) \\ P(T) \\ B(T) \\ r(T) \end{bmatrix}$$

and $\mathbf{G} : \mathbf{R}^4 \to \mathbf{R}^4$.

The identity between h and P enables us to reduce the problem dimensions.

Now, the equilibrium point $\mathbf{Y}^*$ is locally stable if the linear approximation of $\mathbf{G}$ at $\mathbf{Y}^*$ admits a globally stable equilibrium point $\mathbf{Y}^*$ (see, for instance, LAKSHMIKANTHAM – TRIGIANTE (1988)).

But the linear approximation is stable iff all the eigenvalues of the jacobian matrix $\mathbf{G}'(\mathbf{Y}^*)$ are inside the unit disk in the complex plane.

The jacobian matrix is:

$$\begin{bmatrix} 0 & -a'(0)(1-w) & 0 & a'(0)(1-w) \\ -\mu'(0) & 1 & -\mu'(0) & 0 \\ \psi'(0)\mu'(0) & \psi'(0) + a'(0)(1-w) & \psi'(0)\mu'(0) & -a'(0)(1-w) \\ 0 & w & 0 & 0 \end{bmatrix}$$

It is easy to check that two eigenvalues are 0 and the other two eigenvalues are those of the matrix:

$$\mathbf{A} \stackrel{d}{=} \begin{bmatrix} 1 & -\mu'(0) \\ \psi'(0) & \psi'(0)\mu'(0) \end{bmatrix}$$

A simple theorem (see, for instance BARNETT (1983)) allows us to provide a necessary and sufficient condition for having the spectrum of $\mathbf{A}$ in the interior of the unit disk. It must happen that

$$\begin{cases} |\det \mathbf{A}| < 1 \\ |\mathrm{tr}\mathbf{A}| < 1 + \det \mathbf{A} \end{cases}$$

The first condition becomes:

$$\psi'(0)\mu'(0) < \frac{1}{2}$$

or

$$\mu'(0) < \frac{1}{2}\,\phi'(0)$$

while the second is always satisfied under our assumptions.

The economic interpretation of the condition provided above is easy: what's required is that the equilibrium reactivity of the PT is less than half of the analogous parameter for the SP. The reaction behaviour of the NPT appear irrelevant for the nature of this equilibrium.

All of this agrees with FERRARI – LUCIANO – PECCATI (1992) results obtained in the linear case.

3 The model with imitation

We can think about some imitation effects influencing the agents' behaviour: as long as we accept the hypothesis that imitative decisions only regard non-professional traders, they do not affect the negotiations inside a single session.

The only equation that will be influenced by imitation is in fact the one about NPT offered transactions.

Also within the limits of this hypothesis, there is a large number of possible imitation structures. We shall study only two of them: the first one considers that part of non-professional traders' offered transactions which are determined by the last session PT's behaviour, while the second one involves a more generalized pattern of imitation, with each agent potentially looking at every other NPT, and at the PT too.

3.1 Imitation toward the professional trader

We can think of a linear effect of the PT last session behaviour on the NPT actual offered transactions.

The only part of the model describing the evolution from session to session that changes is equation (1). This relation becomes:

$$Q(T) = -a[P(T-1) - r(T)] + \gamma B(T-1) \tag{9}$$

γ is a positive parameter, that may be thought of as the sum of all the analogous constants characterizing the behaviour of each non-professional trader.

Following the same steps of subs. 2.3, we can easily demonstrate that the same equilibrium values hold (but not necessarily the same path to the equilibrium).

As regards local stability, we can again approximate the non-linear system with a linear one. The new jacobian matrix we get is: The jacobian matrix is:

$$\begin{bmatrix} 0 & -a'(0)(1-w) & \gamma & a'(0)(1-w) \\ -\mu'(0) & 1 & -\mu'(0) & 0 \\ \psi'(0)\mu'(0) & \psi'(0) + a'(0)(1-w) & \psi'(0)\mu'(0) & -a'(0)(1-w) \\ 0 & w & 0 & 0 \end{bmatrix}$$

As concerns its spectrum conditions analogous to the ones given in FERRARI – LUCIANO – PECCATI (1992). We have to add the condition $\gamma < 1$ to get stability.

3.2 A pattern of generalized imitation

If the NPT also potentially imitate each other, we can't aggregate their behaviour in a single equation any more.

Each non-professional trader behavioural equation is:

$$q_m = -a_m[P(T-1) - r_m(T)] + \gamma_m B(T-1) + \sum_j e_{mj} q_j(T-1)$$

where γ_m is the imitation parameter characterizing the behaviour of agent m in response to the previous session PT's behaviour, while e_{mj} quantifies the imitative behaviour of agent m toward agent j.

We can write compactly this relation with vectors and matrices:

$$\mathbf{q}(T) = -\mathbf{a}[\mathbf{1}P(T-1) - \mathbf{r}(T)] + \mathbf{g}B(T-1) + \mathbf{E}\mathbf{q}(T-1) \tag{10}$$

where $\mathbf{a} : \mathbf{R}^m \to \mathbf{R}^m$ is the vector function describing the speculative part of non-professional traders behaviour, $\mathbf{g}$ collects the γ_m imitation coefficients toward PT and $\mathbf{E}$ is the matrix of the imitation parameters between non-professional traders.

The dynamical system describing the long run market evolution is the following:

$$\begin{cases} \mathbf{q}(T) = -a[\mathbf{1}P(T-1) - \mathbf{r}(T)] + \mathbf{g}B(T-1) + \mathbf{E}\mathbf{q}(T-1) \\ h(T) = h(T-1) - \mu[B(T-1) + \mathbf{1}'\mathbf{q}(T-1)] \\ \mathbf{r}(T) = (\mathbf{I} - \hat{\mathbf{w}})\mathbf{r}(T-1) + \mathbf{w}P(T-1) \\ P(T) = h(T) \\ B(T) = \psi[h(T) - k] - \mathbf{1}'\mathbf{q}(T) \end{cases}$$

where $\mathbf{w} \in \mathbf{R}^m$ collects the adjustment coefficients w_m and the "hat" denotes diagonalization of the underlying vector.

Any equilibrium point must satisfy:

$$\begin{cases} \mathbf{q}^* = -a[\mathbf{1}P^* - \mathbf{r}^*] + \mathbf{g}B^* + \mathbf{E}\mathbf{q}^* \\ h^* = h^* - \mu[B^* + \mathbf{1}'\mathbf{q}^*] \\ \mathbf{r}^* = (\mathbf{I} - \hat{\mathbf{w}})\mathbf{r}^* + \mathbf{w}P^* \\ P^* = h^* \\ B^* = \psi[h^* - k] - \mathbf{1}'\mathbf{q}^* \end{cases}$$

which can be easily reduced to:

$$\begin{cases} \mathbf{q}^* = -a[\mathbf{1}P^* - \mathbf{r}^*] + \mathbf{g}B^* + \mathbf{E}\mathbf{q}^* \\ h^* = p^* = k \\ B(T) + \mathbf{1}'\mathbf{q}(T) = 0 \end{cases}$$

indeed very similar to the final results in the linear case.

4 Conclusions

The purpose of this paper was to underline some properties of the behaviour of a stock market characterized by different kinds of traders, asymmery of information and some imitation effects among the agents.

Namely it was demonstrated that the equilibrium eventually reached in the long run involves a fixing price equal to the fundamental value as seen by the specialist (that is the market maker deciding the price on the basis of all the transactions offered by other agents), the convergence of all agents' opinions about the fundamental value of the stock and exchanges vanishing.

This result, substantially identical to the one achieved in FERRARI – LUCIANO – PECCATI (1992) in a linear context, is reached in this paper under very general hypotheses on the behavioural equations.

Anyway, the effort to model stock markets in a realistic way should not stop here. Alternative hypotheses may be useful to make comparisons and realize how things go on in the real world. In this direction the consequences of considering the professional trader making a sequence of proposals inside the session, but concluding the negotiations only at the end of it, are already being studied.

On the other hand, the model can be improved in a number of ways if we accept to make it more complex.

Furthermore, at this level of generalization there is no empirical interest in the model: studying how the different functional forms of the relations affect the model, and simulating numerically its time evolution, could be interesting for the understanding of the model behaviour not only asymptotically but within an appropriate time horizon.

References

S. BARNETT (1983): *Polynomials and Linear Control Systems.* Marcel Dekker, New York.

A. CORNAGLIA (1991): 'A Non-linear Model of Stock-Market and Imitation', in A. CORNAGLIA – L. FERRARI – E. LUCIANO – L. PECCATI (1991): *Some Models of imperfect financial Markets*, Quaderni dell'Istituto di Matematica Finanziaria dell'Università di Torino, serie III, n. 62.

L. FERRARI – L. PECCATI (1991): 'Stock-Market Behaviour and Imitation: a Simple Model', in A. CORNAGLIA – L. FERRARI – E. LUCIANO – L. PECCATI (1991): *Some Models of imperfect financial Markets*, Quaderni dell'Istituto di Matematica Finanziaria dell'Università di Torino, serie III, n. 62.

L. FERRARI – E. LUCIANO – L. PECCATI (1992): 'Institutionally Heterogeneous Agents in an Imitative Stock-Market', in this volume.

V. LAKSHMIKANTHAM – D. TRIGIANTE (1988): *Theory of Difference Equations: Numerical Methods and Applications*, Academic Press, New York.

E. LUCIANO (1991): 'Equilibrium in a Financial Market with Asymmetric Information, Imitation and Noise', in A. CORNAGLIA – L. FERRARI – E. LUCIANO – L. PECCATI (1991): *Some Models of imperfect financial Markets*, Quaderni dell'Istituto di Matematica Finanziaria dell'Università di Torino, serie III, n. 62.

N.L. STOKEY – R.L. LUCAS (1989): *Recursive Methods in Economic Dynamics*, Harvard University Press, Harvard.

Small Business Diagnosis Using Statistical Modelling and Artificial Intelligence

Omer van der Horst Jansen
University of Groningen
Postbus 800, 9700 AV Groningen, The Netherlands

1. Introduction

In the research project described in this paper an automated business diagnosis system (called Phalanx) is developed, specifically for use by consultants advising small businesses. An automated business diagnosis system can be defined as a computer program that delivers an opinion of the viability of a company. As a working hypothesis, it is assumed that the use of such a system improves the performance of the consultant; better judgements are made with such a system than without one.

One way to develop an automated business diagnosis system is to make a list of often-occurring problems in firms, and to use a statistical technique to relate each of these problems to observable characteristics of the firm. Another way is to use a knowledge-based system that mimics the behaviour of human consultants. In this project, the diagnosis system is built as a knowledge-based system that is capable of using the result of statistical models to create a diagnosis.

In the next two sections, the context in which the diagnosis system will be used is looked into. In the remainder of this paper, the reasoning process used to reach a diagnosis will be examined.

2. Application of the diagnosis system

The Dutch Small Business Institute (IMK) has been established to advise small to medium-sized businesses on a variety of subjects. When a firm becomes aware of the existence of a problem, often because of its negative impact on actual or expected financial performance, IMK may be requested to send a consultant to assist in finding a solution to the problem.

IMK consultants currently use a financial modelling tool called Finan that assists them with the financial analysis during the consulting process. Finan requires the consultant to enter the firm's balance sheet and profit and loss statement data; it then allows the consultant to calculate the financial effects of a number of scenarios.

Phalanx will extend the services rendered by Finan. It compares the firm's past and forecasted financial performance to a set of norms. If deviations occur, the system searches for the underlying cause (which does not have to be of a financial nature). The result of the search process - the diagnosis - is presented to the user in natural language. Additionally, the diagnosis system may present a number of predefined "scripts", representing alternative courses of action, that may alleviate the problem represented by the diagnosis.

3. Phalanx's position in the problem solving process

Simon (1960) divides the problem solving process into three phases: Intelligence, Design and Choice. In the Intelligence phase, the environment is scanned for signals that may identify problems or opportunities; the problem is identified and described. In the Design phase, a search for possible courses of action to solve the problem is carried out. Alternatives are developed and evaluated. This involves processes to generate solutions, and to test solutions for feasibility. In the Choice phase, one of the alternative courses of action is selected.

Simon's view of the problem solving process can be mapped onto the specific situation as stated below:

Intelligence. A company that finds itself in some kind of trouble contacts IMK (it may have been prompted by its bank or its accountant to do so). A consultant is assigned to the firm. The consultant then tries to develop a "mental map" of the firm in order to determine the nature and causes of the problem. The diagnosis system attempts to make this mental map explicit, which (according to the working hypothesis mentioned in section 1) should accelerate the problem detection process.

Design. After having determined the causes of the problem, the consultant develops a number of alternative strategies designed to alleviate the problem. Each of these strategies has to be checked for financial soundness. The pre-defined scripts offered by the diagnosis system should help the consultant both in developing and testing alternative strategies.

Choice. The consultant selects a number of viable strategies and presents these to the firm's management. The management then has to decide which, if any, of the presented alternatives it will implement.

Phalanx is a support system, meaning that it is not designed to make decisions for its user. It does not support the Choice phase. The user, usually an IMK consultant, will have to decide whether to accept Phalanx's opinion of the firm's condition, or to accept one of Phalanx's possible solutions.

4. Finding problems in financial data: Bouwman's approach

The reasoning mechanism used by the diagnosis system presented here is based on the results of research by Bouwman (1978, 1983). His approach will be discussed in this section; in the next section, an adaptation of his model will be presented.

Bouwman developed a diagnosis model that uses symbolic reasoning techniques. Although the human subjects used in his study were no experts on the subject (financial analysis based on balance sheet data), Bouwman's results are very encouraging. His computer program examined data in the same order as the human subjects, made the same inferences, and reported the same conclusions.

Protocol analysis was used to study the way human subjects evaluated accounting statements, and used the findings of this study to construct a computer program that emulated the human subject's diagnostic process.

The program contains an "internal model of the firm". This is a qualitative model; for example, it might show that the level of profit depends on the level of sales, and that a rise in the level of sales will have a positive effect on the level of profit, without specifying the quantitative relation between the levels of sales and profit.

Bouwman's program processes the available data in a number of steps. In the first step the program attempts to detect the presence of a problem by identifying symptoms. Like the human subjects in the study, the program translates the quantitative data into qualitative terms. Five different operators are used to process each data item: 1. the computation of a simple trend ("increase" or "decrease"), 2. the computation of a more complex trend, 3. the comparison against an industry norm, 4. the comparison with other financial information provided, and 5. the application of an internal heuristic like "earnings should be positive." Bouwman's program then uses heuristics to select the potentially significant items. For example, a "large" increase may be considered significant, while a "small" increase might not. As its result, step 1 delivers a list of significant findings. Only the findings in this list are available for further processing.

In step 2, the items on the list of significant findings are "integrated". If two significant findings pertain to variables directly linked in the internal model of the firm, they are linked together. The pairs created are then linked up again to other significant findings, creating chain and tree structures. Only the terminal nodes of these chains and trees are available for further link-ups. In this way, clusters of significant findings are generated.

In step 3, problem-hypotheses are formulated. Here, the "roots" of clusters are examined. If A, B and C are observed significant findings, and it has been established in step 2 that A causes B and C, then A will be explored further by returning to step 1. Because there may be many clusters, heuristics are used to determine which roots will be investigated. Bouwman's program examines the first root of a cluster that reached a certain minimum size.

The internal model of the firm is used to find causes that might explain the root of the cluster. It then searches for possible causes of these causes, creating a tree structure of causes. In this way a large number of explanatory paths are created, each path being a hypothesis about the nature of the problem.

A problem noted by Bouwman is that the number of problem-hypotheses may be large. The goal of the program is to report as few overlapping problems as possible in its final diagnosis. A possible way to select a hypothesis is to generate multiple trees from different roots, and intersect them. Causes explaining more roots might be considered more likely. The program developed by Bouwman ranks the hypotheses on the basis of their conformance to observed significant findings. If a hypothesis contains a statement contradicting the observations, it will be deemed less likely than a hypothesis adhering to the observations.

Bouwman's model has a number of interesting attributes. It can explain how it reached a conclusion by displaying its "causation tree". It has been implemented in a working computer program. It reports the same findings as the human analysts it simulates. It provides a good starting point for a quantitative approach (Courtney et al., 1987); Cohn (1989) states that qualitative techniques may be used to find possible problems in a given situation; when a problem has been detected, quantitative techniques can be used to focus in on it.

The model fits well into Simon's framework of the problem solving process; it explicitly supports the Intelligence phase. The model can be used to perform a what-if analysis, and its performance should not suffer from occasional missing data items; if a data item is missing, it can be considered either insignificant or significant. In the last case, there are only three to five values the (qualitative) variable can assume, which makes it relatively easy for the user of the model to substitute the missing value with an estimate. .

The model also has drawbacks. For example, its use of qualitative reasoning may lead to the overlooking of emerging trends that are deemed insignificant.

5. A modified problem detection model

Bouwman's model has been adapted for use in a number of diagnosis systems. Courtney et al. (1987) use a variant of the internal model of the firm in a decision support system; Daniels and Feelders (1990) use a constraint-logic programming language to create a diagnosis.

In Phalanx, a number of changes have been made to Bouwman's original model. Phalanx is based on the (quantitative) financial model already used in the Finan package. A linked, but logically separate model, contains qualitative variables that can only take the values -1, 0 and 1, indicating that the value of the corresponding quantitative variable is either too low, "OK", or too high, or decreasing, stable or increasing. Each qualitative variable is assigned a text describing the meaning of the value of the variable.

The value of a qualitative variable is determined by a norm function, a lower bound for the function result, and an upper bound for the function result. The qualitative variable is assigned a value depending on the result of the norm function with respect to the bounds specified. The norm function may access any variable in the quantitative model, allowing a spreadsheet-like flexibility in construction of the model. As an example, all of Bouwman's five operators can be used in the norm function.

To create a diagnosis, a third model similar to Bouwman's internal model of the firm is used. It specifies the direction and sign of each qualitative variable on other qualitative variables. Using simple tree-searching techniques, clusters of cause-effect relations between non-zero qualitative variables are constructed. These clusters represent a problem. They can be printed out in a natural language using the texts assigned to each qualitative variable.

The diagnosis-creating process will be enhanced by allowing the search process to "speculate" about the value of variables with missing data, asking the model user for confirmation when needed. If a terminal node (an "ultimate cause") of a cluster of qualitative variables has not been assigned a value, a sub-model can be presented to the model user to allow additional data to be entered. For example, the diagnosis system might have determined that travelling costs for a firm are high when compared to the industry average. In that case, the model user will be prompted to enter additional data on the subject. Thanks to this property, Phalanx does not saddle its users with the burden to enter large amounts of data for every firm diagnosed.

If a problem type occurs regularly, and a more-or-less standard procedure is available to solve it, a script can be created to include the solution in the diagnosis model. Scripts contain a textual description of the problem which it is designed to solve, an activation function that "fires" when a number of qualitative variables representing the problem is present in the diagnosis, and a procedure (which is similar to a spreadsheet macro or Pascal procedure) that can either change the value of quantitative variables automatically, or assist the user in doing so. The last property allows the user to change the firm's representation in the financial model in a number of steps. For example, a script might be used to evaluate the effects of a change in a firm's legal structure. This script might be triggered by the fact that the company's legal structure differs from that of most of its competitors, and that tax as a percentage of profit is significantly higher than that of its competitors. To ensure the appropriateness of the script, the model can be re-diagnosed to find out if new problems have surfaced.

6. Symptom detection using statistical models

The financial model at the basis of the Phalanx system contains several hundred financial variables. To be able to create a diagnosis, a norm function needs to be specified for most of these variables. Most of these functions and their associated bounds will be specified using data gathered during interviews with IMK consultant. In a number of cases, separate sub models may be used to indicate the presence of symptoms by classifying quantitative variables. As an example, the integration of sub-models estimated using statistical techniques will be discussed.

Many statistical methods can be used to solve classification problems. Altman et al. (1981) describe the use of linear regression techniques, discriminant analysis, probit and logit analysis. An introduction to the linear probability model and logit analysis can be found in Aldrich (1983). Discriminant analysis, probit and logit analysis are well suited to classification problems with dichotomous or polytomous dependent variables, which have to be explained by a number of independent variables.

A large amount of research has been carried out in the area of credit scoring models and business failure prediction. For example, in the United States, Altman (1981) has done research on credit scoring models and financial distress prognosis using ratio analysis. In the Netherlands, research in this area has been carried out by Bilderbeek and Van Frederikslust (Bilderbeek, 1979).

As an example, one of these studies will be shortly presented. In this study, Altman (Altman et al., 1981) used multiple discriminant analysis (MDA) to find a relation among 22 financial indicators and the presence of financial distress in a company. He analysed 33 bankrupted industrial companies from a period spanning from 1946 until 1965. A healthy company was assigned to every bankrupt one from the same industry, of about the same size and from the same time period.

Altman estimated a linear discriminant function in which the following five indicators ultimately provided the best estimate:

- working capital / total assets
- retained earnings / total assets
- earnings before interest and taxes / total assets
- market value of equity / book value of total debt

- sales / total assets

According to Altman, his research reconfirmed the utility of ratio analysis and showed the importance of multivariate analysis techniques. A shortcoming of the model was its inability to predict bankruptcies more than two years in advance.

Altman's function has been widely used to predict bankruptcies. It seems likely that the parameters and variables in the model would have to be changed for business area, country and time period. Research in other countries has confirmed this (Altman, 1988).

In Phalanx, models like the one estimated by Altman may be used to determine whether a symptom is present. If a statistical model predicts failure of the firm within a number of years, this can be treated as a significant fact influencing the firm's ability to raise credit. In this way, the statistical model acts as a link between a variable representing the impossibility to raise new credit, and the independent variables present in the model.

7. Implementation of Phalanx

Phalanx is currently being implemented for personal computers running the Microsoft Windows operating system in the C++ computer language by the author of this paper. It interprets a modelling language in which the diagnosis model is being developed. The separation between the model and its interpreter allows for a great flexibility in the development of the model; for example, a separate model can easily be created for different lines of business.

The selection of Microsoft Windows as an operating platform was prompted both by the removal of memory limitations inherent to MS-DOS-based programs, the quality of the user interface, and the standard facilities allowing integration of Phalanx with other applications.

Implementation of the diagnosis model is currently limited to building an empirically empty, purely financial diagnosis model based on the currently used Finan financial model. Norm functions and their associated bounds will be added later in 1992 by interviewing experienced IMK consultants. The model will also be extended to cover non-financial areas of the firm.

8. Conclusion

Automated business diagnosis systems are still far from commonplace. For some sub-tasks, like the evaluation of a loan or the prediction of company failure, systems are in use. Phalanx represents an attempt to integrate these tasks in a framework supporting both the Intelligence and the Design phase in the problem solving process, using the modelling approach pioneered by Bouwman. If successful, IMK consultants will experiency both an increase in efficiency, because the amount of time needed to analyse a company diminishes, and in effectiveness, because the diagnosis generated by Phalanx will be based on the common knowledge of experienced collegues.

References

Aldrich J.H, Nelson F.D.: "Linear probability, logit, and probit models", Sage University Paper Series on Quantitative Applications in the Social Sciences, series no. 07-045, Sage Pubns., Beverly Hills, 1984

Altman E.I., Avery R.B., Eisenbeis R.A., Sinkey J.F.: "Application of classification techniques in business, banking and finance", JAI Press, Greenwich, 1981

Altman E.I. (ed.): "International Business Failure Prediction Models, North-Holland", Amsterdam, 1988

Bilderbeek J., "Financiële ratio-analyse", Stenfert Kroese, Leiden, 1979.

Bouwman M.J: "Human diagnostic reasoning by computer: an illustration from financial analysis", Management Science Vol. 29 pp653-672, 1983.

Bouwman M.J.: "Financial diagnosis: a cognitive model of the processes involved", Ph.D. thesis, Carnegie-Mellon University, University Microfilms #7818922, 1978.

Cohn, A.G.: "Qualitative reasoning", Advanced Topics in Artificial Intelligence, Lecture Notes in Artificial Intelligence, issue 345, ed. by R.T. Nossum, Springer-Verlag, Berlin, 1987.

Courtney J.F., Paradice D.B., Ata Mohammed N.H.: "A Knowledge-Based DSS For Managerial Problem Diagnosis", Decision Sciences, Vol. 18, pp373-399, 1987.

Daniels H.A.M., Feelders A.J.: "Model-based diagnosis of business performance: a constraint-logic programming approach", Tilburg University, 1990.

Simon H.: "The new science of management decision", Harper, New York, 1960.